YELLOW CREEK
MENNONITE
COOKBOOK

The Yellow Creek Mennonite Church is a body of believers commit-
ted to Jesus Christ, peaceful living, and extending God's kingdom.

We invite others to faith in Christ, we nurture one another in love,
and we celebrate in worship, service, and fellowship.

Baked Oatmeal Pg 167 ✱   *Sugar Free Raisin Bars 170*
                                   Chicken with a cheese flavor
                                                            Pg 68

Stir Fry - 75   1

Honey baked chicken 73

YELLOW CREEK WOMEN'S FUNCTIONS

Over the past years, the women of the Yellow Creek Mennonite Church have been meeting monthly quilting, sewing garments and carpet rags, knotting comforters, etc., for those in need. The first Yellow Creek Mennonite Sewing Circle was organized February 2, 1916. They met in homes until the group was larger, then they started meeting at the church. The mothers always took their children along to the all-day sewing, and the children entertained themselves playing in the classroom sand boxes or playing on the floor next to their mothers. The time arrived in the late 40's and early 50's that some of the younger women started working outside the home and couldn't attend the daytime sewing. Eventually, an evening circle was organized, (later discontinued), as well as projects for their younger daughters. Today the remaining groups are called the Women's Missionary and Service Commission and Girls' Missionary and Service Auxiliary.

Monthly, in the evenings, we have a time of fellowship, along with some sort of program, called Women's Fellowship. Our Yellow Creek Hostess Co. serves meals for banquets, weddings, funerals, public sales and outside groups. Each year the entire congregation is invited to help make noodles for the Michiana Relief Sale. Yellow Creek has many expert cooks and through the years many recipes have been exchanged at these various meetings.

Since October of 1979, we have a monthly new sheet, YELLOW CREEK RIPPLES, in which we try to keep our women (and men) informed of wanted, free, and for sale items; interviews with women from our congregation; library book reviews; household/gardening hints and yes, recipes. Yellow Creek WMSC Council oversees all the above functions.

Yellow Creek Quilters in 1955, 40 years ago. Seated from left to right: Nora Lehman, Grace Stichter, Sadie Pletcher, Mabel Blosser and Savilla Wise. Standing left to right: Dorothy Hartman, Dora Eberly, Ida Pletcher, Goldie Wenger, Martha Leinbach, Fannie Smucker, Elsie Goetz, Pearl Newcomer and Cora Tyson.

Pastors

Yellow Creek Mennonite Church

Serving from 1845-1938
Martin Hoover, John Hoover, Jacob Wisler, Jacob Christophel, Joseph Roher, John Bare, Benjamin Hershey, John Christophel, Christian Christophel, Noah Metzler, Jonas Loucks, Jacob W. Christophel.

Serving from 1924-1995

Allen Christophel	1924-1932
Virgil Weaver	1935-1942
Ralph Smucker	1942-1947
John Moseman	1947-1950
Ralph Smucker	1950-1951
Peter & Rheta Mae Wiebe	1951-1959
John David & Ruth Zehr	1960-1966
Mahlon & Dorothy Miller	1966-1974
Aden & Helen Yoder, Interim	1974-1975
Bob & Marge Detweiler	1975-1989
Wes & Cheryl Bontreger	1990-Present

Associate Pastors & Youth Pastors
Everett Metzler, John David Zehr, Jerry Weaver, James Wenger, Dale Schumm, Clayton Swartzentruber, Otis Hochstetler, Larry Klippenstein, Gary Harder, Paul Christophel, Clifford Miller, Ray Epp, Steve Thomas, Wes Bontreger, Clare & Katie Ann Schumm. Clare is presently serving as Minister of Counseling & Family Life.

The above list of Associate Pastors and Youth Pastors is not necessarily in order of their service, and it may also not be the complete list. No one was deliberately left out. We apologize for any mistakes that may appear.

Yellow Creek Members currently serving on the Mission Field:

Carl & Lois Ramer
Elk Point, Alberta, Canada

Otis & Betty Hochstetler
Conceicao do Araguaia-PA,
Brazil

Max & Susan Ramer
LaPaz BCS,
Mexico

Verda Weaver recently returned
from the Mission Field in Africa.

Dwight & Margaret Hartzler
Sil, Box 1800
Jaya Pura 99018
Irian Jaya, Indonesia

Chris & Lois Luiz
Min Chuan Rd. #44
Hualien 970
Taiwan ROC

It is with great pleasure that we present to you these recipes from the YELLOW CREEK MENNONITE CHURCH.

A sincere thank you to each person that contributed recipes. There is a wide variety of recipes from young and old.

A special "Thank You" to:
Lattanakhone (Lat) Bounmythavong for the artwork on the divider pages.
Florence Hershberger for the lettering on the divider pages and cover.
Roy Martin for the pictures on the Title page and cover.
Shirley Albrecht for the history of our Women's organizations.
Betty Leinbach for gathering and organizing the names of our former Pastors.
Jill Erb for gathering and organizing the names of our Missionaries.

We hope you will enjoy our book as you browse through it and as you try the recipes from your many friends at Yellow Creek.

From the Committee:
Esther Martin, Chairperson
Jill Erb
Beth Fervida
Betty Leinbach
Merianne Shaffer
Lou Thomas

Yellow Creek Mennonite Church
64901 C.R. 11
Goshen, IN 46526

TABLE OF CONTENTS

Appetizers
& Beverages

APPETIZERS & BEVERAGES

Appetizers

CHEESE BALL

1 jar Kraft Old English
1 jar Kraft Roca Blue

3 3-oz. pkgs. cream cheese
Nuts, chopped

Cream together ingredients; roll into a ball. Roll in chopped nuts.

CHEESE BALL

1 jar Old English Cheddar cheese
1 8-oz. pkg. cream cheese
1 T. Accent salt
2 T. onion, cut fine
1/2 pkg. Hidden Valley Ranch
  Dressing Mix

1 T. Worcestershire sauce
1 3-oz. pkg. thin sliced smoked
  ham
1/2 c. nuts (opt.)

Mix all ingredients together. Chill. Roll into ball and roll in nuts, if desired.

Cheryl Bontreger

COCKTAIL MEATBALLS

1-2 lbs. hamburger
Salt
Pepper
Onion powder
1 egg
Bread crumbs

1 tsp. seasoned salt
Sauce:
1 10-oz. jar grape jelly
1 12-oz. bottle chili sauce
1 16-oz. can whole cranberry
  sauce/jelly

Roll hamburger, seasonings, eggs and bread crumbs into bite-size meatballs. Place sauce ingredients in crock pot. Stir. Add meatballs and cook on low for 8-10 hours. (4-pounds hamburger makes 100 meatballs.)

Martha Ramer

COCKTAIL MEATBALLS

1-lb. ground beef
1/2 c. dry bread crumbs
1/3 c. onion, minced
1/4 c. milk
1 egg
1 T. parsley

1 tsp. salt
1 tsp. pepper
1/2 c. shortening
1 12-oz. bottle chili sauce
1 10-oz. jar grape jelly

Mix ground beef, crumbs, onions, milk, egg, parsley flakes, salt and pepper. Shape into small balls. Melt shortening and brown meatballs. Remove from skillet and pour off fat. Heat chili sauce and jelly in skillet, stirring constantly until jelly is melted. Add meatballs. Simmer, uncovered, for 30 minutes.

Renita Graber

CRAB ROLL-UPS

8-10 flour tortillas
2 12-oz. tubs soft cream cheese
Garlic salt

Imitation crab meat sticks
Cocktail sauce

Spread soft cream cheese on tortillas. Sprinkle with garlic salt and add cut up crab meat. Roll up as tight as possible. Place in refrigerator for a couple of hours to set. Cut rolls into 1-inch pieces. Serve with cocktail sauce.

Kathy Kulp

DEVILED EGGS

6 hard cooked eggs
1/4 c. Miracle Whip
1 tsp. prepared mustard

1 tsp. vinegar
Dash of pepper

Slice peeled eggs in half lengthwise and remove yolks. Mash yolks. Add Miracle Whip and seasonings. Fill whites with yolk mixture. For a fancy touch, put the yolk mixture into a cookie press and use the eclair-lady finger tip to fill the whites. Garnish with paprika. Makes 6 servings.

Merianne Shaffer

CHILI CHEESE DIP

1-lb. hamburger
1-lb. Velveeta cheese, cut into
   pieces

1 8-10 oz. can green chilies and
   tomatoes
2 tsp. Worcestershire sauce
1/2 tsp. chili powder

Put ingredients in crock pot on High for 1 hour or on Low for up to 6 hours.

Martha Ramer

CHILI CON QUESO

1 T. salad oil
1/4 c. onion, minced
1 4-oz. can chopped green
   chilies, drained
1/2 tsp. garlic powder

1/3-1/2 c. light cream or milk
1 8-oz. pkg. Velveeta cheese,
   cubed
1 c. Cheddar cheese, grated
Tortilla chips or fresh vegetables

In a small saucepan, heat oil over moderately high heat. Add onion, chilies and garlic; cook 5-7 minutes, stirring frequently, until onion is lightly browned. Reduce heat to low and add 1/3 cup of cream. Add cheeses and stir until mixture is smooth. If necessary, thin sauce with additional cream. Serve in small chafing dish with tortilla chips or fresh vegetables.

Shanda Weaver

Peace is seeing a sunset and knowing who to thank.

CROCK POT HOT DIP

2-lbs. hamburger, browned
1-lb. Colby cheese, shredded
1 15-oz. can tomato sauce
2 cans refried beans with chilies
2 cans jalapeno relish

Combine all ingredients in crock pot. Simmer 2 hours. Serve with taco chips.

Beth Fervida

HAMBURGER DIP

4-lbs. hamburger
2 lg. cans chili (without beans)
1-lb. Velveeta cheese, cubed

Brown hamburger. Add chili. Add cheese and heat until cheese is melted. Serve with tortilla chips.

Dianne Hartman

HOT MEXICANA DIP

1 can condensed bean with
  bacon soup
6-oz. Velveeta cheese (about
  1 c. sm. cubes)
1/2-1 tsp. liquid garlic flavoring
1 c. sour cream
1/4 c. onion, minced
1/4 tsp. bottled hot pepper sauce
Dash of chili powder
Corn chips or crackers

In a saucepan or chafing dish, combine soup and cheese. Heat slowly, stirring constantly, until cheese melts. Stir in sour cream, onion and hot pepper sauce. Heat thoroughly. Sprinkle with chili powder. Serve hot with corn chips or crackers. Meatballs, small hot dogs or sausages are good with this dip. too.

Joan Rhoade

NACHO HOT DIP

1 can stewed tomatoes
1 sm. can green chilies
3-lbs. Velveeta cheese
1 med. onion
1-lb. sausage (Bob Evans)
Milk
Parsley flakes

Brown sausage until well done; drain. Chop onion until fine. Combine tomatoes, chilies, onion and Velveeta, stirring occasionally. Add sausage. Simmer for 1 hour. Add milk to desired consistency. This recipe works great in a crock pot.

Delora Reinhardt

SPICY TACO DIP

1-lb. fresh sausage
1-2 lbs. Velveeta cheese
1 can Cheddar cheese soup
2 c. milk (approx.)
1 lg. jar taco salsa
Taco chips

Brown sausage; drain grease. Mix meat and ingredients in a crock pot. Heat until cheese is melted. Serve over chips or use as a dip.

Ron Huber

COTTAGE CHEESE DIP

16-oz. cottage cheese	1 T. Lawrey's seasoning
1 c. mayonnaise	1 T. dry parsley
1 T. dillweed	1 T. chopped onion or chives

Put cottage cheese in blender until smooth. Add remaining ingredients. Use as dip or with crackers.

Gloria Tyson

DEVILED HAM DIP

12-oz. cream cheese, softened	1/3 c. green pepper, finely
1 can Underwood Deviled Ham	chopped
1 T. Worcestershire sauce	1/3 c. red pepper, finely
	chopped

In a small mixing bowl, combine cream cheese, deviled ham, Worcestershire sauce; beat on medium speed until smooth. Stir in peppers. Cover and refrigerate for 1 hour.

Marilyn K. Miller (Willie)

SHRIMP DIP

1 can shrimp	Salt and pepper
1 12-oz. carton cottage cheese	Worcestershire sauce
1 8-oz. pkg. cream cheese	Garlic salt

Mix all ingredients. Serve with crackers.

Dove Leinbach

SHRIMP SPREAD

1 8-oz. pkg. light cream cheese, softened	2 (4 1/4-oz.) cans shrimp, rinsed and drained (or shredded crabmeat)
1/2 c. low-fat sour cream	3/4 c. tomato, finely chopped
1/4 c. light mayonnaise	3 green onions, sliced
1 c. seafood cocktail sauce	
2 c. light mozzarella cheese, shredded	

In a small bowl, beat cream cheese, sour cream and mayonnaise until smooth. Spread evenly on plate or decorative platter. Spread seafood sauce over cheese mixture. Sprinkle with mozzarella cheese. Top with meat, tomatoes and onions. Refrigerate 1-2 hours. Serve with crackers.

Verna Gongwer

TACO DIP

1 8-oz. pkg. cream cheese, softened	1 can Homel Chili (without meat) Cheddar cheese

Spread cream cheese on plate. Put chili over cream cheese and top with Cheddar cheese. Put in microwave to heat. Serve with chips.

Brenda Gongwer

SPINACH DIP

1 8-oz. carton sour cream
1 c. mayonnaise
1/2 tsp. celery salt
1/2 tsp. dillweed

1/2 tsp. onion salt
1/4 c. green onions, chopped
3 c. frozen spinach, chopped
8-oz. water chestnuts, chopped

Thaw frozen spinach. Squeeze all of the juice from the spinach. Mix with remaining ingredients. Serve with bread.

Renita Graber

VEGETABLE DIP

1 1/2 c. sour cream
1 1/2 c. Hellman's mayonnaise
2 T. minced onion
2 T. parsley flakes

3 tsp. dillweed
2 tsp. Natures seasoning
(by Morton)

Mix all ingredients together. Cover and refrigerate.

Marilyn (G. Keith) Miller

BREAD POT FONDUE

1 round loaf brown bread
(Hawaiian is best)
Filling:
8-oz. Cheddar cheese,
shredded

1 1/2 c. sour cream
1 c. shaved ham, diced
1/2 c. onion, chopped
4-oz. green chilies, chopped
1 tsp. Worcestershire sauce

Slice off top of bread. Hollow out inside of loaf into bite sized chunks; save for later. Combine filling ingredients; fill into hollowed loaf. Replace top of bread. Wrap completely in foil and bake at 350 degrees for 1 1/4 hours. While baking, toast bread cubes on a baking sheet. Serve with a variety of raw vegetables and toasted bread cubes.

Carolyn F. Yoder

PIZZA FONDUE

1 onion, chopped
1/2-lb. ground beef
2 10 1/2-oz. cans pizza sauce
(2 1/2 c.)
1 T. cornstarch

1 1/2 tsp. fennel seed
1/4 tsp. garlic powder
10-oz. Cheddar cheese, grated
1 c. mozzarella cheese
French bread

Brown onion and hamburger. Add pizza sauce, cornstarch, fennel seed and garlic powder. When mixture is thick, add cheese and stir. Dip cubes of garlic bread into pizza fondue.

Becky Schwartzentruber

A good memory is fine--
but the ability to forget is the
true test of greatness.

JOAN'S EGG ROLLS

Marinade:
1 tsp. rice wine
1/4 tsp. salt
1 tsp. cornstarch
1/3-lb. ground meat
Egg Rolls:
Egg roll wrappers
4 c. cabbage, shredded
1/2 c. carrots, shredded
3 c. boiling water
6 T. vegetable oil

1/2 c. bamboo shoots, shredded
1 tsp. salt
1 1/2 tsp. sugar
1/4 tsp. pepper
3 T. soy sauce
3 T. cornstarch
1 T. sesame oil
3 T. water
2 T. flour
6 c. oil for deep frying

Combine marinade ingredients in medium bowl. Add ground meat; mix well. Let stand for 10 minutes. Place cabbage and carrots in 3 cups boiling water in a medium saucepan. Boil 2 minutes. Drain and cover with cold water. Let cool. Drain and squeeze vegetables to remove excess water. Heat vegetable oil in a wok over medium heat for 30 seconds. Add marinated meat. Stir-fry for 2 minutes or until meat is no longer pink. Remove meat with slotted spoon and set aside. Combine vegetable mixture and bamboo shoots in wok. Stir-fry until soft, about 5 minutes. Add salt, sugar, pepper, soy sauce, cornstarch and cooked meat to vegetables; mix well. Remove from heat. Add sesame oil; mix well. Place one egg roll skin on a flat surface with corners at top, bottom, left and right. Combine flour and water in a small cup. Place 1/2 cup of filling just below the center of egg roll skin. Fold bottom corner over filling. Roll once and fold left and right corners over filling. Continue rolling toward top corner. Dab a little flour and water mixture under the top corner. Press firmly to seal. Repeat with remaining egg roll skins and filling. Heat oil in a clean wok over high heat to 350 degrees. Reduce heat to medium. Carefully lower several egg rolls into hot oil with a slotted metal spoon. Deep-fry several at a time for 2 minutes. Turn each egg roll and deep-fry other side for 2 minutes. Egg roll skins should be golden brown. Remove with slotted spoon, draining well over wok. Repeat with remaining egg rolls. Serve hot.

Joan Troyer

GINGER CHICKEN

5-lb. bag chicken wings
1 c. sugar
1 c. soy sauce

1 tsp. garlic powder
1 tsp. ginger
1/2 tsp. red pepper

Spread wings on baking sheet. Bake at 350 degrees for 45-60 minutes (if frozen). In a 5-quart saucepan, combine remaining ingredients. Cook over low heat until sugar is dissolved. Put cooked chicken in sauce, stirring occasionally, until sauce is thick and chicken is coated. Serve hot or cold.

Sherry Kehr

HAM STACK APPETIZER

8-oz. shaved ham   1 tsp. horseradish (opt.)
3-oz. pkg. cream cheese   1 pkg. flour tortillas
1 T. mayonnaise

Mix cream cheese, mayonnaise and horseradish. Spread on tortillas. Put ham on top. Roll tortilla. Refrigerate for at least 1 hour before slicing into bite size pieces for serving. *Chopped black olives are optional.*

Rita Rupp

PARMESAN BREAD

1 loaf French bread   3 T. Miracle Whip
1/2 c. Parmesan cheese   2 tsp. basil
6 T. plain non-fat yogurt   1/2 tsp. garlic powder

Slice bread in half lengthwise. Stir together remaining ingredients. Spread on cut-sides of bread and place on baking sheet. Bake at 450 degrees for 7-10 minutes or until golden brown and bubbly. *I serve this with spaghetti as a side dish.* Makes 12 servings.

Merianne Shaffer

SNACK OYSTER CRACKERS

1-lb. oyster crackers   1 1/4 tsp. dill weed
1 c. oil   1 tsp. lemon pepper seasoning
1 pkg. Ranch-style dressing mix

Place crackers in a large bowl; set aside. Combine oil, dressing mix, dill weed and lemon pepper. Pour over crackers; mix thoroughly. Spread on cookie sheet. Bake at 250 degrees for 1 hour, stirring 3 times. Store in airtight container. Delicious as a snack or great with soups.

Marilyn Miller (Willie)

BACON-STUFFED MUSHROOMS

1-lb. fresh mushrooms   1 c. Colby cheese, shredded
2 T. onion, chopped   2-3 ozs. crumbled bacon or
2 T. butter   bacon bits
1 slice bread, torn into
   small pieces

Remove stems from mushrooms; set aside caps and chop stems. Cook onion and chopped stems in butter until tender; add bread. Remove from heat; stir in bacon and cheese. Mound filling in caps and place in shallow pan. Bake at 400 degrees for 15 minutes. Serve hot.

Rita Rupp

Begin each morning with a talk with God.

13

STUFFED MUSHROOMS

2 T. margarine
2 T. onions
1/2 c. fine bread crumbs
1 tsp. parsley flakes
1/4 tsp. oregano

Dash of garlic salt
1/4 tsp. salt
2 T. Parmesan cheese
1/4 c. sour cream or yogurt
1 pkg. fresh mushrooms

Saute margarine and onions. Mix remaining ingredients with onion mixture. Cut out stems of mushrooms and stuff with mixture. Bake at 375 degrees for 20 minutes.

Barb Croyle

TORTILLA PINWHEELS

5 10-in. flour tortillas
Salsa
Filling:
8-oz. cream cheese, softened
4-oz. diced green chilies, drained

4-oz. chopped black olives, drained
1 c. Cheddar cheese, grated
1/2 c. onion, chopped
Garlic powder (to taste)
Seasoned salt (to taste)

Mix all filling ingredients together. Divide and spread filling among the 5 tortilla shells. Roll up and cover with plastic wrap. Refrigerate several hours or overnight. Unwrap and cut into 1/2-3/4 inch thick slices. Lay pinwheels flat on glass serving plate. Serve with salsa. *If you are diet or cholesterol conscience, light cheeses may be used.*

Carolyn Yoder

Marilyn Miller (Willie) adds 8-ounces sour cream to the filling. Her recipe yields 50 pinwheels.

Beverages

CAPPUCCINO MIX

1 c. instant coffee creamer
1 c. instant hot chocolate mix
2/3 c. instant coffee crystals

1/2 c. sugar
1/2 tsp. cinnamon
1/4 tsp. nutmeg

Combine all ingredients; mix well. Store in an airtight container. To prepare 1 serving, add 3 tablespoons mix to 6-ounces hot water; stir well. Makes 3 cups of dry mix.

Patty Bontrager

FIRESIDE COFFEE

2 c. Nestle's Quick
16-oz. coffee creamer
1 c. instant coffee

1 1/2 c. powdered sugar
1 1/2 tsp. cinnamon
1 tsp. nutmeg

Mix all ingredients and store in airtight container. Use 2 or more heaping teaspoons per cup of hot water.

Mary Martin

HOT APPLE-CINNAMON STICK CIDER

1 gal. cider	1 tsp. cinnamon
1/2 c. dark brown sugar	

Bring ingredients to a boil; simmer for 10 minutes. Put a whole cinnamon stick in each cup for a swizzle stick when serving. Serve when hot.

Marilyn (G. Keith) Miller

CHRISTMAS PUNCH

1 3-oz. pkg. cherry or strawberry jello	3 c. cold water
1 c. boiling water	1-qt. cranberry juice
1 16-oz. can frozen lemonade concentrate	1 28-oz. bottle ginger ale or 7-UP

Dissolve jello in 1 cup boiling water. Stir in lemonade. Add cold water and cranberry juice. Chill. When ready to serve, pour over ice cubes or an ice ring mold in a large punch bowl. Slowly pour in ginger ale or 7-UP. Fruit flavored sherbet may be added.

Joy VanDiepenbos

FROZEN PUNCH

4 c. sugar	1 sm. can orange juice
6-qts. water	1 lg. can pineapple juice
1 sm. can frozen lemonade	5 ripe bananas

Bring sugar and water to a boil; simmer 5 minutes. Cool. Puree bananas in blender. Add bananas and fruit juices to sugar water. Stir together well. Place in freezer. Thaw before serving.

Ruby Panyako

SLUSH PUNCH

2 1/2 c. sugar	4 T. real lemon juice
4 c. water	1 46-oz. can pineapple juice
3-5 ripe bananas, blended in blender	2 c. water
2 sm. cans frozen orange juice	7-UP

Heat sugar and 4 cups water until dissolved; cool. Blend bananas in blender. Mix orange juice according to directions on can. Add lemon juice, pineapple juice and 2 cups water. Mix all ingredients thoroughly and freeze. Blend with 7-UP right before serving.

Barb Croyle

The happiest times we ever spend
are those we share with a special friend.

RASPBERRY MINT CRUSH

1/2 c. fresh mint leaves, slightly packed
1 c. boiling water
1-pt. fresh raspberries, crushed and sweetened with 1/2 c. sugar (or 1 10-oz. pkg. frozen raspberries)

1 (6-oz.) can frozen lemonade
2 c. cold water

Combine mint leaves and boiling water; let stand for 5 minutes. Add crushed berries and frozen lemonade. Stir until dissolved. Strain into pitcher half filled with crushed ice. Add cold water. Stir and garnish with fresh mint leaves. Makes 8 servings.

Rosalind Slabaugh

FRIENDSHIP TEA MIX

1 18-oz. jar orange flavor Tang
1 c. sugar
1/2 c. presweetened lemon aid mix

1/2 c. instant tea
1 3-oz. box apricot jello
2 1/2 tsp. ground cinnamon
1 tsp. ground cloves

Combine ingredients in a large bowl, stirring well. Store in airtight container. To serve, place 1 1/2 tablespoons mix in a cup. Add 1 cup boiling water. Stir well. Serves 50.

Ruth Metzler

RUSSIAN TEA MIX

2 c. Tang
1 pkg. unsweetened lemonade Kool-Aid
1/2 c. sugar

1/2 c. instant tea
1 tsp. cinnamon
1/2 tsp. ground cloves
1/2 tsp. nutmeg

Mix well. Use 2 heaping teaspoons per cup of boiling water.

Mafra Maust

SOMALI TEA

4 c. water
1/4 tsp. ground cardamom
1/4 tsp. ground cinnamon

1/4 tsp. ground cloves
1/3-1/2 c. sugar
2 tea bags

Bring water to boil. Add spices and bring to boil. Add sugar and boil again. Remove from heat. Add tea bags and steep 3 minutes. Milk may be added if desired.

Verda Weaver

The family that prays together, stays together.

Quick Breads, Yeast Breads, & Rolls

QUICK BREADS, YEAST BREADS & ROLLS

Quick Breads

SPICED APPLESAUCE RAISIN BREAD

3/4 c. Fiber One cereal	3 tsp. baking powder
1 1/3 c. flour	3/4 tsp. ground cinnamon
1/2 c. sugar	1/2 tsp. ground allspice
1/2 c. brown sugar, packed	1/2 tsp. salt
1 c. applesauce	1/4 tsp. ground cloves
1/2 c. skim milk	1 egg or 2 egg whites
1/4 c. vegetable oil	1/2 c. raisins

Heat oven to 350 degrees. Grease bottom only of 9 x 5 x 3-inch loaf pan. Crush cereal. Mix all ingredients, except raisins, in large bowl. Beat 30 seconds. Stir in raisins. Pour into pan. Bake for 55-65 minutes or until toothpick inserted in center comes out clean. Cool 10 minutes. Remove from pan. Cool completely before slicing.

Ruth Metzler

BANANA-MOLASSES BREAD

3 ripe bananas	1 3/4 c. flour (may be part wheat
1 egg	flour)
1/3 c. sugar	1/3 c. oats
3 T. molasses	1 tsp. baking powder
2 T. margarine	1 tsp. baking soda
	1/4 tsp. salt

Mash bananas until smooth. Add egg; mix well. Beat in sugar, molasses and margarine. Add dry ingredients. Place into greased 9 x 5-inch loaf pan. Bake at 350 degrees for 50-60 minutes. Cool on rack.

Chris & Lois Leuz-Taiwan

BANNOCK
(The Bread of the North)

1 c. flour	1/4 tsp. salt
1 tsp. baking powder	Cold water or milk

Mix dry ingredients thoroughly before you add the liquid. Stir in enough cold water or milk to make a firm dough. Bake at 375 degrees. *There are many variations to the basic recipe. You can add sugar (1 tablespoon to 1 cup flour), eggs, fruits, raisins, or use your imagination. This recipe is something we learned to enjoy while living in Northern Alberta.*

Carl & Lois Ramer-Canada

CARROT-PINEAPPLE BREAD

3/4 c. oil
1 c. sugar
1 egg
1/2 c. crushed pineapple,
   drained
1 c. carrots, grated

1 1/2 tsp. vanilla
1 1/2 c. flour
1/2 tsp. salt
1/2 tsp. soda
1 tsp. cinnamon
1/2 c. nuts, chopped

Combine oil, sugar and egg; beat well. Add remaining ingredients and mix well. Place in greased bread pans. Bake at 325 degrees for 1 hour and 10 minutes. If you use 3 smaller pans, bake for less time. Test with toothpick in center. If it comes out clean, it is done.

Pat Stahly

BEST CORN BREAD

1/2 c. shortening
1 c. sugar
2 eggs
1 scant tsp. salt

1 1/2 c. flour
1 c. cornmeal
2 tsp. baking powder
1 c. milk

Cream shortening, sugar and eggs. Sift together flour, cornmeal, salt and baking powder. Add alternately with milk to first mixture starting and ending with flour. Bake in a 9 x 13-inch pan at 350 degrees for 30 minutes or until it tests done. Very tender and good.

Rheta Mae Wiebe

CORN BREAD

1 c. cornmeal
1 c. flour
1/4 c. sugar
4 tsp. baking powder

1/2 tsp. salt
1 egg
1 c. milk
1/4 c. shortening (margarine)

Melt margarine in a 9 x 12-inch pan. Add to remaining ingredients. Bake at 425 degrees for 20-25 minutes.

Marilyn (G. Keith) Miller

GEORGIA CORN BREAD

1 1/4 c. all-purpose flour
3/4 c. cornmeal
1/3 c. sugar
1/3 c. pecans, coarsely
   chopped

2 tsp. baking powder
1/2 tsp. salt
1 c. buttermilk
1/4 c. oil
1 egg, slightly beaten

Preheat oven to 450 degrees. Grease bottom and sides of a loaf pan; set aside. Combine dry ingredients in a large mixing bowl. In a separate bowl, combine buttermilk, oil and egg. Add to dry ingredients. Stir just until dry ingredients are moist. Bake for 25 minutes or until golden brown and toothpick inserted in center comes out clean. Run knife around outside to loosen. Serve warm.

Ruby Panyako

SOUPER CORN BREAD

1 can Campbell's New Golden
  Corn Soup
2 eggs
1/4 c. milk

1 12-14 oz. pkg. corn muffin mix
1/4-lb. bulk pork sausage,
  cooked and drained

Preheat oven to 400 degrees. Combine soup, eggs and milk. Stir in muffin mix until blended. Gently fold in sausage. Place mixture into a greased 9-inch square baking pan. Bake for 20 minutes or until lightly browned and toothpick inserted in center comes out clean. Makes 6 servings.

Ruth Metzler

CRANBERRY OATMEAL BREAD

2 c. flour
1 1/2 c. sugar
2 tsp. baking powder
1/2 tsp. soda
1 tsp. salt
1 c. raw cranberries, halved
1/2 c. walnuts

1/2 c. oatmeal
3 T. grated orange peel
1 egg, slightly beaten
1/2 c. orange juice
1/2 c. warm water
1 tsp. vanilla

Mix and sift together flour, sugar, baking powder, soda and salt. Stir in cranberries, walnuts, oatmeal and orange peel. Combine egg, orange juice, water and vanilla. Add to flour mixture, stirring just enough to moisten. Spoon into greased bread loaf pan or 3 mini loaf pans. Bake at 350 degrees until done, 45-60 minutes.

Mary Martin

GLAZED LEMON BREAD

1/3 c. butter, melted
1 c. sugar
2 eggs
1/4 tsp. almond extract
1 1/2 c. flour
1 tsp. baking powder

1/2 c. milk
1 T. grated lemon peel
1/2 c. nuts, chopped
3 T. fresh lemon juice
1/4 c. sugar

Blend butter and 1 cup sugar well; beat in eggs, 1 at a time. Add almond extract. Sift together dry ingredients; add to egg mixture alternately with milk. Blend just to mix. Fold in peel and nuts. Turn into greased 8 1/2 x 4 1/2 x 2 3/4-inch glass* loaf pan. Bake at 325 degrees for about 70 minutes or until loaf tests done in center. Mix lemon juice and 1/4 cup sugar; immediately spoon over hot loaf. Cool 10 minutes. Remove from pan; cool on rack. Do not cut for 24 hours. *If using a metal loaf pan, bake at 350 degrees. *Gary really likes this recipe-it tastes similar to pound cake.*

Merianne Shaffer

LEMON BREAD

4 eggs, beaten
1 pkg. lemon cake mix
1 pkg. instant lemon pudding
mix
1 c. water
1/2 c. oil
1/4 c. poppy seed

Mix first 5 ingredients together on medium speed for 4 minutes. Add poppy seeds after 3 minutes. Grease 2 bread pans or 1 bundt pan. Bake at 350 degrees for 45 minutes.

Shirleen Weaver

POPPY SEED BREAD

1 1/2 tsp. baking powder
3 c. flour
1 1/2 tsp. salt
1 1/2 c. milk
2 1/4 c. sugar
3 eggs
1 1/8 c. oil
1 1/2 T. poppy seeds
1 1/2 tsp. almond extract
1 1/2 tsp. butter flavoring
Glaze:
1/2 tsp. butter flavoring
1/2 tsp. almond extract
3/4 c. sugar
1/2 tsp. vanilla
1/4 c. orange juice

Combine bread ingredients in mixing bowl. Beat with mixer for 2 minutes on High. Pour into 2 greased loaf pans. Bake at 350 degrees for 45 minutes to 1 hour or until toothpick comes out clean. Let cool slightly in pan. Combine glaze ingredients in saucepan; heat until sugar dissolves. Pour glaze over warm loaves. Let cool completely before removing from pan. Can be frozen.

Jill Erb

SWEET POTATO NUT BREAD

1/2 c. butter
1/2 c. shortening
2 2/3 c. sugar
4 eggs
2 c. cold sweet potatoes,
mashed
3 1/2 c. flour
1 tsp. salt
1 1/2 tsp. nutmeg
1 tsp. cinnamon
2 tsp. soda
1 c. nuts
2/3 c. cold coffee

Cream first 3 ingredients; add eggs and sweet potatoes and beat well. Add sifted dry ingredients; mix well. Add nuts and coffee. Bake at 350 degrees for 40-50 minutes or until done.

Orange Butter:
1/4 c. butter
1 c. powdered sugar
1 T. orange juice

Beat ingredients until fluffy.

Beverly Coblentz

ZUCCHINI BREAD

3 eggs
1 c. vegetable oil
2 c. sugar
2 tsp. vanilla
2 c. zucchini, shredded
3 c. flour

1 tsp. baking powder
2 tsp. soda
2 tsp. cinnamon
1 tsp. nutmeg
1 tsp. salt

Beat eggs, oil, sugar and vanilla until thick. Stir in remaining ingredients; mix well. Pour into 2 greased 9 x 5-inch loaf pans. Bake at 350 degrees for 1 hour and 5 minutes or until toothpick comes out clean.

Sandy Owen

ZUCCHINI OATMEAL BREAD

3 eggs
1 c. cooking oil
1 c. sugar
2 c. zucchini, grated
1 c. quick cooking oatmeal
1 tsp. vanilla
2 c. flour

1 tsp. salt
1 tsp. baking soda
1/4 tsp. baking powder
3 tsp. cinnamon
1/2 c. raisins
1/2 c. nuts, chopped

Beat eggs until light and foamy. Add oil, sugar, zucchini, oats and vanilla. Mix slightly, but well. Sift together flour, salt, baking soda, baking powder and cinnamon. Add to batter and mix well. Fold in nuts and raisins. Spoon into greased and floured pans. Bake at 325 degrees for 1 hour.

Linda Hartman

BLUEBERRY BUCKLE

3/4 c. sugar
1/4 c. shortening
2 eggs
1/2 c. milk
1 1/2 c. flour
1/4 tsp. salt
2 tsp. baking powder

1/4 tsp. nutmeg
1-pt. blueberries
1/2 c. sugar
1/3 c. flour
1/2 tsp. cinnamon
1/4 c. margarine

Mix sugar, shortening, eggs and milk until blended. Stir in flour, baking powder, salt and nutmeg. Fold in blueberries. Spread batter into greased 9-inch square pan. Combine remaining ingredients. Sprinkle crumbs over batter. Bake at 375 degrees for 45-50 minutes.

Rita Rupp

Dear Lord, I know that I will make
mistakes most every day.
Keep me from making serious ones
for which someone must pay.

BLUEBERRY COFFEE CAKE

1 egg, well beaten
2/3 c. sugar
1/2 c. oil
1/2 tsp. vanilla
1 1/2 c. flour
2 tsp. baking powder
1/2 tsp. salt
1/2 c. milk

1 1/2 c. blueberries (fresh or
frozen), drained
Topping:
1/2 c. brown sugar
1/3 c. flour
1/2 tsp. cinnamon
1/4 c. margarine, melted
1/2 c. nuts, chopped

Beat together egg, sugar, oil and vanilla until fluffy. Sift dry ingredients together and add alternately with milk. Fold in blueberries. Pour into a greased 9-inch square pan. Combine brown sugar, flour, cinnamon, margarine and nuts. Sprinkle over top. Bake at 350 degrees for 25-30 minutes. Serve warm.

Gloria Landes

BREAKFAST BUNDT CAKE

1 yellow cake mix
1 3-oz. pkg. instant vanilla
pudding mix
3/4 c. oil
4 eggs
1 tsp. vanilla
3/4 c. water

1/2 c. nuts, chopped
1/4 c. sugar
2 tsp. cinnamon
Glaze:
2 c. powdered sugar
1/4 c. milk

Combine cake mix, pudding, oil and water. Add eggs, 1 at a time, blending well after each addition. Beat at High speed for 8 minutes; add vanilla. Combine nuts, sugar and cinnamon; put 1/2 in bottom of greased and floured bundt pan. Add 1/2 of batter, then remaining crumbs. Finish with remaining batter. Bake at 400 degrees for 30 minutes or until done. Turn upside down on plate while cooling. Cream together glaze ingredients; drizzle over warm cake.

Ruby Panyako

CHRISTMAS COFFEE CAKE

3 c. flour
2 c. sugar
3/4 c. shortening
1/2 tsp. salt
1/2 tsp. cloves
1/2 tsp. cinnamon

1/2 tsp. nutmeg
2 tsp. soda
2 c. buttermilk
1/2 c. raisins
1/2 c. nuts

Mix flour, sugar, shortening, salt, cloves, cinnamon and nutmeg. Reserve 3/4 cup mixture for top. Add soda, buttermilk, raisins and nuts to the remaining mixture. Pour into greased and floured 9 x 13-inch pan. Sprinkle top with reserved mix. Bake at 350 degrees for about 45 minutes. *We have this Christmas morning. We put a candle in it and sing Happy Birthday to Jesus.*

John Cunningham Family

COFFEE CAKE

2 1/2 c. flour
1 c. brown sugar
3/4 c. sugar
1 tsp. cinnamon
1/2 tsp. salt
3/4 c. oil
1 tsp. soda
1 egg
1 tsp. baking powder
1 c. buttermilk
1/3 c. nuts, chopped

Combine flour, sugars, cinnamon, salt and oil. Mix to crumb consistency. Save 1/3 for topping. Mix soda and baking powder with remaining crumbs. Beat egg and buttermilk. Add 1/2 liquid with crumbs and beat for 2 minutes. Add remaining liquid and beat 2 minutes more. Spread into a 9 x 13-inch pan. Add chopped nuts to reserved crumb mixture; sprinkle on top. Bake at 350 degrees for 30 minutes. *This was Bob's favorite coffee cake. I often baked it for our Sunday morning breakfast.*

Marge Detweiler

ORANGE COFFEE CAKE

2 c. flour, sifted
2 tsp. baking powder
1/4 tsp. soda
1 tsp. salt
1 egg
1/2 c. sugar
1/2 c. margarine, melted
2/3 c. orange juice
2 T. margarine, melted
1 T. flour
4 T. brown sugar
1/2 tsp. cinnamon

Mix first 8 ingredients for 1 minute. Spread batter into greased 9 x 9-inch pan. Pour 2 tablespoons melted margarine on top. Combine flour, brown sugar and cinnamon; sprinkle over top. Bake at 350 degrees for 30 minutes. *I often frost with powdered sugar frosting using orange juice for the liquid.* Serve warm.

Ruth Zehr

OVERNIGHT COFFEE CAKE

3/4 c. butter, softened
1 c. sugar
2 eggs
1 8-oz. pkg. cream cheese
2 c. flour
1 tsp. baking powder
1 tsp. soda
1/2 tsp. salt
1 tsp. cinnamon or nutmeg
Topping:
3/4 c. brown sugar, firmly packed
1/2 c. walnuts, chopped
1 tsp. cinnamon

Cream butter and sugar until light and fluffy. Add eggs and cream cheese; mix well. Combine dry ingredients and add to batter. Pour into a 9 x 13-inch pan. Combine topping ingredients and mix well. Sprinkle evenly over batter. Cover and chill overnight. Uncover and bake at 350 degrees for 35-40 minutes. Put cold cake in cold oven, turn on heat and time from when the oven reaches 350 degrees.

Sherry Kehr

PECAN COFFEE RING

3/4 c. light brown sugar, packed
2 T. grated orange peel
1 c. pecans, chopped
2 8-oz. pkgs. refrigerated
  biscuits, separated

1/3 c. butter or margarine,
  melted
2 T. orange juice
1 c. powdered sugar

Mix brown sugar, orange peel and nuts in a shallow dish. Dip biscuits in butter, then roll in sugar mixture. Arrange biscuits, slightly overlapped into greased 6 cup mold or ring mold. Bake in preheated 350 degree oven for 30 minutes or until light brown. Invert onto serving dish and remove mold. Beat orange juice into powdered sugar until smooth. Drizzle over hot biscuit ring. Serve warm. Can be made the night before and baked in the morning.

Nina Weaver

CORNMEAL MUFFINS

1 c. flour
1 tsp. baking powder
3/4 tsp. salt
1/2 tsp. baking soda
1/2 c. cornmeal

1/2 c. oatmeal
1 c. buttermilk
1 egg
1/3 c. brown sugar
1/2 c. butter, melted

Mix flour, baking soda, baking powder and salt; set aside. Stir together cornmeal, oatmeal and buttermilk. Add egg, sugar and butter; blend well. Add flour mixture. Bake in greased muffin tins at 400 degrees for 20-25 minutes.

Mafra Maust

FEATHER-LIGHT MUFFINS

1/3 c. shortening
1/2 c. sugar
1 egg
1 1/2 c. cake flour
1 1/2 tsp. baking powder
1/2 tsp. salt

1/4 tsp. nutmeg
1/2 c. milk
Topping:
1/2 c. sugar
1 tsp. cinnamon
1/2 c. margarine, melted

In mixing bowl, cream shortening, sugar and egg. Combine dry ingredients; add to creamed mixture alternately with milk. Fill greased muffin tins 2/3 full. Bake at 325 degrees for 20-25 minutes or until golden. Let cool for 3-4 minutes. Meanwhile, combine 1/2 cup sugar and cinnamon in small bowl. Roll warm muffins in melted margarine, then in sugar mixture. Serve warm. Yields 8-10 muffins.

Karen Leinbach

No problem is too big for God's power;
no person is too small for God's love.

OAT BRAN MUFFINS

2 1/4 c. oat bran cereal
1/4 c. nuts, chopped
1/4 c. raisins or dates
1 T. baking powder
1/4 c. brown sugar

1/4 c. honey or molasses
1 1/4 c. skim milk
2 egg whites
2 T. vegetable oil

Preheat oven to 425 degrees. In a large bowl, combine oat bran cereal, nuts, raisins and baking powder. Stir in brown sugar. Mix milk, egg whites and oil together; blend in with oat bran mixture. Line muffin tin with paper baking cups and fill 2/3 full with batter. Bake 15-17 minutes. Test for doneness with toothpick. It should come out moist, but not wet. Makes 12 muffins.

Ruth Metzler

PEACHY BRAN MUFFINS

1 1/2 c. peach yogurt
2 c. whole bran cereal
1/2 c. raisins
1/3 c. carrots, shredded
1 T. brown sugar
1/4 c. oil

2 egg whites
1 c. flour
1 tsp. baking soda
1 tsp. baking powder
1/2 tsp. cinnamon

Combine yogurt and cereal; mix lightly. Add raisins, carrots, sugar, oil and egg whites; mix well. Combine dry ingredients and add to cereal mixture; stir just until moistened. Spoon into paper-lined muffin cups, filling each almost full. Bake at 400 degrees for 18-20 minutes or until golden brown. Makes 1 dozen.

Phyllis Garber

GRAHAM GEMS

1 c. graham flour
1 c. flour
1 tsp. soda
1/4 c. brown sugar
1/4 tsp. salt

1 egg, beaten
1 c. buttermilk
3 T. margarine, melted
1/2 c. raisins

Mix ingredients; beat only until blended. Put in gem cups and bake.

A kind word is never lost.
It keeps going on and on,
from one person to another,
until at last is comes back
to you again.

PUMPKIN MUFFINS

1 1/2 c. flour
1/2 c. sugar
2 tsp. baking powder
1 tsp. cinnamon
1/2 tsp. ginger

1/2 c. raisins
1 egg, slightly beaten
1/2 c. milk
1/2 c. canned pumpkin
1/4 c. vegetable oil

Combine first 5 ingredients. In separate bowl, combine egg, milk, pumpkin and oil. Add egg mixture to flour. Stir until ingredients are slightly wet. Batter will be lumpy. Grease muffin pan and fill 2/3 full. Bake at 400 degrees for 25 minutes. Makes 1 dozen. *Tip: I use bake cup inserts in muffin pans. Also, sometimes I use mini muffin pans.*

Ruth Metzler

RHUBARB MUFFINS

1 1/4 c. brown sugar
1/2 c. oil
1 egg
2 tsp. vanilla
2 1/2 c. flour
1 tsp. soda
1 tsp. salt
1 tsp. baking powder

1 c. sour milk or buttermilk
1 1/2 c. rhubarb, finely chopped
1/2 c. nuts, chopped (opt.)
Topping:
1 T. butter or margarine, melted
1 tsp. cinnamon
1/2 c. sugar

Mix muffin ingredients well; put into greased muffin tins. Mix topping ingredients; sprinkle on muffins. Bake at 350 degrees for 20-25 minutes. Makes 18-24 muffins.

Lou Thomas

BAKED FRENCH TOAST

6 eggs, beaten
1 1/2 c. milk
1/4 tsp. cinnamon
1 c. coffee cream or half & half
1 tsp. vanilla
1 loaf French bread

Topping:
1/4 c. margarine, softened
1/2 c. brown sugar
1/2 c. pecan pieces
1 T. light Karo syrup

Spray a 9 x 13-inch pan with Pam. Tear French bread into small pieces in pan. Combine eggs, milk, coffee cream, vanilla and cinnamon. Pour over bread and push bread down to cover all pieces. Combine brown sugar, pecans and syrup. Spread evenly over bread mixture. Chill overnight. Preheat oven to 350 degrees. Bake for 40 minutes or until golden brown. Bread will rise while baking. Serve with butter and syrup.

Esther Hostetler

No door is too difficult for the key of love to open.

BLUEBERRY BRAN PANCAKES

1 c. Fiber One Cereal
1 egg or 2 egg whites, beaten
1 1/4 c. buttermilk or skim milk
2 T. vegetable oil
1 c. all-purpose flour
1 T. sugar
1 tsp. baking powder
1/2 tsp. baking soda
1/2 tsp. salt
1/2 c. fresh or frozen (thawed)
   blueberries, well drained

Crush cereal. Mix egg, buttermilk, oil and cereal. Let stand 7 minutes. Stir in remaining ingredients, except blueberries. Beat with wire whisk or fork until smooth. Fold in blueberries. Pour batter by 1/4 cupfuls onto hot griddle. Batter will be thick. If batter is too thick, stir in additional milk, 1 tablespoon at a time until desired consistency. Cook pancakes until puffed and full of bubbles. Turn and cook other side until golden brown. Makes 10 5-inch cakes.

Ruth Metzler

LAVERNE'S PANCAKES

1 tsp. sugar
1 tsp. salt
1 T. shortening (oil)
2 eggs
2 c. milk
2 c. flour
3 tsp. baking powder

Mix dry ingredients together. Add milk, beating to make a smooth batter. Add eggs and oil. Fry on a hot griddle.

LaVerne Coblentz

OATMEAL PANCAKES

1 c. quick cooking oatmeal
1 c. all-purpose flour
2 T. sugar
2 tsp. baking powder
1 tsp. salt
2 eggs, lightly beaten
1 1/2 c. milk
1/4 c. vegetable oil
1 tsp. lemon juice

Combine oatmeal, flour, sugar, baking powder and salt in a mixing bowl. Make a well in the center. Combine egg, milk, oil and lemon juice; pour into well and stir just until moistened. Pour batter by 1/4 cupfuls onto a lightly greased hot griddle; turn when bubbles form on top of pancakes. Cook until second side is golden brown. Serve with maple syrup or applesauce. Yield: 6 servings.

Shirley Albrecht

*Forgive me, Father, for the times
I am anxious. You have promised
to take care of all my needs.*

MANDARIN PANCAKES

1 1/2 c. flour
1/2 tsp. sesame oil
1/4 tsp. salt

3/4 c. boiling water
1 T. sesame oil (approx.)

Place flour, 1/2 teaspoon sesame oil and salt in a medium bowl. Add boiling water. Gradually mix flour and water with a wooden spoon to make a soft dough. On a lightly floured surface, gently knead dough until smooth. Cover with a damp cloth and let rest 15 minutes. Use your hands to shape dough into a long roll about 1-inch in diameter. Add more flour if necessary. Place the point of a sharp cleaver on cutting surface with middle of roll under cutting edge. Chop with a quick downward motion, cutting roll in half. Chop each half into 8 pieces. Roll each into a ball, then pat flat to make a circle. Brush top of 8 circles with sesame oil. Place an unoiled circle on top of each oiled circle. Use a rolling pin to flatten each pair of circles into one 5-inch circle. Roll both sides, changing directions frequently so flat pancake remains a circle. Cover pancakes with a dry towel. Heat an ungreased 8-inch skillet over high heat for 30 seconds to 1 minute. Reduce heat to medium. Place 1 pancake in skillet. When pancake puffs and bubbles appear on surface, turn and cook other side. Cook about 1 minute on one side until pancake is speckled with brown. Turn pancake and cook about 30 seconds until underside is speckled with brown. Remove from skillet, wrap in a clean, dry towel and place in a bread basket. Just before serving, separate each pancake into 2 pancakes, gently pulling apart from edges. Serve warm. Makes 16 pancakes. Serve with MuShu Chicken or Pork.

Joan Troyer

Yeast Breads and Rolls

BAGELS

1 c. water
3 T. sugar
1 pkg. yeast
1 1/2 c. bleached flour

1 1/2 c. whole wheat flour
1 tsp. salt
2 T. olive oil
1 T. cinnamon (opt.)

Dissolve yeast in water with sugar. Add to flour and salt; mix well. Cover and let rise 40 minutes; punch down. Form into bagels. Add olive oil to a large pan of boiling water. Drop bagel into water; lift out when bagel starts to float. Bake on greased cookie sheet at 350 degrees for 10 minutes, then at 400 degrees for 10 minutes.

Sherry Kehr

Love can come from surprising places.

28

AVANTI'S BREAD

2 pkgs. dry yeast
3 c. warm water
3 T. oil
3 eggs

1 T. salt
1 1/4 c. sugar
10-11 c. flour

Dissolve yeast in water. Add remaining ingredients; knead for 10 minutes or until smooth and elastic. Place in greased bowl turning once to bring greased side up. Cover with cloth and let rise in warm, draft-free spot until double (1 1/2-2 hours). After first rising, punch down and turn over; let rise until almost double (30-45 minutes). Cut dough into 9-12 portions. Let rest covered for 10 minutes. Flatten dough, pressing out all the air. Form into loaves (hold the dough by the ends and pull, shaping on the table to elongate and roll between hands). Place on greased and floured sheet. Cover and let rise for 50-60 minutes. Sprinkle flour on top. Bake at 350 degrees for 17-20 minutes.

Lisa Heinz

WHOLE WHEAT BREAD

6 c. scalded milk, cooled
1 c. honey
3 T. yeast
4 c. rolled oats
4 c. whole wheat flour

2 eggs
2 T. salt
1/2 c. Canola oil
Additional whole wheat flour

Add yeast to cooled milk; let soften. Add honey, rolled oats, whole wheat flour, oil, eggs and salt; stir well. Add more whole wheat flour, 1 cup at a time, until dough is stiff. Knead well and place in greased large bowl. Let rise until double. Punch down and let rise again. Form into 4 loaves and place in 4 greased loaf pans. Let rise. Bake at 350 degrees for 50-55 minutes. Remove from pans and let cool on wire racks.

Gretchen Weaver

CINNAMON ROLLS WITH CAKE MIX

1 box yellow cake mix with
   pudding
2 T. yeast
5 c. flour

1 tsp. salt
2 1/2 c. warm water
Butter, melted
Sugar and cinnamon

Place water in large mixer bowl. Mix yeast with cake mix and add to water. Add flour and salt; mix well. Let stand until double, about 1 hour. Punch down and roll out 1/2 of dough. Spread with melted butter and sprinkle with sugar and cinnamon. roll up and slice 1-inch thick. Place on greased cookie sheet. Repeat with remaining dough. Let stand until double, 1-2 hours. Bake at 350 degrees for 15 minutes. Do not overbake. Frost.

Phyllis Garber

WHOLE WHEAT HONEY BREAD

2 T. yeast (2 pkgs.)	1/4 c. honey
1 1/4 c. lukewarm water	1 T. salt
1 c. milk	3 1/2 c. flour
3 T. butter	3 1/2 c. whole wheat flour

Soften yeast in lukewarm water with a squirt of honey added. Scald milk; add honey, butter and salt. Cool to lukewarm; combine with yeast mixture when cooled. Mix flours together and reserve 1 cup. Add remaining flour to yeast mixture. Turn out onto floured board and knead 5 minutes. Use remaining cup of flour as needed (sparingly). Knead as sticky as possible. Cover and let rest 5 minutes. Knead again for 4 minutes. Put into greased bowl, grease bread, cover and let rise until double. Punch down and divide into 2 large or 3 small loaves. Put into greased loaf pans. Use fork to remove air bubbles. Let rise. Bake at 400 degrees for 10 minutes, then reduce heat to 350 degrees for 20 minutes.

Becky Brenneman

CINNAMON ROLLS

1 pkg. dry yeast	3 1/4-3 3/4 c. flour
1/4 c. sugar	1 c. heavy cream
1 c. warm water	1 c. brown sugar, packed
2 T. butter, softened	1/2 c. sugar
1 egg	2 tsp. cinnamon
1 tsp. salt	1/2 c. butter, softened

In a large bowl, dissolve yeast and 1/2 teaspoon sugar in 1/4 cup warm water (105-115 degrees). Add remaining sugar and water, butter, egg, salt and 1 1/2 cups flour. Beat until smooth. Stir in enough remaining flour to form a soft dough. Turn onto a lightly floured surface; knead until smooth and elastic. Place in a greased bowl; turn once to grease top. Cover and let rise in a warm place until doubled, about 1 hour. Meanwhile, combine heavy cream and brown sugar; pour into a greased 13 x 9-inch baking pan. Set aside. Combine 1/2 cup sugar, cinnamon and 1/2 cup butter; set aside. Punch down dough and turn onto a lightly floured surface. Roll into a 15 x 8-inch rectangle. Spread sugar, cinnamon and butter filling over dough. Roll up from the long side; seal seam. Slice into 15 rolls, 1-inch thick. Place cut side down on top of cream and brown sugar mixture. Cover with a towel and let rise until nearly doubled, about 30-45 minutes. Bake at 375 degrees for 15-20 minutes or until browned. Cool 3 minutes. Invert pan onto a serving plate.

Lawrence Troyer

Life is fragile--handle it with prayer.

COOKIE COFFEE ROLLS

1 pkg. dry yeast	1 c. shortening
1/4 c. warm water	2 eggs, beaten
1/4 c. flour	1 c. scalded milk, cooled
1/2 tsp. lemon extract	1 T. cinnamon
1/4 c. sugar	1 c. sugar

In a large bowl, combine flour, salt, lemon extract and 1/4 cup sugar. Cut in shortening. Dissolve yeast in water. Combine eggs, milk and yeast and add to flour mixture. Mix lightly. Refrigerate several hours. Divide dough in half and roll out. Mix together sugar and cinnamon and sprinkle on dough. Roll up and cut. Bake at 400 degrees for 10 minutes.

Phyllis Weaver

CREAM CHEESE DANISH

Dough:	Cream Cheese Filling:
1/2 c. warm water	2 8-oz. pkgs. cream cheese
2 pkgs. dry yeast	3/4 c. sugar
1 tsp. sugar	1 egg
1 c. sour cream	1/8 tsp. salt
1/2 c. butter	2 tsp. vanilla
1/2 c. sugar	Glaze:
1 tsp. salt	2 c. powdered sugar
4 c. flour	4 T. milk
2 eggs	2 tsp. vanilla

Dough: Combine water, yeast and sugar; set aside. Heat sour cream on low just until barely bubbly. Add butter, sugar and salt, stirring until dissolved. Cool to lukewarm. Beat eggs; combine with yeast mixture. Add flour, mixing well. Cover and refrigerate over-night.

Cream Cheese Filling: (make the next morning) Beat together well cream cheese and sugar. Add egg, salt and vanilla; mix well. Divide dough into 4 equal portions. Roll out each portion on floured surface into a 12 x 8-inch rectangle. Spread 1/4 of cream cheese mixture into center of each rectangle. Fold dough over and pinch edges together. Place on a greased baking sheet pan. Slit each roll on top 1/2 way through dough at 2-inch intervals resembling a braid. Cover and let rise until double. Bake at 350 degrees for 12-15 minutes. Do not overbake.

Glaze: Mix together powdered sugar, milk and vanilla. Spread over loaves while still warm. Refrigerate leftover Danish.

***God meant the Bible to be bread for our daily use,
not just cake for special occasions!***

NEVER FAIL ROLLS

1/2 c. sugar
2 pkgs. yeast
2 c. flour
1/4 tsp. salt

2 c. warm water
2 eggs, beaten
1/2 c. cooking oil
4 1/2 c. flour

Mix sugar, yeast, 2 cups flour and salt. Stir in warm water. Add eggs, oil and remaining flour. Mix well and let rise 40 minutes or until double. (Mixture will be sticky. Either knead in some flour or use plenty to roll it out.) Roll and shape dough any way you desire (cinnamon rolls, dinner rolls, etc.) Let rise in pan for 40 minutes. Bake at 350 degrees for 15 minutes.

Mafra Maust

POTATO ROLLS

1 1/2 c. warm water
1 pkg. dry yeast
2/3 c. sugar
1 1/2 tsp. salt

2/3 c. shortening
2 eggs
1 c. lukewarm mashed potatoes
7-7 1/2 c. flour

Mix water and yeast. Stir in sugar, salt, shortening, eggs and potatoes. Add flour. Knead until soft and elastic. Place in a greased bowl. Cover with a damp cloth. Place in refrigerator 1 1/2-5 hours (dough will keep up to 5 days in refrigerator). Shape into sweet rolls, dinner rolls or doughnuts. Let rise until double. Bake at 400 degrees for 12-15 minutes.

Rosalind Slabaugh

STICKY BUNS

1 tube biscuits
2 1/4 T. butter

9 tsp. brown sugar
9 tsp. corn syrup

Preheat oven to 350 degrees. Grease muffin tin. Place 1/4 tablespoon butter in each cup. Top with 1 teaspoon brown sugar and 1 teaspoon corn syrup. Place biscuits on top. Bake for 10-12 minutes. Use knife to loosen biscuits; invert onto plate. Makes 9 servings. Soak muffin tin while you eat.

Jonathan Yoder

ENGLISH MUFFIN BREAD

5 c. flour + 1 c.
1 T. sugar
2 tsp. salt
1/4 tsp. baking soda

2 pkgs. Rapid Rise yeast
2 c. milk
1/2 c. water

Combine 5 cups flour and remaining dry ingredients. Heat water and milk to 105-115 degrees. Add to dry ingredients. Beat well. Add remaining cup of flour and mix in. Put in 2 loaf pans sprayed with Pam. Let rise 30-45 minutes. Bake at 400 degrees for 25-30 minutes.

Lou Thomas

SWEET ROLLS

1 c. warm water
5 T. yeast
1-qt. milk
3/4 c. sugar
4 tsp. salt
1 c. butter

8 eggs
5 c. + unbleached flour to make
   soft dough
Butter
Cinnamon and sugar

Scald milk; add sugar, salt and butter. Let cool until warm; place in large mixing bowl. Add yeast, which was softened in warm water. Add eggs and 5 cups flour; beat well. Stir enough flour into the dough to be able to knead. Knead dough until smooth and not sticky. Place in greased dishpan and let rise until double. Punch down and roll out. Brush with butter and sprinkle with cinnamon and sugar. Roll up and cut into 1/2-inch slices. Place on greased cookie sheets and let rise. Bake at 375 degrees for 15-20 minutes. Ice when cool.

Gretchen Weaver

WALNUT WALK-A-WAYS

1 pkg. dry yeast
1/2 c. warm water
2 c. flour
1/8 tsp. salt
3/4 c. butter
1 egg

Filling:
3-oz. cream cheese
1/2 c. sugar
1 tsp. orange rind
Nuts (opt.)

Soften yeast in water. Combine flour and salt; cut in butter. Add egg and yeast mixture. Mix until blended. Roll half of dough on a floured surface to 9 x 13-inches. Beat cream cheese, sugar and orange rind until fluffy. Spread half on each 9 x 13-inch dough. Start rolling on long side in jelly roll fashion. Place seam side down on greased cookie sheet. Cut each roll lengthwise half way through. Bake at 375 degrees for 20-25 minutes. Drizzle powdered sugar icing over when cool. *I add walnuts to the filling.*

Nelda Nussbaum

FLAT BREAD

1 loaf frozen bread dough
1 tsp. oil

Garlic salt or cinnamon and
   sugar

Thaw bread dough. Heat oven to 350 degrees. Put dough on cookie sheet or pizza pan. Rub oil over dough; prick all over with a fork. Sprinkle with garlic salt (or sprinkle with cinnamon and sugar). Bake to your liking, chewy or crispy (10-20 minutes). *Makes a good snack for children.*

Anabel Hartman

YEAST ROLLS OR CINNAMON ROLLS

1/2 c. mashed potatoes
3 T. fat
1/8 tsp. salt
1/2 c. sugar

1 c. scalded milk
1 egg
1 pkg. dry yeast
4 c. flour (approx.)

Scald milk to boiling point. Place potatoes, fat, salt and sugar in blender. Pour on milk and blend. Cool until lukewarm in large bowl. Add yeast and egg. Stir in about half the flour. Beat smooth and continue adding flour until dough no longer clings to bowl. Rolls will be nicer if dough is not too stiff. Knead the dough in the bowl into small ball. Grease lightly and let rise to top of bowl. Roll out in thirds and cut desired size for bread rolls and for cinnamon rolls. Roll out in to a rectangle; spread with butter, cinnamon and brown sugar. Roll up and cut into slices. Bake at 350 degrees for 15 minutes. Frost with powdered sugar frosting.

Grace Weldy

FRENCH BREAD

2 pkgs. yeast
2 1/2 c. lukewarm water
 (105-115 degrees)
1 T. salt
2 T. shortening

2 T. sugar
7 c. flour, sifted
1 egg, beaten
1 T. water
Sesame seed

Dissolve yeast in 1/2 cup lukewarm water. Add salt, shortening, sugar and 2 cups warm water; stir well. Add sifted flour. Knead well for 10-12 minutes. Let stand for 1 hour or until double in size. Punch down and let rise 1 hour. Divide dough into 2 equal parts; roll in rectangular size. Roll up from long side. Pinch ends together. Place on greased cookie sheets. Let rise 1 hour. Just before baking, make cuts with sharp knife across top. Brush with beaten egg and 1 tablespoon water. Cover with sesame seeds. Bake at 400 degrees for 20-30 minutes.

Sara Frey

ANGEL BISCUITS

1 pkg. dry yeast
3 T. warm water
5 c. flour
1/4 c. sugar

5 tsp. baking powder
1 tsp. salt
1 c. shortening
1 1/4 c. warm buttermilk

Preheat oven to 400 degrees. Mix yeast and water; set aside. Mix dry ingredients; cut in shortening until it resembles course crumbs. Mix yeast and buttermilk; stir into dry ingredients. Knead a few times. Roll 1/2-inch thick. Cut biscuits and place on greased cookie sheet. Bake 15-18 minutes.

Marlene Sutter

POTATO BREAD

1-qt. mashed potatoes (approx.)	3 T. yeast
3 c. milk, scalded	1 c. potato water, cooled to
1 stick butter	105-115 degrees
1/3 c. honey	4 eggs
3 tsp. salt	Unbleached flour

Peel and boil potatoes until tender. Drain, save water and mash potatoes. Stir in milk, butter, honey and salt. Combine yeast with cooled potato water. Combine with potatoes (make sure potatoes are not hot, but you don't want them cold either), eggs and 5 cups flour. Beat well. Add more flour until ready to knead. Knead well. Place in greased dish pan. Let rise and form into 4-6 loaves. Place in greased pans. Let rise again. Bake at 350 degrees for 40 minutes. Remove from pans and cool on wire racks. *This is Verl's favorite bread.*

Gretchen Weaver

BUTTER FLAKE ROLLS

2 pkgs. yeast	1/2 c. butter or shortening,
1/4 c. sugar	softened
1 1/2 c. buttermilk, warmed	4 1/2 c. flour
but not hot	1/2 tsp. soda
1 tsp. salt	

Dissolve yeast and sugar in warm buttermilk; let stand about 10 minutes. Add salt, butter and flour sifted with soda. Beat until smooth. Knead well, about 10 minutes. Cover with towel and let rise until double in bulk. Divide and roll very thin, about 1/4-inch thick. Cut with 2-inch biscuit cutter. Brush with melted butter. Pile up 4 or 5 circles. Place cut edges down in greased muffin pans. Let rise until very light. Bake at 400 degrees for 15-20 minutes. Makes about 2 dozen rolls.

Sara Frey

CORNMEAL BUNS

1/2 c. cornmeal	1 T. yeast
1/2 c. salt	1/4 c. warm water
2 tsp. sugar	2 eggs
1 stick butter	Unbleached flour
2 c. milk	

Cook cornmeal and milk together in saucepan until thick (like mush). Stir in salt, sugar and butter; let cool. Add yeast softened in water and eggs. Beat thoroughly. Add flour to dough until ready to knead. Knead well. Place in greased bowl; cover and let rise. Punch down. Roll out dough into 1-inch thickness. Cut in 2-3 inch circles. Place on ungreased cookie sheet; let rise. Bake at 375 degrees for 15 minutes. *I usually add some whole wheat flour.*

Gretchen Weaver

FINE BISCUITS

2 c. flour

4 tsp. baking powder

2 tsp. sugar

1/2 tsp. salt

1/2 tsp. cream of tartar

1/2 c. butter or margarine

2/3 c. milk

Stir together flour, baking powder, sugar, salt and cream of tartar. Cut in butter until particles are fine (pea size). Add milk. Mix with fork to form soft dough. Turn out onto floured surface; knead until smooth. Roll out and cut in desired shape.

Grace Weldy

BAKERWOMAN

Bakerwoman runs the bakery on the corner, right down from where you live. She is most welcoming - not too skinny, not too organized. She spends her nights baking bread for the people - measuring, kneading, warming, rising, shaping. Some people follow the scent in the early hours of the morning before the doors officially open and they find she has something ready. She trusts that every day you will come by - the scent is irresistible. And when you stop by the door is open - not one of those pneumatic air doors that take all the challenge and creativity out of passing thru - but the old fashioned door that lets you see thru the window first, then has the old copper knob with filigree that you get to turn, and the hinges that squeak a little so she knows you are coming through. The inside warmth and smell and bakened beauty is overwhelming. She knows this so she comes around from behind the counter, envelopes you in the floury, yeasty self and hugs you so you feel kind of like the jelly in a Bismarck. And then she gives you your bread for that day - sometimes it's a bread stick with caraway seed, sometimes flat bread from hand stoned wheat, or a caramel roll with pecans or a jelly roll or sometimes a wonderful loaf for sandwiches. Only enough, of course, for that day. Who wants day old bread? And as you're leaving, she puts something else in your hand - it's a recipe card with the picture of what she's just given you on it. That's so you won't forget what you've just received - and in case you meet someone today who can't seem to make it to the store, you can bake her bread with them.

Casseroles

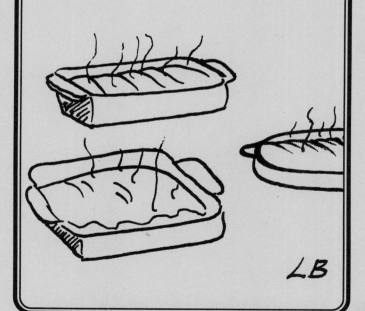

CASSEROLES

5 CAN CASSEROLE

1 10-oz. can boned chicken
1 can mushroom soup
1 can chicken rice soup
1 sm. can Pet milk
1 can chow mein noodles

Bake at 350 degrees for 45 minutes. Can put crumbs on top last 20 minutes. A quick and easy meal if you're limited on time.

Marge Detweiler

7-LAYER SUPPER CASSEROLE

4-5 med. potatoes, sliced
1 can mushroom soup
3/4 c. mayonnaise
3/4 c. sour cream
1-2 c. chunked ham
1 lg. onion, chopped
1-2 carrots, sliced
2 c. cabbage, chopped
1 c. cheese, shredded

In a separate bowl, mix together mushroom soup, mayonnaise and sour cream; set aside. Place sliced potatoes in a large casserole dish. Pour soup mixture over potatoes spreading evenly. Layer in ham chunks, onion and carrots ending with cabbage on top. Bake, covered, at 350 degrees for 1 hour. Uncover and sprinkle with cheese; bake 30 minutes longer.

Karen Graybill

BRAZILIAN RICE & BEANS

Rice:
1 onion, minced
1 clove garlic, minced
2 T. oil
2 c. uncooked rice
1 tsp. salt
4 c. boiling water
1/2 tsp. turmeric (opt.)

Beans:
1-lb. dry pinto beans
1 ham bone
1 bay leaf
2 bacon strips
1 onion, chopped
2 cloves, garlic, minced
2 tsp. salt (or less)
1/4 tsp. pepper

Saute onion, garlic, and oil in saucepan until onion is clear. Add rice and stir fry for 2 minutes. Add salt and boiling water. Bring to a boil. Reduce heat. Cover and simmer 20 minutes. Turn off heat. Never stir. Keep rice covered 10 minutes more. Flake with fork into serving dish. Keep warm; set aside. Pour water over beans to cover 2-inches above beans. Soak overnight; drain water. Add 1 ham bone, bay leaf and enough water to cover beans plus 1-inch. Cook in crock pot for 3 hours. Fry bacon in skillet. Saute 2 minutes with onion and garlic cloves. Add to beans; add salt and pepper. Cook 15 minutes to blend flavors. Serve over rice.

Betty Hochstetler

MEXICAN BEANS & RICE

1-lb. hamburger
1 can refried beans
1 sm. jar salsa

1/2 pkg. taco seasoning
2 c. rice, cooked
8-oz. Cheddar cheese

Brown hamburger; drain. Add refried beans, salsa and taco seasoning. Place rice in bottom of casserole dish. Top with hamburger-bean mixture. Top with Cheddar cheese. Bake at 350 degrees for 30 minutes. Serve with sour cream.

BREAKFAST PIZZA

1-lb. bulk sausage, browned
  and drained
1 pkg. Pillsbury crescent rolls
1 c. hashbrowns, thawed
1/8 c. onion, chopped fine

1 c. Cheddar cheese, shredded
5 eggs
1/4 c. milk
2 T. Parmesan cheese

Cook sausage; drain and set aside. Place crescent rolls on 12-inch pizza pan, points in center. Spoon on cooked sausage. Sprinkle with potatoes and onion. Top with Cheddar cheese. Mix together eggs and milk; pour over crust. Sprinkle with Parmesan cheese. Bake at 375 degrees for 25-30 minutes.

Amy Martin

BROCCOLI CASSEROLE

1 whole chicken
2 pkgs. frozen broccoli spears
1/4-lb. Velveeta cheese
1/2 tsp. pepper

1 can cream of mushroom soup
1 can cream of chicken soup
2 cans waters chestnuts, sliced
Buttered bread crumbs

Boil chicken; cut into bite size pieces. Place broccoli in bottom of casserole dish; top with chicken. In a saucepan, bring cheese, pepper, mushroom soup, chicken soup and water chestnuts to a boil. Pour over broccoli and chicken; top with buttered bread crumbs. Bake at 350 degrees for 30 minutes.

Marilyn (G. Keith) Miller

HAM & BROCCOLI SKILLET

1/2 stick butter
Garlic powder (to taste)
1 8-16 oz. pkg. broccoli
1 c. milk

1 T. cornstarch
1/2 c. Parmesan cheese
1 1/4 c. macaroni, uncooked
2-3 c. ham

Melt butter; add garlic to cover pan. Cut ham and broccoli; add to butter and cook until tender. Add cornstarch and Parmesan cheese to milk. Add milk mixture to skillet and cook until cheese has melted. Add cooked macaroni and mix well.

Shanda Weaver

CARROT CASSEROLE

12 carrots
4 T. butter
4 T. flour
1/2 c. onion
1/4 tsp. salt
1/4 tsp. celery salt

1/2 c. Velveeta cheese, diced
1 tsp. mustard
1/8 tsp. pepper
Crushed potato chips or
    bread crumbs

Dice carrots; cook until tender but not too soft. Make white sauce with butter, flour and milk. Add onion, salt, pepper, mustard and cheese. Put all ingredients into casserole. Top with crushed potato chips or bread crumbs. Bake at 350 degrees for 30 minutes.

Dorcas Snyder

SWEET-SOUR CARROTS

2 bags carrots
1 med. onion, sliced thin
1 med. green pepper
1 can tomato soup
1 c. sugar

3/4 c. cider vinegar
1/2 tsp. mustard
1 tsp. Worcestershire sauce
Salt and pepper (to taste)

Slice carrots and cook in small amount of salt water until tender but firm. Boil soup with sugar, vinegar, oil and seasonings until thick (10 minutes). Drain carrots; add onions and green pepper. Pour sauce over vegetables and refrigerate. May also be served warm.

Marilyn (G. Keith) Miller

CHICKEN CASSEROLE

1 pkg. hash browns
4 c. hot water
1 1/2 tsp. salt
2 c. chicken

1 c. celery
1 c. cheese
1 can cream of chicken soup

In a 2 1/2-quart dish, soak potatoes, water and salt for 15 minutes; drain. Add hash brown mixture to chicken, celery, cheese and soup. Bake, uncovered, at 350 degrees for 35-40 minutes.

Joy Vandiepenbos

CHICKEN-ALMOND CASSEROLE

3 c. chicken, cooked
2 cans cream of chicken soup
1 c. mayonnaise
2 c. rice, cooked
2 T. onion, chopped
2 c. celery, diced

6 eggs, hard cooked
2 T. lemon juice
1 c. almonds, slivered
1 sm. can water chestnuts, sliced
1 tsp. salt
2/3 c. cornflakes, crushed

Mix all ingredients thoroughly. Place in a 9 x 13-inch pan. Cover top with crushed cornflakes. Bake at 350 degrees for 30 minutes. Serves 10-12 people.

Florence Nussbaum

CHICKEN CASSEROLE

1/2 c. onion, chopped
1/3 c. celery, chopped
1/3 c. margarine
1/2 pkg. herb bread stuffing
2 c. cooked chicken, diced
1 c. water
2 eggs, beaten

1 10-oz. can cream of chicken
  soup
1/3 c. mayonnaise
3/4 tsp. salt
1/4 tsp. garlic powder
1 1/2 c. milk

Saute first 3 ingredients until tender; add to next 3 ingredients. Stir until blended. Pour into a 2-quart or 8 x 12-inch greased casserole. Combine eggs, chicken soup, mayonnaise, salt, garlic powder and milk; mix thoroughly and pour over chicken mixture. Bake at 350 degrees for 30-45 minutes.

Lou Thomas

ALMOND CHICKEN WITH APRICOT

1/4 c. apricot or peach jam
1/2 T. onion, finely chopped
2 tsp. soy sauce
1 tsp. vinegar
1/4 tsp. dry mustard

6 skinless, boneless chicken
  breast halves
1/2 c. almonds, sliced
1 T. butter, melted

Stir together first 5 ingredients. Put chicken halves in greased 13 x 9 x 2-inch baking pan. Pour sauce on top. Press almonds on top of chicken. Drizzle with melted butter. Bake at 350 degrees for 50 minutes or until almonds are golden brown and chicken is done. Makes 6 servings.

Merianne Shaffer

CHICKEN ENCHILADA CASSEROLE

1 c. onion, chopped
1/4 c. margarine or butter
1/4 c. flour
2 1/2 c. water
1 T. chicken bouillon
8-oz. sour cream

3 c. chicken, chopped
2 c. Cheddar cheese, shredded
1 4-oz. can chopped green
  chilies
1/2 tsp. chili powder
10 8-in. flour tortillas

Cook onion in butter; stir in flour. Mix chicken bouillon and water; add to flour mixture and cook until thickened. Remove from heat; add sour cream. In a large bowl, combine 1 cup of sour cream sauce with chicken; add 1 cup cheese, chilies and chili powder. Mix well. Dip each tortilla into remaining hot sour cream sauce to soften. Put a portion of chicken mixture in center of tortilla and roll up like a crepe. Arrange, seam side down, in a lightly greased 13 x 9-inch dish. Spoon remaining sauce over enchiladas; sprinkle with remaining cheese. Note: Can use 2 1/2 c. regular chicken broth instead of water and bouillon. Bake at 350 degrees for 25 minutes. *Good to make the night before.*

Shanda Weaver

CHICKEN DIVAN

2 10-oz. pkgs. broccoli
4-6 c. cooked chicken, chopped
10 3/4-oz. can cream of chicken
  soup
10 3/4-oz. can cream of
  mushroom soup

1/2 c. mayonnaise
1 tsp. lemon juice
1 c. cheese, grated
1 c. bread crumbs

Cook broccoli according to package directions. In a 8 x 12-inch dish layer broccoli and chicken. Combine soups, mayonnaise and lemon juice; pour over chicken. Sprinkle with cheese and bread crumbs. Bake at 350 degrees for 35-40 minutes.

Jill Erb

AMISH DRESSING

2-qts. bread, crumbled
1/4 c. carrots, cooked and diced
1/2 c. celery, finely chopped
3 eggs, beaten
1 c. diced potatoes, cooked
  and salted

1 chicken, finely chopped
1/4 c. parsley, finely chopped
2 c. milk
1/4 c. butter

Brown bread in butter in skillet, turning often. Mix all ingredients. Put 1/4 c. butter in baking pan; brown. Pour dressing in. Bake at 350-375 degrees until brown all over.

Marilyn (G. Keith) Miller

TURKEY DRESSING

1 c. celery, chopped
1/2 onion, chopped
2 T. chicken bouillon
1/4 c. margarine

5 eggs
1 loaf bread, cubed
1-lb. pkg. stuffing mix
Turkey giblets

Cook giblets in water until tender. Remove neck meat from bones and chop finely. Add chicken bouillon to broth for flavor. Saute onions and celery in margarine. Pour broth over bread cubes. Add celery, onion, chopped meat and slightly beaten eggs. (*More liquid will be needed to make sure all bread is soaked. To check, press a spoon into dressing. It should fill with liquid.) Stuff turkey with dressing. Do not pack tightly as dressing swells as it bakes. Bake remaining dressing in a greased baking dish. Bake at 350 degrees for 1 hour. *Use broth for better flavor.

Betty Leinbach

*God could not be everywhere,
therefore, He created mothers.*

SAUSAGE CORN DRESSING

1-lb. bulk sausage	5 slices bread
5 stalks celery	2 cans creamed corn
1 onion	Sugar (to taste)

Fry sausage, celery and onion; drain. Add bread (which has been moistened with water and broken up), corn and sugar. Mix well. Bake at 375 degrees for approximately 45 minutes or until brown.

Carol Martin

CORN BREAD-SAUSAGE NUT STUFFING

1 8 or 9-in. corn bread, baked and crumbled	2 eggs, lightly beaten
1-lb. country style sausage	1 c. pecans, chopped
3-4 ribs celery	2 (4-oz.) cans water chestnuts, chopped (reserve liquid)
1 lg. onion	1/2 tsp. ground sage
1 sm. carrot, grated	1/4 tsp. ground thyme
1/4 c. parsley, shopped	1/4 tsp. ground marjoram
1-2 cloves garlic, minced	1/4 tsp. ground savory
2 tsp. salt	Milk and liquid from chestnuts to make 1 1/2 c.
1/2 tsp. pepper	

Brown sausage; remove from drippings. Add vegetables, parsley and garlic to drippings. Cook over low heat until tender. Mix all ingredients together. Bake at 350 degrees for 45 minutes.

Becky Schwartzentruber

LUNCHEON CHICKEN SQUARES

3 c. cooked chicken, chopped	3 tsp. lemon juice
3 c. celery, chopped	3 c. rice, cooked
3 10-oz. cans cream of chicken soup	Topping:
	2 c. cornflakes
3 c. mayonnaise	1/4 c. butter, melted
1/4 c. green onions, sliced	1/2 c. slivered almonds

Combine all ingredients, except topping. Spread in well buttered 9 x 13-inch pan. Mix topping and sprinkle over chicken. Bake at 350 degrees for 40-50 minutes or until browned and bubbly. Let stand 10 minutes before serving. Cut into squares.

Shirley Albrecht

Ask, and it will be given you; seek, and you will find;
knock, and it will be opened to you.
For everyone who asks receives, and he who seeks finds,
and to him who knocks it will be opened.
Matthew 7:7-8

CHICKEN AND NOODLE CASSEROLE

1 box Betty Crocker Beef
Romanoff Hamburger Helper
1 sm. can mushrooms, drained
1 can cream of mushroom soup
2 c. cooked chicken, diced
1 stick margarine, melted
1 stack Ritz crackers, crushed

Prepare noodles as directed on package. Combine with mushroom soup, drained mushrooms and chicken. Put into buttered 8 x 12-inch casserole dish. Combine melted margarine and crackers; sprinkle on top of casserole. Bake at 350 degrees for 20-30 minutes.

Kathy Leinbach

CHICKEN POT PIE

2 cans cream of broccoli soup
1 c. milk
1/4 tsp. dried thyme leaves,
crushed
1/4 tsp. pepper
2 c. cooked chicken, cubed
16-oz. pkg. frozen broccoli,
cauliflower and carrots
1 c. potatoes, cooked
1 10-oz. can Hungry Jack Flaky
Biscuits

Combine first 4 ingredients in a 3-quart baking dish. Stir in vegetables and chicken. Bake at 400 degrees for 15 minutes or until mixture begins to bubble. Cut each biscuit into quarters. Remove dish from oven and stir. Arrange biscuit pieces over hot mixture. Bake at 400 degrees for 15 minutes or until biscuits are golden brown.

Jill Erb

CHICKEN STUFFED PASTA SHELLS

15-20 jumbo pasta shells,
cooked
3-4 chicken breasts, boiled
1 c. peas (can also use corn)
1 onion, diced
Salt and pepper (to taste)
1 can cream of mushroom soup
8-oz. Cheddar cheese

Saute chicken, onion, peas, salt and pepper in butter. Stuff into shells. Put in single layer in casserole dish. Cover with cream of mushroom soup mixed with 1/2 can of water. Cover with cheese. Bake, covered, at 350 degrees for 25 minutes. Uncover and bake 5 minutes more.

Karen Leinbach

CHICKEN & RICE CASSEROLE

2 c. chicken
1 1/2 c. instant rice
1 onion, chopped
1 c. celery, chopped
1 can cream of chicken soup
1 can mushroom soup
Milk
1/2-lb. frozen peas (or other
vegetables)
1 T. butter

Cook and cut up chicken. Toss together chicken, rice, onion, celery and soups. Add a little milk, peas (or other vegetables) and melted butter. May put crushed potato chips on top. Bake at 350 degrees for 30 minutes.

Rosemary Martin

CHICKEN RICE CASSEROLE

1 3-lb. chicken, cup up
1 can cream of celery soup
1 can mushroom soup
1 env. dry onion soup mix
2 c. rice, uncooked
3 c. milk

In a 13 x 9 x 2-inch greased baking dish, mix soups. Gradually add milk and dry rice. Lay chicken pieces in mixture. Sprinkle dry onion soup mix on top. Bake at 350 degrees for 1 1/2 hours.

Ruth Tyson

CHICKEN & SAUSAGE JAMBALAYA

1 1/2 c. vegetable oil
2 chickens, cut up and seasoned
2-lbs. sausage, cut into 1 1/2-in.
  pieces
2 1-lb. cans tomatoes
5 c. long grained rice
10 c. water
4-lbs. onions
5 cloves garlic
1 bunch green onions
1 bell pepper
Salt
Black pepper
Red pepper

Brown seasoned chicken in hot oil preferably in a 12-quart black iron pot (or at least a cast aluminum pot). Next, brown sausage well. Remove meat and most of the oil. Add onions, garlic, bell pepper and green onions. (It is extremely important to brown these vegetables well. You may have to add a little water from time to time to keep them from sticking.) Put chicken and sausage back into pot along with all the water and tomatoes. Add salt and pepper. When mixture comes to a rolling boil, add rice. When it reaches a good boil again, lower heat and let all the water boil out. Stir well, lower heat and cover. After 15 minutes, uncover and stir well once more and cover again. Do not keep stirring. Leave undisturbed over low heat for 45 minutes. (Excess stirring makes the rice mushy.) Serves 16-20 people.

Gloria Yoder

CHICKEN SUPREME

1 chicken, cooked, boned and
  cut into small pieces
6 c. bread, cubed
3/4 c. butter or margarine,
  melted
1/2 c. flour
3 c. broth (approx.)
1 1/4 tsp. sage
1/4 c. evaporated milk or cream
3/4 tsp. salt
1/3 c. onion, chopped
1/3 c. celery, chopped
1 10-oz. pkg. frozen peas
Buttered bread crumbs

Make a thin gravy with margarine, flour and broth. Add onions, celery and seasonings. Pour gravy over bread cubes; stir in peas and chicken. Put in a 9 x 13-inch pan. Pour milk over top. Sprinkle with buttered bread crumbs. Bake at 350 degrees for 30 minutes.

Bertha Goetz

SPICY CHICKEN & CORN

1 T. margarine
1-lb. skinless and boneless
  chicken
1 med. onion, chopped
1 med. green pepper, chopped
1/2 tsp. dried oregano leaves
1/2 tsp. paprika

1/4 tsp. black pepper
1/4 tsp. red pepper
1 can Campbell's New Golden
  Corn Soup
1 16-oz. can stewed tomatoes
1 c. rice, cooked

In skillet, cook 1/2 of chicken until browned, stirring often. Remove and set aside. Repeat with remaining chicken. In skillet, cook onion and green pepper with oregano, paprika, black pepper and red pepper until tender crisp, stirring often. Stir in soup, tomatoes and rice. Heat to boiling. Return chicken to skillet; cover. Cook over low heat 5 minutes or until chicken is no longer pink, stirring often. Garnish with fresh parsley, if desired. Makes 4 servings.

Ruth Metzler

"GARBAGE CAN" TURKEY

1 10-gal. galvanized can
1 2 x 2-in. wooden stake,
  2 ft. long
10-lbs. charcoal brickettes

Heavy duty aluminum foil,
  18-in. wide
10-12 lb. turkey, thawed, washed
  and dried
1 shovel

Light entire 10-pounds charcoal in a pile. Let burn for about 20 minutes until white. While coals are heating, drive stake into ground, leaving 12-inches extending above ground. Wrap stake with foil. Spread additional foil on ground around stake to make an area about 3 feet. Place turkey on stake through open butt end with the neck up. Invert a metal garbage can over turkey. Make sure top and sides of container do not touch bird. Shovel one layer of burning coals over top area of garbage can. Shovel remainder of coals evenly around base of can, touching can all the way around. Let cook 1 1/2-2 hours undisturbed. Carefully remove hot ashes from top and sides of can. Lift off can carefully and remove turkey from stake. Carve and serve.

Gloria Yoder

24 HOUR EGG OMELETTE

5 slices white bread
1/2-lb. cheese, grated
1/2 tsp. salt
4 eggs, slightly beaten

2 c. milk
1/2 tsp. dry mustard
Dash of pepper

Butter 1 side of bread; cut in 1-inch cubes. Place bread in well greased 8 x 11-inch casserole; sprinkle with cheese. Beat together eggs, milk, salt, pepper and mustard. Pour over bread. Refrigerate, covered, overnight. Bake, covered, at 325 degrees for 1 hour or until set. Uncover the last 15 minutes of baking time.

Rheta Mae Wiebe

TASTY EGG RECIPE "FOR A CROWD"

Light cream   Eggs
Butter   Salt and pepper

Put into each section of a muffin pan 1 teaspoon light cream and a small piece of butter. Place into 350 degree oven to heat through. Remove from oven and break 1 large egg into each section of pan. Sprinkle eggs with salt and pepper. Return pan to oven. Bake 15-20 minutes or until eggs are just "set."

Vera Brubacher

EGG ROLLS

3-lb. head of cabbage   3 med. onions
1 pkg. egg rolls wrap   1 T. sugar
1 1/2-lbs. ground pork   2 tsp. salt

Cook ground pork; drain off fat. Shred cabbage and onions; steam and let cool. Squeeze out excess water. Mix pork, cabbage, onions, salt and sugar together. Wrap mixture in egg roll wrap. Fry in deep hot oil until golden brown.

Tanh Bounmythavong

HAMBURGER CASSEROLE

3 c. potatoes   1 1/2 c. peas
2 c. carrots, sliced   1 can mushroom soup
1-lb. hamburger   1/2 soup can milk
Onion, sliced   Salt and pepper (to taste)

Peel and slice potatoes; salt and pepper to taste. Parboil carrots. Brown hamburger; drain. Layer potatoes, onion, carrots and hamburger twice. Top with peas. Season with salt and pepper. Mix soup and milk; pour over casserole. Cover and bake at 350 degrees for 1 hour.

Ruth Bauman

QUICK CHEESEBURGER BAKE

1-lb. ground beef   1/4 c. milk
3/4 c. onion, chopped   2 c. original Bisquick or reduced
1 can condensed Cheddar   fat mix
   cheese soup   3/4 c. water
1 c. frozen mixed vegetables,   1 c. Cheddar cheese, shredded
   if desired

Heat oven to 400 degrees. Generously grease a 13 x 9 x 2-inch baking dish. Cook beef and onion in a 10-inch skillet until beef is brown; drain. Stir in soup, vegetables and milk. Stir baking mix and water in baking dish until moistened; spread evenly into baking dish. Spread beef mixture over batter. Sprinkle with cheese. Bake 30 minutes. Makes 8-10 servings.

Ruth Metzler

HAMBURGER CORN CASSEROLE

1 1/2-lbs. hamburger	2 c. noodles
1 c. onion, chopped	1/2 tsp. Accent
1 1/2 c. corn (plus liquid)	1/4 tsp. pepper
1 can cream of chicken soup	Topping:
1 can cream of mushroom soup	1 c. bread cubes
1 c. sour cream	3 T. butter, melted
1/4 c. pimento, chopped	Parsley flakes
3/4 tsp. salt	

Cook noodles. Brown hamburger; add remaining ingredients. Spread into a greased 9 x 13-inch casserole dish. Top with bread cubes, melted butter and parsley flakes. Bake at 350 degrees for 30 minutes or until heated through.

Shirleen Weaver

BEEF MACARONI SKILLET

1-lb. ground beef or turkey	1 tsp. salt
1 med. onion, chopped	1/8 tsp. pepper
3 c. tomato juice	1 tsp. dry mustard
1 T. Worcestershire sauce	1 c. elbow macaroni, uncooked
1 T. vinegar	

Brown beef or turkey and onion in a 12-inch skillet; drain. Add tomato juice, Worcestershire sauce, vinegar, salt, pepper, mustard and macaroni. Bring to a boil. Reduce heat. Cover and simmer for 20 minutes or until macaroni is tender, stirring occasionally. More tomato juice may need to be added. Serves 5-6.

Mary Rhoade

HEARTY BEEF 'N POTATO CASSEROLE

4 c. frozen potato rounds (1/2 of 30-oz. bag)	1 med. tomato, chopped (opt.)
	1 10 3/4-oz. can cream of celery soup
1-lb. ground beef, browned	1/3 c. milk
1 10-oz. pkg. frozen chopped broccoli, thawed	1 c. Cheddar cheese, shredded
1 2.8-oz. can Durkee French Fried Onions	1/4 tsp. garlic powder
	1/8 tsp. black pepper

Place potatoes on bottom and up sides of 8 x 12-inch casserole. Bake, uncovered, at 400 degrees for 10 minutes. Place browned beef, broccoli, 1/2 can French fried onions and tomatoes in potato shell. Combine soup, milk, 1/2 cup cheese and seasonings; pour over beef mixture. Bake, uncovered, at 400 degrees for 20 minutes. Top with remaining cheese and onions. Bake, uncovered, 2 or 3 minutes longer. Preparation time: 15 minutes. Makes 6 servings.

Connie Davidhizer

SOMBRERO PIE

1/2-lb. ground beef
1/2-lb. ground pork
1 lg. onion, sliced
2 1/2 c. tomato juice
1 10-oz. pkg. frozen corn
1 or 2 T. chili powder
1 tsp. salt
1/4 tsp. pepper
Cornmeal Pastry:
1 c. flour
1/4 c. cornmeal
1/2 tsp. salt
1/3 c. + 1 T. shortening
3 T. cold water

In a large skillet, cook meat and onions until meat is brown and onions are tender; drain off fat. Stir in remaining ingredients. Heat to boiling, reduce heat and simmer for 10 minutes. Heat oven to 400 degrees. Pour mixture into ungreased 11 1/2 x 7 1/2 x 1 1/2-inch baking dish. Cover with pastry. Seal edges of baking dish. Bake 30-35 minutes. Makes 4-6 servings.

For pastry: Measure flour, cornmeal and salt into bowl; cut in shortening thoroughly. Sprinkle in water, 1 tablespoon at a time. Mix until all flour is moistened. Gather into a ball. Roll in a 12 x 8-inch rectangle on slightly floured cloth covered board. Fold lengthwise in half, cut slits on folded edge. Lay pastry over casserole and seal to edges of baking dish. If using self-rising flour, omit the salt.

Ruby Panyako

LAZY BEEF STROGANOFF

1 env. dry onion soup mix
1 can cream of celery soup
1 can cream of mushroom soup
1/3 can of water
1 can mushrooms, undrained
2-2 1/2-lbs. stew meat, uncooked
1/2 c. sour cream

Mix all ingredients, except sour cream. Bake, covered, at 275 degrees for 3-4 hours. Stir in sour cream just before serving. Serve over noodles or rice.

Patty Bontrager

BEEF STEW

2-lbs. beef stew meat
8 carrots
2 c. celery
2-3 c. potatoes
1 med. can whole tomatoes
1 T. salt
1 T. sugar
3 T. tapioca quick pudding
1 lg. onion

Mix all together. Bake at 300 degrees for 2 1/2 hours while at church. (May cut recipe in half.)

Delora Reinhardt

*Prayers should be the key of the day
and the lock of the night.*

HAMBURGER AND VEGETABLE CASSEROLE

6 med. potatoes
1 1/2-lbs. hamburger

Onion, chopped
2 cans vegetable soup

Fry hamburger and onion just enough to pour off some of the grease (not completely browned). Put half of hamburger in bottom of baking dish. Place peeled and sliced potatoes on top. Add remaining hamburger. Pour cans of soup on top. Bake at 350 degrees for 1 1/2 hours. Serves 6.

Edna Hochstetler

KRAUT CASSEROLE

1 pkg. med. noodles
1 c. milk
1 can cream of mushroom soup

1-lb. sauerkraut
1 can corn beef
Mozzarella cheese

Rinse sauerkraut. Mix all ingredients together. Top with cheese. Bake at 350 degrees for 1 1/2 hours.

Annabelle Snyder

BOILED KIELBASA AND KRAUT

4 or 5 med. whole potatoes,
  pealed
3 or 4 whole onions, peeled
4 or 5 cloves of garlic, peeled
1 1/2-qts water
1 1/2-lbs. fresh sauerkraut

3-lbs. kielbasa
1 tsp. oregano
1/4 tsp. red pepper flakes
  (more or less)
2 tsp. black pepper

Put potatoes, onions and garlic in large saucepan or dutch oven with water; boil 20 minutes. Add sauerkraut, kielbasa, oregano, red pepper flakes and black pepper. Simmer over low heat for an additional 30 minutes. Makes 4-5 servings.

Nina Weaver

SAUSAGE IN SAUERKRAUT

2 c. macaroni, uncooked
1-lb. pork sausage
1 16-oz. can tomatoes with
  liquid, cut up

1 c. sauerkraut
1 tsp. sugar
4-5 T. Cheddar cheese,
  shredded

Cook macaroni. Brown sausage in skillet; drain, reserving 1 tablespoon drippings. Add tomatoes and sauerkraut to pork and cook for 2 minutes. Drain macaroni; stir into skillet along with cheese. Put into a greased 8-inch square baking dish. Bake, uncovered, at 350 degrees for 20 minutes. Makes 4-6 servings.

Arlene Hartman

The Lord wants our precious time,
not our spare time.

49

LASAGNA

1-lb. hamburger
1 lg. can Ragu Spaghetti Sauce
1-lb. cottage cheese
2 eggs, unbeaten
Salt
Pepper
1/3 c. Parmesan cheese
1-lb. mozzarella cheese, grated
Lasagna (for 3 layers)

Brown hamburger. Add spaghetti sauce and simmer 10 minutes. Mix together cottage cheese, eggs, salt, pepper and Parmesan cheese. In a 9 x 13-inch baking dish, layer <u>uncooked</u> lasagna, sauce, cottage cheese mixture and 1/3 of grated mozzarella cheese. Keep layering until ingredients are all in dish. This can be refrigerated overnight or baked immediately. Bake at 350 degrees for 45-55 minutes. Let stand 15 minutes, then cut and serve. Serves 6-8.

LASAGNA

1/2-lb. sweet Italian sausage
3-oz. pkg. pepperoni
30-oz. jar spaghetti sauce
1/2-1 lb. lasagna noodles, cooked
1 med. onion, chopped
1 can mushrooms
1/2 c. butter
2 8-oz. pkgs. mozzarella cheese

While noodles are cooking and sausage is browning, saute onions and mushrooms sprinkled with garlic in butter and enough water to cover. Spread small amount of sauce in bottom of cake pan. Layer with 1/2 of noodles, top with drained mushrooms, onions and pepperoni. Next layer on 1 package (8-oz.) mozzarella cheese. Layer on more sauce with sausage, remaining noodles, remaining sauce and top with remaining cheese. Bake 40-45 minutes, covered the first 20 minutes.

Deb Krawiec

LASAGNA ROLLS

1 c. ricotta cheese
2 eggs, beaten
2-oz. mozzarella cheese, shredded
4 T. Parmesan cheese, grated
1/4 tsp. oregano
1/4 tsp. basil
Dash of garlic powder
8 lasagna noodles, cooked and drained
2 c. tomato sauce

Combine ricotta cheese, eggs, mozzarella cheese, 2 tablespoons Parmesan cheese and seasonings; mix well. Place cooked lasagna noodles on damp towel and spoon equal amounts of cheese mixture onto noodles. Spread evenly and roll up. Place in sprayed casserole dish. Spoon tomato sauce over roll-ups and sprinkle with remaining Parmesan cheese. Bake at 350 degrees for 35-40 minutes.

Dianne Kehr

BEST LASAGNA

1-lb. ground round	1/2 tsp. crushed red pepper
1 sm. onion, diced	1/4 tsp. garlic salt
1 28-oz. can tomatoes	1 bay leaf
1 12-oz. can tomato paste	2/3 of 16-oz. pkg. lasagna
1 T. sugar	noodles (about 12-14 noodles)
1 1/2 tsp. salt	2 eggs
1/2 tsp. oregano leaves	1 15-oz. container ricotta cheese
1/2 tsp. thyme leaves	1 16-oz. pkg. mozzarella cheese,
	diced

In a 5-quart dutch oven over high heat, cook ground beef and onion until all pan juices evaporate and meat is well browned, stirring frequently. Add tomatoes and its liquid, tomato paste, sugar, salt, all herbs, garlic salt and bay leaf. Heat to boiling, stirring to break up tomatoes. Reduce heat to low; simmer 30 minutes or until sauce is properly thickened, stirring occasionally. Discard bay leaf. Prepare noodles; drain. In a 13 x 9-inch pan, arrange 1/2 of noodles overlapping to fit. Combine eggs and ricotta cheese; spoon 1/2 of mixture over noodles; sprinkle with 1/2 of mozzarella cheese and top with 1/2 of sauce. Repeat. Bake at 375 degrees for 45 minutes or until heated through. Remove from pan after 10 minutes for easier serving.

Gloria Tyson

CHICKEN CHEESE LASAGNA

1 onion, chopped	1 tsp. dried basil
1 garlic clove, minced	1 tsp. dried oregano
1/2 c. butter	1/2 tsp. white pepper
1/2 c. flour	2 c. ricotta cheese
1 tsp. salt	1 T. fresh parsley
2 c. chicken broth	9 lasagna noodles, cooked
1 1/2 c. milk	2 c. cooked chicken, cubed
4 c. mozzarella cheese,	1-2 c. frozen spinach, thawed
shredded	and drained
1 c. Parmesan cheese	

In saucepan, saute onion and garlic in butter. Stir in flour and salt; cook until bubbly. Stir in broth and milk; bring to boil. Stir in 2 cups mozzarella cheese, 1/2 c. Parmesan cheese and spices; set aside. Combine ricotta cheese, parsley and remaining mozzarella cheese; set aside. Spread 1/4 of cheese sauce in greased 13 x 9-inch dish; cover with 1/3 noodles. Top with 1/2 ricotta mixture, 1/2 of spinach and 1/2 of chicken. Repeat all layers. Sprinkle with remaining Parmesan cheese. Bake, uncovered, at 350 degrees for 35-40 minutes. Let stand 15 minutes.

Verna Gongwer

MEXICAN LASAGNA

1-lb. ground beef
1 12-oz. jar thick & chunky salsa
6 tostada shells
1 c. refried beans

1 c. sour cream
4-oz. Cheddar cheese, shredded
Lettuce, shredded (for garnish)

Brown beef; drain. Stir in 1/2 cup salsa. Spread 1/4 cup salsa in 10-inch pie plate. Top with 3 tostadas. Top with 1/2 of each of the beans, meat mixture, sour cream and cheese. Repeat layers. Cover with foil. Bake at 350 degrees for 30 minutes. Top with lettuce, remaining salsa and sour cream. Makes 6-8 servings.

Gloria Yoder

RANCH-STYLE BAKED LENTILS

2 c. lentils, dry
2 tsp. salt
5 c. water (divided)
1-lb. ground turkey

1 env. dry onion soup mix
1 c. catsup
1 tsp. mustard
1 tsp. vinegar

Wash lentils and cook with 4 cups water and salt for approximately 20 minutes. Brown turkey. Stir soup, catsup, mustard, vinegar and water. Gently stir in lentils. Place in 2-quart greased casserole dish and bake, covered, at 400 degrees for 35 minutes.

Phyllis Garber

LEONARD'S ONE-DISH MEAL

1/2-1 lb. lean ground beef
12-oz. lean bacon, cut in
  small pieces
1 c. onion, chopped
1/2 c. celery, chopped
1/4 c. green pepper, chopped
1/2-lb. smoked sausage, sliced
  1/4-in. thick
1 16-oz. can kidney beans,
  drained
1 16-oz. can pork & beans,
  drained

1 16-oz. can lima beans, drained
1 16-oz. can Northern beans,
  drained
1 c. chili sauce
1/4 c. brown sugar
1 T. liquid smoke
3 T. white vinegar
1 tsp. salt
1 T. Worcestershire sauce
Dash of black pepper

Brown ground beef in skillet. Drain off fat; place beef in slow cooker. Brown bacon pieces; remove to paper towel. Drain fat from skillet; lightly brown onions, celery and green pepper. Add bacon, onions and pepper to slow cooker; stir in remaining ingredients. Cover, cook on Low for 4-6 hours. *Variations: Instead of bacon, I've used ham and instead of sausage, hot dogs. One could also divide ingredients into 2 casseroles and bake, uncovered, at 350 degrees for 1-1 1/2 hours.* Yield: 12 servings.

Shirley Albrecht

LIMA BEAN CASSEROLE

20-oz. frozen lima beans
1 1/4 c. brown sugar
1 lg. onion, chopped
1 green pepper, chopped

1/2-lb. bacon, browned
1 can tomato soup
3 tsp. dry mustard
1 tsp. salt

Boil lima beans; drain saving 1/2 cup broth. Mix all together. Bake 1 hour.

Marilyn Miller (Willie)

MASHED POTATO CASSEROLE

10-12 potatoes, peeled and
   diced
8-oz. Philadelphia cream cheese
Butter

Paprika
8-oz. sour cream
1 tsp. garlic salt
1 tsp. onion salt

Boil and mash potatoes. Add small amount of milk for mashed potatoes. Mix softened cheese, garlic and onion salt. Mix cheese mixture with potatoes. Put into baking casserole, dot with butter and sprinkle with paprika. Bake at 350 degrees for 45 minutes. *This can be made and refrigerated several days ahead of serving time.*

Marilyn (G. Keith) Miller

CREAMY POTATO CASSEROLE

4-5 med. potatoes
4 hard boiled eggs, chopped
1 onion, diced

1 sm. carton sour cream
1 stick butter
Salt and pepper (to taste)

Cook potatoes and dice. Mix all ingredients together. Cover and bake at 350 degrees for 30 minutes. Stir half way through cooking time.

Deb Krawiec

SAUSAGE AND CREAMED POTATOES

1-lb. sausage links
1 med. size onion
6-8 potatoes
2 T. flour

1 1/2 tsp. salt
1/4 tsp. pepper
1 c. milk

Cut sausage links in 1/2-inch lengths. Chop onion fine. Mix meat and onion together and fry until slightly browned. Add water to cover; cook 10 minutes. Cut potatoes in quarters. Add to meat and season. Cover and cook until vegetables are done. Make a paste of flour and milk. Add to mixture and cook until thickened. *Cooked fresh or frozen peas may be added for variety.* Serves 6-8.

Lois Blosser

Seven days without prayer makes one weak.

PIZZA CASSEROLE

1-lg. ground beef
2 T. onion, chopped
1/4 tsp. garlic powder
1 can tomato soup
6 T. water

1 tsp. oregano
1/2 tsp. salt
4 c. noodles, cooked
1/2 c. cheese, shredded

Brown beef with onions, garlic powder and salt; drain. Cook noodles; drain. Blend together all ingredients, except cheese. Put into casserole dish and top with cheese. Bake at 350 degrees for 30 minutes. Makes 4-6 servings.

Marilyn Stauffer

QUICK QUICHE

1 c. Swiss cheese, shredded
1 c. mushrooms, sliced
1/2 c. flour
1/2 tsp. salt
1/2 tsp. pepper

4 eggs
1 1/2 c. milk
2 tsp. Worcestershire sauce
1 3-oz. can French fried onions
1/2 c. green onions, sliced

This recipe forms its own crust. Grease a 9-inch pie plate; set aside. In a large bowl, toss together first 5 ingredients. In a small bowl, beat eggs, milk and Worcestershire sauce; stir into dry ingredients, mixing well. Pour into pie plate. Microwave on Medium 14-15 minutes, turning several times. Remove cover and sprinkle with onions. Cook on High 5-6 minutes or until center is set. Let stand 5 minutes. Makes 6 servings. 275 calories per serving. For regular oven, bake at 350 degrees for 30-35 minutes.

QUICHE

1 9-in. unbaked pastry shell
6 slices bacon (1/3-lb.), fried
   and crumbled
3/4 c. Swiss cheese (3-oz.),
   shredded

1/4 c. onion, minced
3 eggs
1 12-oz. can evaporated milk
1/4 tsp. sugar
1/8 tsp. cayenne red pepper

Heat oven to 425 degrees. Sprinkle bacon, cheese and onion in pastry-lined pie pan. Beat eggs slightly; beat in remaining ingredients. Pour cream mixture into pie pan. Place on the lowest shelf of oven and bake for 10 minutes. Reduce temperature to 300 degrees and bake 30 minutes longer. A knife inserted 1-inch from edge will come out clean when done. Let stand 10 minutes before cutting. Makes 6 servings.

Merianne Shaffer

*If you walk with the Lord,
you'll never be out of step.*

54

REUBEN QUICHE

1 9-inch pastry shell
1 T. caraway seed
8-oz. corn beef, shredded
1 T. Dijon mustard
3/4 c. sauerkraut, squeezed
and drained (unwashed)

2 c. Swiss cheese, shredded
1 c. light cream (half & half)
1 tsp. onion, grated
1/2 tsp. dry mustard
2 eggs

Sprinkle caraway seed over pie crust. Prick crust with fork and bake at 375 for 7 minutes. Fill crust with corn beef. Spread mustard over meat. Top with sauerkraut and cheese. Mix eggs, cream, onions and dry mustard together. Pour into pie shell and bake 40 minutes. Let stand 4 minutes before cutting.

Barb Croyle

RICE CASSEROLE

1 c. long grain rice, uncooked
1 can condensed onion soup

1 4-oz. can mushrooms,
undrained
1 stick margarine

Mix ingredients. Bake in covered casserole at 350 degrees for 1 hour.

Lou Thomas

SAUSAGE SWEET POTATO BAKE

1-lb. bulk sausage
2 med. raw sweet potatoes
3 med. apples
2 T. brown sugar

1 T. flour
1/4 tsp. cinnamon
1/4 tsp. salt
1/2 c. water

Brown bulk sausage; drain excess fat. Peel and slice potatoes and apples. Layer sausage, sweet potatoes and apples into a 2-quart casserole dish. Combine all other ingredients and pour over layers. Cover and bake at 375 degrees for 50-60 minutes or until done. Serves 4-6. *Note: May use cut up turkey sausage. If using turkey sausage, delete salt.*

Donnabelle Hoover

IRISH-ITALIAN SPAGHETTI SAUCE

1 onion, chopped (opt.)
2 T. salad or olive oil
1-lb. ground beef
1 tsp. salt
1/2 tsp. chili powder
1/2 tsp. Tabasco sauce

1/4 tsp. black pepper
1 10 1/2-11 oz. can cream of
mushroom soup
1 10 1/2-11 oz. can tomato soup
1 8-oz. bag spaghetti

Brown meat; drain grease. Add remaining ingredients, except soups; simmer for 15 minutes. Add soups; simmer for 45 minutes to 1 hour. *Note: For larger amount, add extra soup, keeping amounts of each equal.*

Ron Huber

SWEET POTATO & APPLE CASSEROLE

1/3 c. brown sugar, packed
1/2 tsp. ginger
1/8 tsp. salt
2-lbs. sweet potatoes,
  cooked and peeled

2 lg. cooking apples
3 T. butter or margarine,
  melted (or less)
1/4 c. pecans, chopped
1/2 c. coconut, shredded (opt.)

In a small bowl, combine sugar, ginger and salt. Cut sweet potatoes in 1/2-inch thick slices; arrange 1/2 in greased baking dish. Cover with sliced apples. Sprinkle 1/2 of brown sugar mixture over apples. Top with remaining sweet potato slices. Sprinkle with remaining brown sugar mixture. Spread 2 tablespoons melted butter over layers. Cover and bake at 375 degrees for 35 minutes. Remove from oven. Combine pecans, coconut and remaining 1 tablespoon butter. Sprinkle over potatoes. Return to oven and bake 10 minutes longer or until lightly browned.

Donnabelle Hoover

EASY MANICOTTI WITH CHEESE

32-oz. jar spaghetti sauce
1 c. water
8 -oz. manicotti, uncooked
15-oz. ricotta cheese
8-oz. mozzarella cheese

1/4 c. Parmesan cheese
1/4 c. parsley flakes
1/2 tsp. salt
1/4 tsp. pepper

Bring spaghetti sauce and water to a boil; reduce heat and keep warm. Mix together ricotta, mozzarella, Parmesan, parsley, salt and pepper. Spoon mixture into uncooked manicotti. Pour 1 cup sauce on bottom of 13 x 9 x 2-inch pan. Arrange filled manicotti in a single layer over sauce. Pour remaining sauce over manicotti. Cover with foil and bake at 400 degrees for 40 minutes. Remove foil and bake 10 minutes longer.

Wes & Cheryl Bontreger

MANICOTTI WITH CHEESE FILLING

12 manicotti shells
2-lbs. ricotta or cottage cheese
1/4-lb. mozzarella or American
  cheese, shredded
1/2 tsp. salt

1-qt. spaghetti sauce
1/2 c. Romano or Parmesan
  cheese
2 eggs, slightly beaten
1/3 c. parsley, chopped

Mix cheeses, eggs, parsley and salt thoroughly. Boil water and add approximately 6 manicotti at a time so water continues to boil. Cook 3 minutes; drain and set aside. Continue with remaining manicotti shells. Heat spaghetti sauce; add 1 cup water. Pour 1/2 sauce in bottom of 13 x 9-inch pan. Fill each shell with cheese mixture. Arrange shells in baking pan and pour remaining sauce on top. Bake at 400 degrees for 25 minutes. Sprinkle with grated cheese. Serves 6-8.

Barb Croyle

SPAGHETTI PIE

6-oz. spaghetti, cooked
and drained
2 T. olive oil
2 lg. eggs, well beaten
3/4 c. Parmesan cheese,
fancy shredded

1 c. ricotta cheese
1 c. spaghetti sauce
1/2-lb. hamburger, browned
1/2 c. mozzarella cheese,
shredded

Preheat oven to 350 degrees. Lightly grease a 10-inch pie plate. Toss hot spaghetti with oil. Combine eggs and parmesan cheese; stir into spaghetti. Pour spaghetti mixture into pie plate. Form into a "crust." Spread ricotta over crust. Spread meat over ricotta. Top with spaghetti sauce. Bake, uncovered, for 25 minutes. Top with mozzarella. Bake 5 minutes more or until cheese melts. Remove from oven and let cool 10 minutes before cutting. Makes 4-6 servings.

Sherry Kehr

SPAGHETTI PIZZA CASSEROLE

8-oz. spaghetti
4 T. margarine
2 eggs
1 c. Parmesan cheese
1-lb. ground beef
1 onion

1 green pepper
1/4-lb. pepperoni
1 can mushrooms, drained
32-oz. jar spaghetti sauce
8-oz. pkg. mozzarella cheese

Cook spaghetti; drain. While hot, add margarine, eggs and Parmesan cheese. Pour mixture into a buttered 9 x 13-inch baking dish; pat down with hand. Spread 1/2 jar of spaghetti sauce over mixture. Add meat, mushrooms, pepperoni and remainder of sauce. Bake, uncovered, at 350 degrees for 45 minutes. Remove from oven; add grated mozzarella cheese. Place in oven until cheese melts. Take out and let stand at least 10 minutes before cutting and serving. Serves 6-8. *Can freeze unbaked; thaw and bake.*

Betty Leinbach

SPAGHETTI WITH ZUCCHINI

12-oz. lean ground beef or
turkey
1 tsp. minced garlic (from a jar)
2 1/2 c. water

1 26-oz. jar low fat pasta sauce
2 med. size zucchini (1-lb.)
8-oz. spaghetti, uncooked

Crumble ground meat into a large, deep non-stick skillet. Add garlic and cook, stirring a few times, 3 minutes or until meat is no longer pink. Stir in water and pasta sauce. Bring to a boil. Scrub zucchini and cut in bite size chunks. Break spaghetti into thirds. Stir zucchini and pasta into skillet. Cover and boil 14 minutes, stirring 3 or 4 times, or until pasta is firm-tender. Serves 4.

Ruth Metzler

SPAGHETTI PIZZA DELUXE

1 7-oz. pkg. spaghetti
1/2 c. skim milk
1 egg, beaten
1/2-lb. ground beef
1 med. onion, chopped
1 med. greenpepper, chopped
2 cloves garlic, minced
1 15-oz. can tomato sauce
1 tsp. Italian seasoning
1 tsp. any salt free herb
   seasoning
1/4 tsp. pepper
2 c. fresh mushrooms, sliced
2 c. mozzarella cheese,
   shredded

Cook spaghetti as directed on package; drain. In a medium bowl, blend milk and egg; add spaghetti and toss to coat. Spray a 15 x 10-inch jelly roll pan with vegetable cooking spray. Spread spaghetti mixture evenly in prepared pan. In a large skillet, cook beef, onion, green pepper and garlic until beef is no longer pink; drain. Add tomato sauce and seasonings; simmer 5 minutes. Spoon meat mixture evenly over spaghetti. Top with mushrooms and cheese. Bake at 350 degrees for 20 minutes. Let stand 5 minutes before cutting.

Evelyn Stichter

SMOKED SAUSAGE AND PASTA

1/2-lb. smoked sausage (comes
   in a ring)
1/4 c. onion, chopped
2 c. broccoli
2 carrots, cut into matchsticks
1/2-lb. Mostaccioli Rigati,
   cooked
1/2 c. Parmesan cheese
1/2-1 c. mozzarella cheese,
   shredded
1/2 tsp. oregano
Parsley

Cut sausage into thin slices and cut each slice into 3 slivers. Heat in a large skillet until slightly browned; add broccoli and carrots. Stir fry 2-3 minutes, stirring constantly. Stir in cooled Rigati. Sprinkle Parmesan, mozzarella, oregano and parsley on top. Do not stir. Cover skillet and cook on lowest heat for 5 minutes to melt cheeses. The Mostaccioli Rigati is a tubular pasta. I've tried spaghetti, macaroni and other pasta forms, but the Mostaccioli tastes better in this recipe.

Merianne Shaffer

TACO CASSEROLE

1-lb. ground beef
2 c. tomato sauce
1 taco seasoning mix
2 1/2 c. corn chips
1 can refried beans
1/2 c. Cheddar cheese,
   shredded

Crush 2 cups corn chips; put in bottom of 11 x 7 1/2-inch pan. Brown beef. Add 1 1/2 cups tomato sauce and taco mix. Spoon meat over chips. Combine remaining sauce and refried beans; put on meat mixture. Bake at 375 degrees for 25 minutes. Put cheese and remaining chips on top; bake 5 minutes longer.

Barb Croyle

SQUASH CASSEROLE

1 1/2-lbs. squash
1 carrot, grated
1 med. onion, chopped
1 can cream of chicken soup

3/4 c. sour cream
1/2 stick margarine
1/2 pkg. Pepperidge Farm
  Herb Stuffing

Peel and cut up squash; cook until partially done. Put in a 1 1/2-quart casserole. Stir together onion, carrot, soup and sour cream. Add to squash. Melt margarine and stir into stuffing. Put on top of squash mixture. Bake at 350 degrees for 45 minutes.

Lou Thomas

CHEESY TACO CASSEROLE

2 c. macaroni, uncooked
1-lb. hamburger
1 1/4-oz. pkg. taco seasoning
  mix
1 15-oz. can tomato sauce
1 15-oz. can kidney beans

1/4 c. milk
2 1/2 c. Cheddar cheese,
  shredded
1 2.8-oz. can French fried onions
1 c. lettuce, shredded
1 med. tomato

Cook macaroni; drain and set aside. In a large skillet, brown meat. Add taco seasoning, tomato sauce and beans. Simmer, uncovered, for 5 minutes. Stir milk and most of cheese into hot macaroni. In a large buttered baking dish, layer 1/2 macaroni, 1/2 meat mixture and 1/2 onions. Repeat with macaroni and meat. Bake, uncovered, at 375 degrees for 20 minutes. To serve, top with remaining cheese and onions, and lettuce and tomatoes.

Barb Croyle

TAGLORENE

1 green pepper, chopped
1 onion, chopped
1 clove garlic, minced
2 tsp. olive oil
1 8-oz. can tomato sauce
1-lb. lean ground beef

1 can cream style corn
1 12-oz. pkg. noodles
1/2-lb. cheese (your choice)
1 can pitted ripe olives
1 T. Worcestershire sauce
Salt and pepper

Saute pepper, onion and garlic in olive oil. Add beef and cook until pink is gone. Add tomato sauce. Mix and cook briefly. Add corn, cooked noodles, olives and seasonings. Add half of grated cheese, with the rest on top. Bake at 350 degrees until bubbly. Save olive juice and use for rewarming leftovers - if any! Serves 10-12.

Florence Hershberger

It is good to give thanks to the Lord,
to sing praises to thy name. O Most High.
Psalm 92:1

TORTILLA BAKE

1 1/2-lbs. sausage and beef
2 c. cottage cheese
2 T. flour
1 tsp. oregano
1 tsp. basil

1/4 tsp. garlic
10 lg. tortilla shells
1 1/2 c. cheese
3 c. spaghetti sauce

Brown meat (total of 1 1/2-pounds); drain. Stir in cottage cheese, flour and 1/2 cup spaghetti sauce. Divide mixture onto tortilla shells. Roll up and place in cake pan. Mix remaining spaghetti sauce, oregano, basil and garlic. Pour over tortillas. Bake at 375 degrees for 35-40 minutes. Put cheese on the last 3 minutes just so it melts.

Sandy Owen

TOSTADA GRANDE

1-lb. ground beef
2 T. (1/2 pkg.) taco or chili
   seasoning mix
1 8-oz. can tomato sauce
1 4-oz. can diced green chilies,
   drained

1 8-oz. can crescent dinner rolls
   or refrigerated biscuits
1 c. refried beans
4-oz. cheese, shredded
1/2 head lettuce
1 lg. tomato, chopped
1 sm. onion, chopped

In a large skillet, brown beef; drain. Stir in seasoning, tomato sauce and chilies; heat until hot and bubbly. Simmer, uncovered, for 15 minutes. Lightly grease a 9 or 10-inch pie plate. Separate rolls or biscuits; arrange in pie plate. Press over bottom and up sides to form crust. Spread beans over dough; top with meat mixture. Bake at 375 degrees for 18-22 minutes or until crust is golden brown. Sprinkle immediately with cheese. Garnish with lettuce, tomatoes and onions. Makes 4-6 servings.

Marilyn Miller (Willie)

TATOR TOT CASSEROLE

1 1/2-lbs. hamburger
1 med. onion, cut up
1 lg. can green beans

1 can mushroom soup
Tator tots

Fry meat and onions together until meat is brown. Add mushroom soup and green beans. Mix together and put in casserole dish. Cover with tator tots and bake at 350 degrees for 1 hour.

Ruth Bauman

*"The Lord is near to all who call upon Him,
to all who call up Him in truth." Psalm 145:18*

TRASH CAN MEAL

Galvanized trash can
Bricks
Grill
Potatoes
Cabbage

Onions
Carrots
Sweet corn in husks, silks
  removed
Smoked sausage links

Put bricks in bottom of trash can; cover with a grill (on top of bricks). Cover with about 10-inches of water. Then layer: potatoes (on top of the grill), cabbage (cut in quarters), whole onions, carrots, sweet corn in husk, smoked sausage (Eckrich). Put on camp fire or charcoal for 2 hours. Don't open lid until after 2 hours. Absolutely delicious! Set garbage can on cement blocks and put fire between blocks.

LaVerne Coblentz

EASY TUNA NOODLE CASSEROLE

6-oz. egg noodles
1 9-oz. can tuna
10-oz. can cream of broccoli
  soup

1 c. Cheddar cheese, grated
1/2 c. milk
1/2 c. seasoned bread crumbs

Cook noodles; drain. Combine tuna, cream of broccoli soup, 1/2 cup grated cheese and milk in saucepan; heat until almost boiling. Mix noodles into sauce mix and pout into a medium-sized greased casserole dish. Sprinkle remaining cheese and bread crumbs over top. Cover and bake at 350 degrees for 20 minutes. Serves 4-6.

Brent Reinhardt

HOT TURKEY SALAD CASSEROLE

2 c. cooked turkey
1 1/2 c. celery, diced
1/2 c. almonds, chopped (opt.)
1/2 tsp. salt
2 T. onions, minced

2 T. lemon juice
1 c. mayonnaise
1/2 c. American cheese, grated
1 c. potato chips, crushed

Combine all ingredients, except cheese and potato chips. Pour into a greased casserole. Top with grated cheese and potato chips. Bake at 375 degrees for 20-25 minutes or until cheese is melted and chips are golden brown.

Arlene Hartman

Help me to live from day to day,
in such a self-forgetting way
that even when I kneel to pray,
my prayer may be for others.

WET BURRITOS

1-lb. hamburger	1/2 c. hot water
1 med. onion	1 c. refried beans
1 can mushroom soup	1/2 c. salsa
1 1/2 c. sour cream	1 pkg. soft tortilla shells
1 pkg. taco seasoning	3-4 c. cheese

Fry hamburger and onion; drain. Add taco seasoning, water, refried beans and salsa; heat through. Mix soup and sour cream. Pour 1/2 of soup mixture in a 9 x 13-inch pan. Lay out tortilla shells. Divide hamburger on shells (about 3-4 tablespoons). Roll up and place side by side in pan. Top with remaining soup mixture. Bake at 350 degrees for 20 minutes. Place shredded cheese on top. Bake another 10 minutes. *I use a mixture of Colby and mozzarella cheese.*

Marge Detweiler

WET BURRITOS

2 c. sour cream	Lettuce, chopped
1-lb. hamburger	Tomatoes, chopped
1 med. onion	1 sm. can mushrooms
1 med. green pepper	1 can mushroom soup
1 pkg. taco seasoning	1 16-oz. can refried beans
Black olives, chopped	1 pkg. soft tortilla shells (big size)

Mix sour cream and mushroom soup. Put 1/2 of mixture in bottom of 9 x 13-inch pan. Fry hamburger, onions and green pepper; add mushrooms, taco seasoning and beans. Cook to heat through. Divide hamburger mix into shells. Roll up and place on top of sour cream mixture in pan. Top with remaining mixture and cheese. Bake at 325 degrees for 20-25 minutes.

Marlene Sutter

WET BURRITO CASSEROLE

16-oz. sour cream	1 sm. can diced mushrooms
1 can cream of mushroom soup	1 pkg. taco seasoning
1-lb. hamburger	16-oz. can refried beans
1 med. onion, chopped	1 pkg. soft flour tortillas
1 med. green pepper, chopped	4 c. cheese, shredded

Mix sour cream and mushroom soup. Put 1/2 of mixture in bottom of 9 x 13-inch pan. Fry hamburger, onion and green pepper; drain. Add mushrooms, taco seasoning and beans to hamburger. Divide mixture onto tortillas. Roll up and place on sour cream mixture in pan. Top with remaining sour cream mixture and sprinkle with cheese. Bake at 350 degrees for 30 minutes.

Jill Erb

One who uses the Bible as his guide
never loses his sense of direction.

ZUCCHINI CASSEROLE

3 precooked chicken breasts, chopped in chunks
6 c. unpeeled zucchini, diced
1 c. onion, diced
1 c. carrot, shredded
1 can cream of chicken soup
1 8-oz. carton sour cream
1/8 tsp. garlic powder
1 pkg. chicken flavor stuffing mix
1/2 c. butter
1 c. Cheddar cheese, grated (opt.)

Combine zucchini and onion in medium saucepan; add water to cover and bring to boil. Boil for 5 minutes; drain and cool. Combine carrots, soup, sour cream and garlic powder in a large bowl. Add zucchini-onion mixture and chicken; mix. Spread in buttered 13 x 9-inch baking dish. To prepare topping, melt butter in skillet; add bread stuffing and seasoning packet; toss well. Sprinkle stuffing over casserole. Top with cheese. Bake at 350 degrees for 1 hour or until golden brown. Yield 6-8 servings.

Amy Martin

ZUCCHINI CASSEROLE-PENNSYLVANIA STYLE

1 c. Bisquick
3 c. zucchini, sliced
1/3 c. oil
3 eggs, well beaten
1 c. white American cheese, grated
1 tsp. salt
1/2 tsp. garlic powder
1/2 c. Parmesan cheese

Mix all ingredients together; pour into a greased casserole. Sprinkle Parmesan cheese on top. Bake at 350 degrees until zucchini is tender, 35-45 minutes. Serves 6.

Kathy Leinbach

ZUCCHINI AND CORN CHIPS

4-6 zucchini, sliced lengthwise
Corn chips
Monterey Jack cheese
Colby cheese
Hamburger

Peel and parboil zucchinis; drain. Brown hamburger; drain. Line bottom of baking dish with crushed corn chips. Put layer of zucchini, then hamburger, Colby cheese, more zucchini and top with Monterey Jack cheese. Bake at 350 degrees for 20-30 minutes. *Sausage instead of hamburger is also good.*

Carol Martin

Trust in the Lord with all thine heart;
and lean not unto thine own understanding.
In all thy ways acknowledge Him,
and He shall direct thy paths.
Proverbs 3:5-6

ZUCCHINI LASAGNA

1 lg. or 2 med. zucchini
1-lb. ground beef
1 sm. onion, chopped
1 c. tomato sauce
1 med. tomato, chopped
Pinch of oregano
Pinch of basil
1 c. ricotta cheese
1 c. cottage cheese
3/4 c. mozzarella cheese, grated

Brown beef; drain fat off. Add onion, tomato, tomato sauce and seasonings. Simmer 10-12 minutes. In oblong dish, layer zucchini, meat mixture and cheese, ending with meat and cheese on top. Bake in a 350 degree preheated oven for 30 minutes. Makes 6 servings.

Phyllis Stauffer

ZUCCHINI SKILLET SUPPER

4 c. zucchini
1 onion
2 c. canned tomatoes, with juice
3/4 c. fresh mushrooms
Cook chicken cubes or ground turkey, browned
Salt and pepper
Oregano
Parmesan cheese

Thinly slice zucchini to make 4 cups; add onion. Add tomatoes and juice, mushrooms and chicken or ground turkey. Add salt, pepper and oregano to taste. Simmer until well heated. Sprinkle with Parmesan cheese.

Ruby Panyako

A CHRISTIAN IS:

A mind through which Christ thinks
A heart through which Christ loves
A voice through which Christ speaks
A hand through which Christ helps
A life through which Christ lives.

Beef, Chicken, & Pork

BEEF, CHICKEN & PORK

Beef

AFTER CHURCH STEW

1 1/2-lbs. beef (1 1/2-in. cubes) 4 med. carrots, quartered
2 tsp. salt 2 med. onions, sliced
1/2 tsp. basil leaves 1 10 3/4-oz. can tomato soup
1/4 tsp. pepper 1/2 soup can water
2 stalks celery, sliced diagonally 3 med. potatoes, cubed

Place beef (no need to brown) in a 3-quart casserole. Sprinkle beef with salt, basil and pepper. Place celery, carrots and onions on top of beef. Combine soup and water. Pour over meat and vegetables coating all pieces. Cover tightly. Bake at 300 degrees for 3 hours. Add potatoes; bake 45 minutes longer. Serves 4-5.

Mary Rhoade

BAR B QUE

1 c. catsup 1 T. Worcestershire sauce
1 c. water 1 1/2-lbs. hamburger
1 1/2 T. vinegar 1 c. oatmeal
2 T. sugar

Fry hamburger with onion; add oatmeal. Add remaining ingredients. Bake at 350 degrees for 1-2 hours. *This is my mother's recipe.*

Phyllis Weaver

BBQ MEATBALLS

1-lb. ground beef 1 T. onion
1 egg 3 T. brown sugar
1 c. cracker crumbs 1/4 c. catsup
1 tsp. salt 1/8 tsp. nutmeg
1/4 tsp. pepper 1 tsp. dry mustard

Combine meat, egg, 3/4 cup crumbs, salt, pepper and onion; mix well. Mix together sugar, catsup, nutmeg and mustard. Add half sauce to meat mixture; mix well. Shape into 12 balls and place in muffin paper in muffin pan. Top with remaining sauce and sprinkle with remaining crumbs. Bake at 400 degrees for 30 minutes.

Barb Croyle

Add a little flour to your hamburger
to keep it from falling apart while grilling.

65

CABBAGE ROLL-UPS

1 head of cabbage
1-lb. hamburger
1 c. rice, uncooked
1 30-oz. jar spaghetti sauce
1 c. cracker crumbs
2 eggs
Parmesan cheese, grated

Steam head of cabbage; remove leaves. Combine hamburger, rice, cracker crumbs and eggs. Form meat mixture into egg size balls. Wrap meat mixture in cabbage leaf and secure with toothpick. Repeat until all meat mixture is used up. Put cabbage rolls in a casserole dish in a single layer. Pour spaghetti sauce over cabbage rolls and sprinkle with cheese. Bake at 350 degrees for 1-1 1/2 hours.

Tami Martin

ITALIAN BEEF

3-4 lb. rump roast
1 lg. onion, quartered
1/2 c. vinegar
3 cloves garlic
1 jar sweet cherry peppers (with juice)
3 c. water
Dry Italian dressing

Mix all ingredients in roasting pan. Bake at 300 degrees for about 3 hours. Slice thin; return to pan with juice. Cover and continue baking on low heat (175-200 degrees) for 1 1/2 hours. Serve as sandwiches on French bread.

MARINADE SAUCE FOR MEAT

1/3 c. soy sauce
2 T. catsup
2 T. oil
3/4 tsp. pepper
1/2 tsp. oregano
1/8 tsp. garlic powder

Mix ingredients together. Pour over meat and let marinate overnight in refrigerator. *Delicious on grilled steaks. I use on pork, beef, lamb and chicken. I also spread on hamburger patties to be grilled just before putting on the grill. I don't add the oil to my recipe.*

Gretchen Weaver

MEAT LOAF

1 1/2-lbs. hamburger
1/4 c. onion, chopped
1/4 c. oatmeal
1 c. bread crumbs
1/2 tsp. salt
1 T. sugar
1 egg, slightly beaten
1/2 c. tomato juice
1/2 c. water
1 T. barbecue sauce
1/2 tsp. liquid smoke
1 T. vinegar
Topping:
1/4 c. catsup
3 T. brown sugar
2 tsp. prepared mustard
2-3 drops liquid smoke

Mix all meat loaf ingredients thoroughly. Put into 9 x 5-inch baking dish that has been sprayed with Pam. Mix topping ingredients and spread over top of meat loaf. Bake at 350 degrees for 1 hour.

Lou Thomas

MEAT LOAF LORETTA

1-lb. hamburger
1/2 c. bread crumbs
1/2 c. milk
1 tsp. salt
1/2 tsp. pepper
2 T. parsley
1/2 c. onion, chopped
1 clove garlic, minced

1/2 tsp. oregano
1/4 tsp. basil
1/2 tsp. paprika
1/8 tsp. fennel
1/3 c. catsup
1 T. brown sugar
1 tsp. dry mustard

Combine hamburger, bread crumbs, milk, salt, pepper, parsley, onion, garlic, oregano, basil, paprika and fennel. Pat mixture into a loaf pan; bake at 350 degrees for 45 minutes. Combine catsup, brown sugar and dry mustard; spread on top of loaf. Bake 10 minutes more.

Wanda Balsley

POOR MANS STEAK

1-lb. hamburger
3/4 c. saltine cracker crumbs
3/4 c. milk
1 med. onion, diced
Salt and pepper

Topping:
1 can cream of chicken,
   mushroom or celery soup
2 soup cans milk

Mix above ingredients; press into a cake pan and chill overnight. Cut into squares; flour and fry. Drain and place back in pan. In a small bowl, whip soup with milk. Pour over meat (it will be runny). Bake at 350 degrees for 1 hour.

Grace Weldy
Deb Krawiec

ROAST

3-4 lb. beef roast
1 1.4-oz. pkg. Mrs. Grass Dry
   Onion-Mushroom Soup Mix

2 T. oil

Coat roast with flour and brown in oil in a heavy dutch oven. Sprinkle dry soup mix on top until it is covered (1/3 of a package). Put lid on and bake at 300 degrees for 1 1/2 hours. I don't add any water. If the temperature is low, it will make its own liquid and won't be dry.

Merianne Shaffer

SLOW COOK ROUND STEAK, ITALIAN STYLE

1 1/2-2 lb. round steak
1 15 1/2-oz. jar spaghetti sauce
1/2 tsp. leaf oregano

1 4-oz. can mushrooms
1 10-oz. pkg. frozen French
   style green beans

Cut meat into serving pieces. Arrange in a crock pot. Combine spaghetti sauce and oregano; pour over meat. Add mushrooms and green beans. Cook on Low heat for 8-10 hours.

Phyllis Kehr

SALISBURY STEAK-ONION GRAVY

1 10 1/2-oz. can condensed
   onion soup
1 1/2-lbs. ground beef
1/2 c. fine dry bread crumbs
1 egg, slightly beaten
1/4 tsp. salt

Dash of pepper
1 T. flour
1/4 c. catsup
1/4 c. water
1 tsp. Worcestershire sauce
1/2 tsp. prepared mustard

In a bowl, combine 1/3 cup soup with beef, crumbs, egg, salt and pepper. Shape into 6 oval patties. In a skillet, brown patties; pour off fat. Gradually blend remaining soup into flour until smooth. Add to skillet remaining ingredients; stir to loosen browned bits. Cover and cook over low heat for 20 minutes or until done, stirring occasionally. Serves 6.

Gloria Landes

SAUERKRAUT & BEEF

1 lg. jar sauerkraut
1-lb. arm roast (or other beef
   cut in small pieces)
1 lg. onion, chopped
1 lg. green pepper, chopped

2 T. catsup
1 tsp. paprika
Pinch of garlic powder
Salt (to taste)

Cook in crock pot on Low for 10-12 hours.

Sandy Miller

SLOPPY JOES

2-lbs. ground beef
Onion
Green pepper
1-2 cans pork & beans
   (Van Camps)

1 can mushrooms, drained
1-2 18-oz. bottles barbecue
   sauce (Hunts Hickory Flavor)

Brown ground beef, drain. Cook onion and green pepper with ground beef. Add mushrooms, beans and barbecue sauce. Heat to boiling then simmer for 20-30 minutes.

Rosemary Martin

SLOPPY JOE

5-lbs. hamburger
2 med. onions
4 stalks celery
1 can celery soup
1 can tomato soup
1 c. catsup
3/4 c. chili sauce

1 1/2 c. brown sugar
3/4 c. water
3 T. Worcestershire sauce
2 T. salt
2 tsp. pepper
2 tsp. Beau Monde

Brown hamburger, onions and celery. Add remaining ingredients; simmer 1-2 hours.

Dianne Hartman

Chicken

BROCCOLI CHEESE CHICKEN

1 T. margarine
4 skinless, boneless chicken
  breasts
1 can Campbell's Broccoli
  Cheese Soup

1/3 c. milk
1/8 tsp. pepper
2 c. broccoli flowerets

In skillet over medium heat, cook chicken in hot margarine for 10 minutes or until browned on both sides; drain off fat. Stir in soup, milk and pepper. Heat to boiling. Add broccoli. Reduce heat to low. Cover; simmer 10 minutes or until chicken is fork tender and broccoli is done, stirring occasionally. Serves 4. Preparation time: 5 minutes; Cooking time: 25 minutes.

Sherry Kehr

CHICKEN-BROCCOLI CREPES

10-oz. pkg. frozen broccoli
2 T. butter
2 T. flour
1/4 tsp. salt

1 1/2 c. milk
3/4 c. Swiss cheese
2 c. chicken, chopped
12 basic crepes or flour tortillas

Melt butter in saucepan. Blend in flour and salt. Add milk; cook until thick and bubbly. Add cheese; set aside. Combine chicken, broccoli and 1 cup cheese sauce. Spoon 1/4 cup filling in center of crepes. Roll up; place seam side up in baking dish. Pour remaining cheese sauce over crepes. Cover and bake at 375 for 20-30 minutes.

Beth Fervida

CHICKEN WITH A CHINESE FLAVOR

6 chicken breast halves, boned
  and skinned
1 T. oil
3 1/2 T. soy sauce

3 1/2 T. vinegar
1/2 c. brown sugar
1 onion, finely chopped
1 can cream of mushroom soup

Combine oil and soy sauce in fry pan. Fry chicken on medium-high heat for 3 minutes, turning once or twice. Put chicken in roast pan. Combine remaining ingredients and pour over chicken. Bake at 350 degrees for 35 minutes. Can serve over rice.

Nina Weaver

Don't have time to marinate meat? Put meat in freezer bags, add sauce and freeze. Meat marinates in the freezer.

CHICKEN COR-DON-BLEU

3 lg. chicken breasts, skinned,
  boned and halved
6 thin sliced boiled ham
3 slices mozzarella cheese,
  halved
1 med. tomato, seeded and
  chopped
1/2 tsp. dried sage, crushed
1/3 c. fine dry bread crumbs
2 T. Parmesan cheese, grated
2 T. parsley
4 T. butter, melted

Pound chicken slightly with meat mallet to 5 x 5-inches. Place ham slice and 1/2 cheese slice on each cutlet. Top with tomato and dash of sage. Tuck in sides and roll up jelly roll style. Combine bread crumbs, Parmesan cheese and parsley. Dip chicken in melted butter and then roll in crumbs; place in shallow baking dish. Bake at 350 degrees for 45 minutes.

Marge Detweiler

CHICKEN CRESCENT ALMONDINE

3 c. chicken, cooked
1 can cream of mushroom soup
1 8-oz. can water chestnuts,
  drained and chopped
1 4-oz. can mushrooms, drained
2/3 c. mayonnaise
1/2 c. celery, chopped
1/2 c. onion, chopped
1/2 c. sour cream
2/3 c. Swiss cheese, shredded
1/2 c. almonds, slivered
2-4 T. butter, melted
8-oz. pkg. crescent rolls

Combine first 8 ingredients in medium pan and cook over medium heat. Pour into lightly greased 9 x 13-inch baking dish. Separate crescent rolls into 4 squares; lay over hot mixture. Combine Swiss cheese, almonds and butter. Pour over dough. Bake at 375 degrees for 20-25 minutes.

Jan Ramer (Brian)

CHICKEN CRESCENTS

1 8-oz. pkg. crescent rolls
2 c. cooked chicken, deboned
3-oz. cream cheese with chives
2 T. butter
2 T. milk
1/2 tsp. salt
1/8 tsp. pepper
1 egg, beaten
Sesame seeds

Blend together cream cheese and butter. Add remaining ingredients, except crescent rolls, beaten egg and sesame seeds. Place together 2 crescent rolls to make a square; fill with 1/2 cup chicken mixture. Fold and pinch rolls closed. Put on lightly greased cookie sheet. Brush with beaten egg and sprinkle with sesame seeds. Bake at 350 degrees for 20 minutes or until brown. Serve with a brown gravy.

Sue Klaassen

CHICKEN ENCHILADAS

2 c. cooked chicken, chopped
1 c. green pepper, chopped
(opt.)
8-oz. picante sauce
8-oz. cream cheese
8 flour tortillas
3/4-lb. Velveeta cheese
1/4 c. milk

Stir chicken, green pepper, 1/2 cup picante sauce and cream cheese in pan over low heat until smooth. Spoon 1/3 cup chicken mixture onto each tortilla; roll up and place in greased baking dish. Stir Velveeta cheese and milk in pan over low heat until melted. Pour over tortillas; cover with foil. Bake at 350 degrees for 20 minutes. Pour remaining picante sauce over tortillas. Makes 4-6 servings.

Brenda Gongwer

CHICKEN MARMALADE

2 T. cornstarch
2 c. water
2 chicken bouillon cubes
1/2 c. orange marmalade
1 tsp. lemon juice
1 T. margarine
6 skinless chicken breasts
Rice

Stir together cornstarch, water, cubes, marmalade and lemon juice. In skillet, cook chicken in margarine. Remove. Pour cornstarch mixture in skillet; stir until thickened. Return chicken to skillet; cover and cook 5 minutes. Serve over rice.

Dwight and Margaret Hartzler

CHICKEN PAPRIKA

1/4 tsp. garlic
1 tsp. paprika
1 chicken, cut up into fryer pieces
2 med. or 1 lg. onion, sliced
2 tsp. paprika
2 c. chicken broth
1/4 c. water
1 T. cornstarch
1/4 tsp. salt
1 c. yogurt
2 T. flour
1/4 c. parsley flakes (or less)

Mix garlic and 1 teaspoon paprika together. Sprinkle over chicken pieces and brown in small amount of oil in skillet. Add onions, 2 teaspoons paprika and chicken broth. Cover and simmer for 35 minutes. Remove chicken pieces. Blend together water, cornstarch and salt; stir into skillet. Stir together yogurt, flour and parsley. Mix into skillet. Return chicken pieces to skillet. Heat thoroughly, but do not boil. Serve with brown rice or noodles.

Gretchen Weaver

Dice bacon before frying for more even, neater pieces.

CHICKEN SUPREME

8 slices bacon, partially cooked
4 whole chicken breasts, halved, skinned and boned
8 slices dried beef

2 cans cream of mushroom soup
1 c. sour cream (can use fat free)
Fresh mushrooms

Wrap 1 slice of bacon around each piece of chicken with dried beef inside chicken breast. Place side by side in greased baking dish. Mix soup and sour cream together; pour over chicken. Bake at 275 degrees for 2 hours. Garnish with fresh mushrooms.

Marilyn Miller (Willie)
Pat Stahly

COMPANY CHICKEN

1 pkg. dried beef
Chicken breasts, deboned
Bacon

1 can cream of mushroom soup
1 c. sour cream

Place dried beef on bottom of shallow baking dish. Lay deboned chicken breasts on top of dried beef. Pour mixture of soup and sour cream over meat. Cover and bake at 350 degrees for 1 1/2-2 hours. Before serving place strips of crisp bacon on top of chicken. Serve over rice.

Sue Klaassen

ESCALLOPED CHICKEN

1 c. rich milk
4 c. chicken broth
1/2 c. butter (part chicken fat)
3/4 c. flour

1/8 tsp. celery salt
5 c. cooked chicken, diced
2 c. fine dry bread crumbs

Heat milk and broth. Blend in butter and flour. Cook until smooth. Into greased baking dish, place a layer of chicken, a layer of gravy and a layer of bread crumbs. Repeat layers. Bake at 350 degrees for 30 minutes.

Bea Yoder

FINGER LICKING CHICKEN

1 4-5 lb. chicken, cut up
1 can chicken soup
1 can celery soup

1 can mushroom soup
2 T. rice, uncooked

Put celery soup, chicken soup, mushroom soup and uncooked rice in bottom of roaster. Stir lightly to blend soups. Lay each piece of chicken in soup, dotting each piece with butter. Season with salt carefully. Bake at 300-350 degrees until done. *Gravy is already made and very delicious.*

Ruth Metzler

FORGOTTEN CHICKEN

1 can cream of celery soup	1 1/2 c. rice
1 can cream of mushroom soup	Chicken pieces
1/2 c. milk	1 env. dry onion soup mix

Combine soups, milk and rice; place in bottom of buttered oblong pan. Roll chicken in dry onion soup mix and place on top of soup mixture. Cover with foil and bake at 350 degrees for 1 1/2 hours.

Connie Davidhizar

GOLDEN GLAZED CHICKEN

1/4 c. margarine	2 tsp. curry powder
1/2 c. honey	1 tsp. salt
1/4 c. Dijon mustard	1/8 tsp. garlic powder
2 T. prepared mustard	Chicken
2 tsp. lemon juice	

Boil all ingredients; pour over chicken. Bake at 350 degrees until done.

Katie Ann Schumm

HONEY BAKED CHICKEN

3-lbs. chicken	2 T. prepared mustard
1/3 c. margarine, melted	1 tsp. salt less!
1/3 c. honey	1 tsp. curry powder

Combine margarine, honey, mustard, salt and curry powder. Pour over chicken. Bake 1 1/4 hours, basting every 15 minutes, until chicken is tender and nicely browned. Serve with rice.

Ruby Panyako

INDIAN CHICKEN CURRY (One Dish Meal)

1/2 c. onion, finely chopped	1/2 tsp. Worcestershire sauce
1/2 c. celery, finely chopped	Salt and pepper (to taste)
1/4 c. shortening	1 tsp. curry powder
1/3 c. enriched flour	4 c. cooked chicken, diced
2 c. chicken broth	4 c. hot cooked rice
1 c. tomato juice	

Lightly brown onion and celery in shortening. Add flour and blend. Add broth; cook until thick, stirring constantly. Add tomato juice, Worcestershire sauce, seasonings and chicken; heat thoroughly. Serve over cooked rice. Makes 8 servings.

Ruth Zehr

When making lasagna, don't precook noodles.
Simply add more sauce, cover pan with foil
and cook slightly longer.

LATTICE TOP CHICKEN

1 can condensed cream of
   potato soup
3/4 c. milk
Pinch of seasoned salt
2 c. cooked chicken, cubed
1 can green beans

1 c. cooked carrots, chopped
1 c. Cheddar cheese, shredded
3/4 c. rice
1 4-oz. pkg. refrigerator
   crescent rolls
French fried onions (opt.)

Combine soup, milk, seasoned salt, chicken, vegetables and 1/2 cup cheese. Place in 8 x 12-inch baking dish. Bake, covered, at 375 degrees for 20 minutes. Unwrap crescent rolls; separate into 2 rectangles. Press together perforated cuts and cut into lengthwise strips. Place strips on casserole to form lattice top. Bake, uncovered, 15 minutes longer. Top lattice with remaining cheese and bake, uncovered, for 3-5 minutes. Serves 4-6.

Jane Schrock

LEMON CHICKEN

Boneless chicken, cooked
Lemon sauce:
1 part squeezed lemon juice

2 parts sugar (or more if sour)
Dash of salt
Cornstarch

Mix lemon sauce ingredients, adding enough cornstarch to thicken. Boil 1 minute. Pour over chicken. Serve with rice or baked potato.

Lois Leuz

SPANISH RICE & CHICKEN

2 1/2-3 lbs. chicken, cut up
1 tsp. salt
1 tsp. celery salt
1 tsp. paprika
1 c. rice, uncooked
3/4 c. onion, chopped
3/4 c. green pepper, chopped

1/4 c. fresh parsley, minced
   (or 1-2 T. dried)
1 1/2 c. chicken broth (or
   1-2 chicken bouillon cubes
   and water)
1 c. tomatoes, chopped
1 1/2 tsp. salt
1 1/2 tsp. chili powder

Place chicken in greased 13 x 9-inch baking pan. Combine garlic salt, celery salt and paprika; sprinkle over chicken. Bake, uncovered, at 425 degrees for 20 minutes. Remove chicken from pan. Combine rice, onion, green pepper and parsley; spoon into pan. In a saucepan, bring broth, tomatoes, salt and chili powder to a boil. Pour over rice mixture; mix well. Place chicken pieces on top. Cover and bake for 45 minutes or until chicken and rice are tender.

Phyllis Kehr

When making soup, drop a lettuce leaf
into pot to absorb excess grease.

STIR-FRIED CHICKEN AND RICE

or less   *black pepper*

4 T. oil, divided
2 c. broccoli flowerets   *other veg.*
1 c. matchstick carrot strips   *cauli? snowpeas*
1/2 c. walnuts, coarsely
  chopped
1 clove garlic, minced
4 chicken breast halves, boned,
  skinned and cut into thin strips *(less)*

2 T. soy sauce
2 T. water
1 tsp. ginger *?*
1/2 tsp. sugar   *or I TBS. Honey*
2 c. water
~~2 chicken bouillon cubes~~ *broth or water*
1 c. regular rice, uncooked

In a large skillet, heat 2 tablespoons oil over medium-high heat. Add broccoli, carrots, walnuts and garlic; stir-fry 2 minutes. Remove vegetables. Add remaining 2 tablespoons oil to skillet. Add chicken; stir-fry 1 minute or until chicken turns white. Add soy sauce, 2 tablespoons water, ginger and sugar; stir-fry 2 minutes. Remove chicken with slotted spoon. ~~Add 2 cups water and bouillon cubes to skillet;~~ bring to a boil. Stir in rice; cover tightly and simmer 20 minutes. Stir in chicken and vegetables. Heat thoroughly; let stand, covered, 5-10 minutes.

Merianne Shaffer

STIR-FRY CHICKEN

2 chicken breasts
2 T. oil
4 lg. fresh mushrooms (do
  not boil)
Pea pods
2 sm. onions
2 carrots

2 tsp. chicken bouillon
5 T. warm water
2 T. soy sauce
1 tsp. cornstarch
1/2 tsp. sugar
1/4 tsp. garlic

Stir-fry chicken in oil in wok or electric skillet. Boil water and add crispy vegetables; boil rapidly for 1-2 minutes. When chicken is done, add onions and all crispy vegetables (already boiled). Be careful not to over fry vegetables, especially mushrooms. Dissolve bouillon in water; add remaining ingredients, stirring well. Add sauce; coat chicken and vegetables well. Serve over rice. *Add or delete vegetables as your family likes.*

Sandy Miller

EASY TACO CHICKEN

Chicken breasts, boneless and
  skinless
2 cans cream soup (any kind,
  mix and match)

1 pkg. taco seasoning
Cheese, shredded

Place chicken breasts in bottom of baking dish. Mix soups and taco seasoning; pour over chicken. Bake until chicken is done. Sprinkle with cheese and return to oven until cheese melts.

Dove Leinbach

SWEET AND SOUR CHICKEN

2 T. vegetable oil
1 onion, chopped
3 T. catsup
3 T. sugar
2 tsp. soy sauce

2 T. lemon juice
Dash of black pepper
4 chicken breasts, halved
1 T. cornstarch
2 T. water

Saute onion in oil over medium heat. In a small bowl, combine sugar, catsup, soy sauce, lemon juice and pepper. Add to pan with onion. Add chicken. Bring to a boil; cover and simmer 35 minutes or until chicken is done. Remove chicken to serving platter. Dissolve cornstarch in water. Add to pan with sauce. Bring to a boil and stir until thick. Pour over chicken.

Marilyn Stauffer

SWEET 'N SOUR CHICKEN

1-lb. boneless chicken, cut
   into cubes
2 T. oil
1 garlic clove, minced
1 c. green pepper strips
1 c. carrot strips
1 1/4 c. chicken broth
1/2 c. soy sauce

3 T. vinegar
3 T. brown sugar
1/2 tsp. ground ginger
1 20-oz. can chunk pineapple
   in juice
1 1/2-2 c. Minute Rice
1 10-oz. jar maraschino cherries,
   drained and cut in half

Saute chicken in oil until lightly browned. Add garlic and vegetables; stir fry 3-5 minutes. Add broth, soy sauce, vinegar, sugar, ginger and pineapple with juice. *(I mix all of this together and then add to skillet.)* Bring to a full boil. Stir in rice. Cover, remove from heat and let stand for 5 minutes. Add cherries and stir. Makes 4-6 servings.

Sherry Kehr

ZESTY BAKED CHICKEN

1/2 tsp. paprika
1/2 tsp. dried basil
1/4 tsp. garlic
6 chicken breast halves, skinned
   and boned

3/4 c. plain low-fat yogurt,
   divided
2 tsp. soy sauce
1 T. flour
2 T. Parmesan cheese, grated

Combine first 3 ingredients. Sprinkle over both sides of chicken. Place in 13 x 9 x 2-inch baking dish. Combine 1/4 cup yogurt and soy sauce. Brush half over chicken. Bake at 350 degrees for 10 minutes. Turn chicken over, brush with remaining yogurt mixture and bake another 10 minutes. Combine remaining 1/2 cup yogurt and flour; stir well. Spoon over chicken. Sprinkle with cheese. Bake another 15 minutes or until chicken is done.

Grace Ramer

TURKEY PATTIES

1 1/4-lb. ground turkey
1/4 c. catsup
1/3 c. oatmeal
1 egg (or 1/4 c. egg substitute)

1 1/4 tsp. Worcestershire sauce
1/2 tsp. poultry seasoning
1/2 tsp. onion powder

Mix all together and make into patties. Grill outside or broil in oven.

Diane Miller

Pork

BBQ SPARE RIBS

2 pkgs. country style spare ribs
1/3 c. vinegar
1/4 c. catsup
2 T. salad oil

2 T. soy sauce
1 T. Worcestershire sauce
1 tsp. mustard
1 tsp. salt

Mix ingredients together. Place meat in a crock pot. Pour sauce over top. Turn on low and cook 6-12 hours. *If you turn the crock pot on just before bed, the meat will be tender and ready to eat at noon the next day.*

Barb Croyle

CHEESE HAM RING-AROUND

1 1/2 c. fresh or frozen broccoli, uncooked
1 T. parsley flakes
2 T. onion, finely chopped
2 T. table mustard
1 T. margarine
1 tsp. lemon juice

8-oz. Cheddar cheese, shredded
1 1/2 c. ham (or turkey ham), chunked
1 8-oz. can Pillsbury Refrigerated Quick Crescent Dinner Rolls
Parmesan cheese, grated

Heat oven to 350 degrees. Cook and drain broccoli. In a large mixing bowl, combine parsley, onion, mustard, margarine and lemon juice; blend well. Add cheese, broccoli and ham; mix lightly and set aside. Separate crescent dough into 8 triangles. On greased cookie sheet, arrange triangles, point toward the outside, in a circle with bases overlapping. The center opening should be about 3-inches in diameter. Spoon ham filling in a ring evenly over bases of triangles. (Some filling may fall onto cookie sheet.) Fold points of triangles over filling and tuck under bases of triangles at center of circle. Sprinkle with Parmesan cheese. Bake at 350 degrees for 25-30 minutes or until golden brown. To make ahead, cover and refrigerate for up to 3 hours. Bake 30-35 minutes.

Sandy Owen

A smile is a language understood by all persons.

GINGERED HAM SLICES

5-lb. canned ham, sliced
  1-in. thick
1 c. ginger ale
1 c. orange juice
1/2 c. brown sugar

2 T. salad oil
3 tsp. wine vinegar
2 tsp. dry mustard
1/2 tsp. ground ginger
1/4 tsp. ground cloves

Slash fat edge of ham. Combine remaining ingredients. Pour over ham in shallow dish. Refrigerate overnight spooning marinade over ham several times. Broil ham slices over low coals about 15 minutes on each side, brushing frequently with marinade. (Just heat through if using canned ham.)

Lisa Heinz

HAM, PINEAPPLE & RICE

3 T. brown sugar
3 T. butter, melted
Pineapple slices
Ham slices
2 1/2 tsp. flour
1/2 tsp. salt

1/8 tsp. pepper
1 1/2 tsp. minced onion
1 1/3 c. Minute Rice
1 c. milk
1 c. water

Blend brown sugar and butter. Pour into a 9 x 9-inch pan. Cover bottom of pan with pineapple, then ham. Place in hot oven (400 degrees). Meanwhile, combine remaining ingredients in saucepan. Bring to a boil. Reduce heat, cover and simmer 5 minutes, stirring occasionally. Spread over pineapple and ham. Cover and bake 10 minutes.

Dove Leinbach

PORK CHOPS & HASH BROWNS

6 thin pork chops
Vegetable oil
Seasoned salt
1 lg. can French fried onion rings
1 can mushroom soup
1 c. Cheddar cheese

1 24-oz. pkg. frozen hash browns
1/2 c. milk
1/2 c. sour cream
1/2 tsp. pepper
Dash of salt

Brown chops in vegetable oil. Season with seasoned salt. Mix soup, milk, sour cream, pepper and dash of salt; stir well. Stir in hash browns, 1/2 cup cheese and 1/2 can French fried onions. Spoon into 9 x 13-inch baking dish. Lay pork chops on top. Bake, covered, at 350 degrees for 40 minutes. Remove from oven and top with remaining cheese and onion rings. Bake, uncovered, for 5-10 additional minutes.

Sandy Miller

PORK CHOPS & SAUERKRAUT

4 pork chops
2 T. cooking oil
1 c. onion, chopped
1 14 1/2-oz. can chicken broth
1/2 tsp. caraway seed

1/4 tsp. celery seed
1 16-oz. can sauerkraut, drained
1 red apple, cored and chopped
4 bacon strips, cooked and
   crumbled (opt.)

In a skillet, brown pork chops in oil; drain. Stir in onion, pepper, broth, caraway seed and celery seed. Cover and cook over medium heat for 45-50 minutes. Add sauerkraut and apple. Cover and simmer 10-15 minutes or until heated through. Before serving, sprinkle with bacon, if desired.

Evelyn Troyer

SALTED PORK

Bacon, unsliced
Flour

Pack a chunk of unsliced bacon in salt as long as you like. When you wish to use, soak in water overnight, slice and roll in flour. Fry. Very good.

SAUSAGE BREAD

1 frozen bread loaf, thawed
1/2-lb. sausage
1/4 c. onion, chopped
1/4 c. green pepper, chopped
6 slices mozzarella cheese

Pizza sauce:
1 8-oz. can tomato sauce
1 tsp. oregano
1 tsp. basil
1/4 tsp. garlic powder

Roll out thawed dough into a large rectangle. Place cheese end to end down the center. Brown sausage, onion and green pepper. Place this over cheese. Fold 1 side of dough over meat, then the other side over the first to seal. Bake at 350 degrees for 16-18 minutes. *For a softer crust, brush with butter after baking.* Pour pizza sauce over sausage bread and serve.

Jan Ramer (Brian)

---

*You'll never shed another tear
while cutting onions if you try this:*

*Before peeling, cut the root end of the onion
and run cold water on the cut while you
rub area with your thumb.*

FAVORITE RECIPES

Recipe Name   **Page #**

Salads, Dressings, & Soups

SALADS, DRESSINGS & SOUPS

Salads

APRICOT SALAD

1 can crushed pineapple
1 1/2 c. water
1 6-oz. box apricot jello

1 8-oz. pkg. cream cheese
2 T. milk
1 12-oz. carton Cool Whip

Boil pineapple, water and jello. cook until syrupy; cool. Cream cream cheese and milk with beater. Add to cooled, thickened jello mixture. Fold in Cool Whip. *(I use most of it, but not the whole 12-ounces.)* You can freeze this until ready to use.

Dorothy Miller

APRICOT SALAD

2 3-oz. pkgs. apricot jello
2 c. boiling water
1 8-oz. pkg. cream cheese
1 c. milk

1 20-oz. can crushed pineapple,
   undrained
1 can apricots, diced
4-oz. whipped topping

Dissolve gelatin in boiling water; set aside. Beat softened cream cheese until smooth; stir in gelatin and milk. Add pineapple and diced apricots; mix well. Chill. When mixture begins to thicken, fold in whipped topping. Chill for at least 2 hours. Serves 10.

Marilyn Stauffer

MIXED BEAN SALAD

1 can green string beans
1 can yellow string beans
1 can dark red kidney beans
1 can lima beans (or frozen)
Green or red pepper
1/2 c. onion, finely chopped

Dressing:
1/2 c. vinegar
3/4 c. sugar
1/3 c. salad oil
Salt and pepper

Mix vinegar, sugar, oil, salt and pepper. Pour over drained vegetables which have been mixed in a large bowl. Refrigerate 24 hours.

Grace Weldy

BROCCOLI SALAD

1 bunch broccoli, washed
   and cut up
1 med. onion, chopped
10 slices bacon, fried
   and crumbled

1 c. sunflower seeds
Dressing:
1 c. Miracle Whip
1/2 c. sugar
1 T. vinegar

Pour dressing over first 4 ingredients. Refrigerate.

Grace Weldy

BROCCOLI SALAD

Dressing:
1 c. mayonnaise
1/2 c. sugar
2 tsp cider vinegar

Salad:
2 med. bunches broccoli, cleaned and broken
1/2 c. raisins
1/2 c. red onion, sliced
8 slices bacon, cooked and crumbled

Mix dressing ingredients; refrigerate 6-8 hours or overnight. When ready to serve, combine remaining ingredients. Stir in dressing and serve.

Dianne Kehr

CHINESE CABBAGE SALAD

1 med. or 2 sm. heads Napa cabbage, chopped
2 bunches green onions, chopped
1/3 c. sesame seeds (or desired amount)
1/3 c. slivered almonds

2 pkgs. Ramen noodles (without flavor packet)
Dressing:
1/3 c. rice vinegar
1/4 c. sugar
1/2 c. oil
2 T. soy sauce

Mix green onions and chopped Napa cabbage; chill. In a small amount of margarine, brown sesame seeds, almonds and broken Ramen noodles each separately. Wrap each separately in foil; do not chill.

For dressing: Boil vinegar, sugar, oil and soy sauce for 1 minute; chill. Toss all ingredients together. *This recipe does not keep well as leftovers, so if it is just for 2 people, you may want to halve recipe.*

Barb Croyle

CRANBERRY RELISH

12-oz. cranberries
1 green apple
2 oranges
1 c. walnuts

1/2 c. orange marmalade
1/4 c. raisins (opt.)
1/4 c. brown sugar

Core apple but do not peel. Grate the zest off the oranges and save. The white membrane tends to be bitter, so peel it off oranges. Coarsely grind cranberries, cored apple, and peeled oranges. Add orange zest and remaining ingredients. Refrigerate for 3 hours to blend flavors before serving.

Merianne Shaffer

So there abide faith, hope and charity,
these three; but the greatest of these is charity.
1 Cor. 13:13

CRANBERRY SALAD

2 12-oz. pkgs. fresh cranberries
4 or 5 apples, peeled
3 oranges
Grated peel of 1 orange (opt.)
2 1/2 c. sugar

2 3-oz. pkgs. raspberry jello
2 c. boiling water
1 c. cold water
Nuts, chopped

Put cranberries, apples and oranges through the grinder. Add sugar; stir to dissolve. This should make about 6 cups relish. Divide into 3 freezer boxes and freeze. To make salad, dissolve jello with boiling water. Add cold water. Add 1 portion (2 cups) frozen relish, partially thawed. Chopped nuts may be added. Pour in ring mold or bowl.

Mary Martin

FLORIDA LETTUCE SALAD

1 head lettuce
1 bunch green onions
1 bag slivered almonds
1 pkg. chicken flavor Ramen
 noodles

Dressing:
1 or 2 T. vinegar
1 T. sugar
1/4 c. oil
1/2 tsp. pepper
1 tsp. salt
Seasoning packet from noodles

Saute almonds in margarine. Combine lettuce, chopped green onion, almonds and mashed noodles. Combine dressing ingredients; mix well. Pour over salad right before serving.

Jill Erb

FROZEN MINT SALAD

8-oz. butter mints
3-oz. lime jello
20-oz. can crushed pineapple

2 c. boiling water
10-oz. Cool Whip
2 c. sm. marshmallows

Dissolve jello in water; add mints. Add pineapple with juice. Chill 6-7 hours. Add Cool Whip and marshmallows. Freeze.

Patty Bontrager

FRUIT SALAD

3 red apples
3 oranges, chopped
1/2 c. celery, chopped
1/3 c. nuts, chopped

3 T. honey
3 T. lemon juice
1/2 c. raisins

In serving bowl, toss apples, oranges, celery, raisins and nuts. In a small bowl, combine honey and lemon juice. Drizzle over fruit salad and serve. Makes 6-8 servings.

Donnabelle Hoover

HARVEST APPLE SALAD

1/3 c. sugar
3/4 c. water
2 T. flour
3 T. lemon juice
3 T. butter
1 c. pineapple chunks, drained

4 c. apples, diced
1 c. celery, diced
1/2 c. pecans, chopped
1 c. red or white grapes, halved
1 c. miniature marshmallows

Combine sugar, water, flour, lemon juice and butter. Cook over low heat until thickened; cool. Combine remaining ingredients; pour dressing over fruit. Serve or refrigerate to serve the next day.

Marilyn Stauffer

FRUIT SALAD

1 lg. can mixed fruit
Mandarin oranges
Pineapple chunks
Apples
Grapes

Bananas
1 sm. box instant vanilla
   pudding
1 1/2 c. Cool Whip

Drain mixed fruit; mix with remaining fruit. Add dry pudding mix. Let stand in refrigerator 8 hours. Add Cool Whip several hours before serving.

Beverly Coblentz

QUICK FRUIT SALAD

1 21-oz. can peach pie filling
3 firm bananas, sliced

2 c. strawberries, halved
1 c. seedless grapes

Combine all ingredients in a bowl. Refrigerate until serving. Serves 6-8.

Patty Bontrager

GARDEN SALAD

1 sm. can peas
1 can white corn
1 can French style green beans
1 sm. jar pimentos
1/2-1 c. celery, cubed
1/2-1 c. onion, diced

Dressing:
1 c. sugar
3/4 c. vinegar
1 tsp. salt
1/2 tsp. pepper

Bring dressing ingredients to a boil; cool and pour over vegetables. Let stand overnight. *Delicious!*

Dorothy Miller

Lord, help me to remember that nothing is going to happen to me today that you and I together can't handle.

GRANDMA'S ORANGE SALAD

1 11-oz. can mandarin oranges
1 8-oz. can crushed pineapple
Water
1 6-oz. box orange gelatin
1-pt. orange sherbet, softened
2 bananas, sliced

Drain oranges and pineapple; save juices and set aside. Add water to juice to make 2 cups. Heat to a boil and add gelatin. Stir in sherbet until smooth. Chill until partially set (watch carefully). Fold in fruit. Pour into 6 cup mold. Makes 8-10 servings.

Beth Fervida

HELEN'S SALAD

1 lg. can crushed pineapple
1 lg. can mandarin oranges
Water
2/3 c. little pearl tapioca
1 c. sugar
1 lg. box orange jello

Drain juice from pineapple and oranges; add water to make 6 cups. Bring water and juices to a boil; add tapioca. Boil 10 minutes. Let stand 10 minutes. Add sugar and jello; let cool. Add to fruit. Refrigerate until set. Add whipped topping, as desired.

Lois Blosser

ICE CREAM SALAD

1 pkg. orange jello
1 c. boiling water
1-pt. vanilla ice cream
1 sm. can crushed pineapple

Dissolve jello in boiling water. Add ice cream and stir. When ice cream is melted, add pineapple. Chopped nuts and miniature marshmallows may be added. Chill until firm. *Variations: Lime jello may be used or strawberry jello and strawberry ice cream. Good to the last bite!*

Lois Blosser

ITALIAN SALAD

2 c. cauliflower
2 c. broccoli
3-4 lg. carrots
1 sm. onion
4-5 lg. stalks celery
2 green peppers
2 cucumbers, peeled
and seeded
1 can black olives
1 jar green olives
1 can water chestnuts
Marinade:
1 c. oil
1 c. sugar
1 c. vinegar
2 env. Good Seasons Italian
Dressing Mix
Salt and pepper (to taste)

Chop all vegetables, olives and water chestnuts. Combine ingredients for marinade; add chopped ingredients. Stir well and marinate in refrigerate at least 24 hours before serving.

Kathy Kulp

JELLO VEGETABLE SALAD

1 pkg. Knox gelatin
1/4 c. cold water
1 1/4 c. boiling water
1 tsp. salt
1/2 c. sugar
1/4 c. ReaLemon juice
1/4 c. vinegar

1 sm. onion, chopped
1 c. cabbage, shredded
2 T. green pepper, chopped
1/4 c. olives, chopped
1/2 c. carrots, chopped
1 c. celery, chopped

Soften gelatin in cold water; dissolve in boiling water. Add salt, sugar, lemon juice and vinegar. Chill until set lightly. Put in mold of choice. Serves 10.

Erma Hartman

LIME JELLO RING DELITE

1 6-oz. pkg. lime jello
1-pt. sour cream (or low fat yogurt)

1 c. crushed pineapple, drained
2 c. boiling water

Dissolve jello in boiling water; cool. Add low fat yogurt or sour cream; whip or blend into jello. Add pineapple and pour into mold. To make this lo-cal, use non fat yogurt and sugar free jello.

Gloria Tyson

LIME SALAD

1 3-oz. pkg. lime jello
1 c. boiling water
1/2 c. salad dressing
1/4 c. light cream

1 8-oz. can crushed pineapple, undrained
1 c. cottage cheese
1/2 c. nuts

Dissolve jello in water. Chill until slightly thick. Blend salad dressing and cream. Stir into jello. Add remaining ingredients. Put in mold or dish and chill.

Ruth Bauman

MACARONI SALAD

1 1/2 c. elbow macaroni, uncooked
1/2 sm. onion, finely chopped
1/3 c. sweet pickle relish
1/2 tsp. salt
1/2 tsp. garlic salt

3/4 c. salad dressing
1/3 c. bacon bits
1/2-1 tsp. parsley flakes
1/3 c. carrots, chopped (adds color)

Cook macaroni for 7 minutes. Add remaining ingredients. Refrigerate until ready to serve.

Delora Reinhardt

MACARONI SALAD

1-lb. macaroni, uncooked	Dressing:
Several stalks of celery, diced	1 c. oil
Green peppers, diced	1 c. vinegar
Tomato chunks (or cherry	4 T. sugar
tomatoes)	1 tsp. salt
Cheese cubes (your favorite)	2 T. oregano
Pepperoni	1 tsp. pepper
1 can black olives, sliced	1 env. Italian Dressing Mix
Dill pickle chunks	

Bring 2-3 quarts water with 1 teaspoon salt added to a rolling boil; add uncooked macaroni. Bring to a rolling boil again. Add 2-3 tablespoons oil so it doesn't run over; cover. Turn off burner and let stand until macaroni is soft, approximately 20-25 minutes. Rinse in cold water. Pour dressing over macaroni and remaining ingredients; chill. Keeps well in refrigerator.

Carolyn F. Yoder

PASTA SALAD

2 c. colored macaroni,	2 c. cherry tomatoes
uncooked	1 can black olives, drained
1 cucumber, thinly sliced	1/4 c. Parmesan cheese
3 carrots, thinly sliced	1/2 c. Italian dressing
2 c. sm. broccoli pieces	

Cook macaroni; drain and rinse immediately with cold water (very important). Drain well. In bowl, mix macaroni with cucumbers, carrots, broccoli, cherry tomatoes (cut in halves or fourths), olives (cut in halves) and Parmesan cheese. Pour dressing over all. Let set for 1 hour in refrigerator to allow flavors to mix. *You can add other ingredients like: cheese, pepperoni and kidney beans.*

Gretchen Weaver

MANDARIN JELLO SALAD

1 (6-oz.) can orange juice	2 11-oz. cans mandarin oranges,
concentrate	drained
1 lg. box orange jello	1 3 3/4-oz. box lemon instant
2 1/2 c. boiling water	pudding mix
1 13 1/2-oz. (or lg.) can crushed	1 c. cold milk
pineapple	1 1/4 c. Cool Chip

Dissolve gelatin in boiling water; add undrained pineapple and orange concentrate. Chill until partially set. Fold in oranges. Pour into a 13 x 9-inch pan. Chill until firm. Beat pudding with milk until smooth. Fold in whipped cream and spread over gelatin.

Delora Reinhardt

POTATO SALAD

Potatoes	Dressing:
Eggs, hard boiled	Mayonnaise (enough to moisten)
Onion, chopped	1 T. mustard
Celery	1 T. horseradish
Parsley	1 tsp. sugar
	2 tsp. vinegar
	Salt and pepper

Cook potatoes in skins. Peel when cool; slice or chop. Mix dressing ingredients (use 1 teaspoon each mustard and horseradish if fewer potatoes; more sugar and vinegar if larger amount). Mix dressing into potatoes. Add chopped onion, celery and parsley to taste. Arrange sliced hard boiled eggs on top. *Can also decorate with tomato wedges, green pepper rings and lettuce leaves.*

Lois Leuz

POTATO SALAD

4 lg. potatoes, grated	1 T. prepared mustard
1 sm.-med. onion, chopped	3 or 4 lg. hard cooked eggs,
1/2 tsp. celery seed	chopped
2 c. Kroger salad dressing	Paprika
1/3 c. sugar	

Cook potatoes with peelings on; grate when cold. Add chopped onion and celery seed. Mix together salad dressing, sugar and mustard; stir into potatoes. Add eggs and mix. Sprinkle paprika on top.

Doris Reinhardt

POTATO SALAD WITH COOKED DRESSING

8 c. potatoes, cooked and diced	2 tsp. butter
(approx.)	1 tsp. salt
2 med. onions, chopped	1 tsp. dry mustard
2 lg. or 3 med. eggs	1/2 c. vinegar
1 c. sugar	

In a large bowl, mix cooked and diced potatoes with chopped onion; set aside. Combine eggs, sugar, butter, salt, mustard and vinegar. Stir constantly until it comes to a full boil and thickened. Pour over potatoes and onion mixture.

Thelma Mishler

Let my house be a house of prayer, a happy home, a haven where my every task is offered there in service, Lord, to thee.
Amen.

RAW RED BEET SALAD

1 red beet	1 tsp. sugar
1 T. vinegar	1/4 tsp. salt
1 T. oil	1 green onion, sliced

Peel and shred raw beet. Mix together with remaining ingredients. Chill.

Betty Hochstetler

RAW SQUASH SALAD

2 c. raw squash, shredded	1 sprig parsley, chopped
2 T. lemon juice	1 green onion, chopped
1/4 c. cream	1/4 tsp. cinnamon

Mix together, chill and serve.

Betty Hochstetler

CRUNCHY SPINACH SALAD

2-qts. fresh spinach	1 onion, sliced
1 16-oz. can bean sprouts, drained	Dressing:
	1/2 c. brown sugar
1 8-oz. can sliced water chestnuts, drained	1/2 c. vegetable oil
	1/3 c. vinegar
4 eggs, hard boiled	1/3 c. catsup
6 strips, bacon, crumbled	1 T. Worcestershire sauce

Beat dressing ingredients with a beater. Top just prior to serving.

Carolyn Graber

EMILY'S SPINACH SALAD

2/3 c. vegetable oil	1/2 tsp. curry powder
1/4 c. wine vinegar	1/2 tsp. salt
2 tsp. lemon juice	1/2 tsp. seasoned pepper
2 tsp. soy sauce	1 pkg. fresh spinach, torn
1 tsp. sugar	5 bacon strips, cooked
1 tsp. dry mustard	2 hard boiled eggs, sliced
1/4 tsp. garlic powder	

Combine oil, vinegar, lemon juice, soy sauce, sugar, mustard, garlic powder, curry powder, salt and seasoned pepper in a jar. Cover tightly and shake to mix well. Put torn spinach in a bowl. Before serving add dressing and toss. Garnish with bacon and egg slices. *Options: Add 2 cups bean sprouts, 1 8-ounce can water chestnuts or 1 small onion.*

Linda Hartman

*Please, Lord, fill my mouth with worthwhile stuff
and nudge me when I've said enough.*

SPINACH SALAD

1/2 c. oil
1/4 c. apple cider vinegar
1/2 c. sugar
2 T. Worcestershire sauce

1 10-oz. pkg. fresh spinach
1/2 c. onions (or leeks), chopped
1/4-lb. bacon, chopped, fried
and drained

Mix oil, vinegar, sugar and Worcestershire sauce in blender. Refrigerate. Chop spinach and dry with paper towels. Put in bowl. Add onions and cooled bacon. Pour dressing over; mix well. Serve immediately.

Gretchen Weaver

STRAWBERRY JELLO SALAD

1 lg. (6-oz.) pkg. strawberry jello
1 #2 can crushed pineapple
3/4-pt. whipping cream

1 16-oz. carton small cottage
cheese

Bring jello and pineapple with juice to a full boil. Cool to room temperature. Add whipping cream (whipped stiff) and cottage cheese. Add pecans, if desired.

Marilyn Miller (Willie)

TACO SALAD

1-lb. hamburger
1 med. onion
1 1/2 T. flour
1 tsp. salt
1/2 tsp. oregano
1 tsp. chili powder
1 15-oz. can kidney beans

2 c. tomato sauce (or catsup)
1-lb. taco chips (or corn chips)
1/2 head lettuce, shredded
8-oz. cheese, shredded
4 tomatoes, chopped
1 c. onion, chopped

In skillet, brown hamburger and onion; stir in flour. Add salt, oregano, chili powder, kidney beans and tomato sauce or catsup. Place corn or taco chips, sauce, lettuce, onion, cheese and tomatoes on plate in order given. *Delicious!*

Esther Martin

QUICK TACO SALAD

3/4-lb. lean ground beef
1/2 c. onion, chopped
1 pkg. Rice-A-Roni (beef flavor)
1/2 c. salsa
1 tsp. chili powder

4 c. lettuce, shredded
1 med. tomato, chopped
1/2 c. Monterey Jack or
Cheddar cheese, shredded
1/2 c. tortilla chips, crushed

In a large skillet, brown ground beef and onion; drain. Remove from skillet; set aside. In same skillet, prepare Rice-A-Roni as directed on package. Stir in meat mixture, salsa and chili powder; continue cooking over low heat until heated through. Arrange lettuce on serving platter. Top with rice mixture, tomato and tortilla chips. Serves 5.

Marlene Sutter

Dressings

BLENDER MAYONNAISE

1 lg. egg
2 tsp. lemon juice
1/2 tsp. dry mustard
1/2 tsp. salt
1 tsp. vinegar
1 c. soybean oil

Put egg in blender. Add salt, mustard and lemon juice. Put on lid and blend on High speed. Remove center lid and slowly add half of oil while keeping blender on. Add vinegar and remaining oil. Makes a little more than 1 cup. Keeps no longer than 1 week.

Gretchen Weaver

COLESLAW, POTATO OR MACARONI SALAD DRESSING

3/4 c. sugar
2 T. vinegar
2 tsp. table mustard
1/2 tsp. celery seed (opt.-
can use real celery)
1 c. Miracle Whip
1 tsp. salt

For Coleslaw: Shred cabbage and add onion. For Macaroni Salad: Cook 5 cups macaroni, use real celery, add onion and chopped boiled eggs. Sprinkle with parsley flakes for color; serve. For Potato Salad: Use real celery and add chopped boiled eggs and diced potatoes. Makes 5-6 cups.

Sandy Owen

FRENCH ITALIAN SALAD DRESSING

1/2 c. vegetable oil
1/4 c. cider vinegar
1/2 c. catsup
3 T. sugar
3/4 tsp. salt
1/8 tsp. pepper
1/2 tsp. dry mustard
1/2 tsp. paprika
1/2 tsp. oregano
1/8 tsp. garlic powder
1 1/2 tsp. dry onions

Blend well all ingredients in a blender. Chill in refrigerator.

Gretchen Weaver

FRENCH SALAD DRESSING

3 cans tomato soup
3 c. oil
2 1/2 c. white sugar
1 1/2 c. vinegar
1 1/2 tsp. pepper
3 tsp. salt
3 tsp. paprika
1 1/2 tsp. dry mustard
1/2 tsp. Worcestershire sauce
1/2 tsp. onion powder
1/2 tsp. celery salt

Mix together and refrigerate.

Ruby Panyako

POPPY SEED DRESSING

1 c. vegetable oil
1/3 c. cider vinegar
1/3 c. honey

2 T. poppy seeds
1/2 tsp. salt

Blend well in blender. Chill before serving.

Gretchen Weaver

Soups

BEEF BARLEY SOUP

1 sm. can canned beef
1 can mushroom pieces, drained
1/2 c. onions, chopped
1/3 c. margarine
1/3 c. flour
3 c. water (or 2 13 3/4-oz. cans
  condensed beef broth)

2 c. milk (or add milk to beef
  broth to make 5 c. total liquid)
1/2 c. quick pearled barley
2 tsp. Worcestershire sauce
3 T. parsley, chopped (or 1 T.
  dry parsley)
1/8 tsp. pepper

In a large saucepan, saute onions and mushrooms in margarine. Stir flour into mixture; simmer and stir until browned. Gradually add broth and milk; add remaining ingredients. Simmer 10-12 minutes until barley is tender, stirring occasionally. Additional water or milk may be added if soup becomes too thick upon standing.

Barb Croyle

BROCCOLI SOUP

1 lg. can (49 1/2-oz.) chicken
  broth
1 lg. pkg. frozen chopped
  broccoli
1 1/2 sticks margarine
3/4 c. flour

Salt
Pepper
Dry mustard
1 c. milk
1 16-oz. jar Cheez Whiz

Cook frozen broccoli and chicken broth until tender. Melt margarine; blend in flour, salt, pepper and dry mustard to taste. Blend in milk, cooking until thick white sauce consistency. Add white sauce to broccoli mixture. Add Cheez Whiz. Simmer and serve.

Delora Reinhardt

*"Thanks be to God, who gives us the
victory through our Lord Jesus Christ."
1 Cor. 15:57*

BROCCOLI CHEESE SOUP

6 c. water
6 chicken bouillon cubes
3 c. potatoes, diced
3 stalks celery, diced
1/2 c. carrots, diced
1/4 c. onion, diced

1-lb. bag frozen broccoli
(or fresh)
1 16-oz. jar Cheez Whiz
3 c. milk
1/4 c. cornstarch
Pepper

In a dutch oven, boil water and bouillon cubes. Add diced vegetables and boil another 15 minutes. Add broccoli and boil another 15 minutes. Add Cheez Whiz and let melt. Mix cornstarch in milk and add to soup. Stir often while it thickens or it will stick to bottom. Sprinkle with pepper. *May substitute California Blend vegetables.*

Dianne Hartman

BROCCOLI CHEESE SOUP

1 med. onion, diced
3 T. butter or margarine
6 c. water
6 cubes chicken bouillon
2 c. frozen broccoli

8-oz. fine noodles
1 tsp. salt
1-lb. Velveeta cheese
6 c. milk

Saute onion in butter; add water and chicken bouillon cubes. Bring to a boil. Add broccoli and cook until tender. Add noodles and salt; cook 3 minutes. Add milk and cheese; simmer until cheese is melted.

Lou Thomas

CREAMY BROCCOLI NOODLE SOUP

2-3 c. fresh or frozen broccoli
1-2 c. ham, chopped (opt.)
1 med. onion, chopped
1 can mushroom soup
1 can Cheddar cheese soup

2 c. milk
1 c. ham broth and/or water
1/4-lb. Velveeta cheese
2-3 c. thin noodles

Put cheese and mushroom soups in crock pot and begin heating on High. Add Velveeta cheese in chunks. Saute onion and chopped ham; add to crock pot. Boil or steam broccoli just until tender; add to soup. Add milk and broth (or water) and stir until smooth. Cook noodles; drain. Stir noodles into soup and continue to heat until cheese is melted. Turn to Low heat until served. Don't boil.

Karen Graybill

Praise God for Mother's gentle hand and love we cannot understand. Praise him who sent us from above the blessing of a Mother's love.

CABBAGE AND BEEF SOUP

1-lb. ground beef
1/2 tsp. garlic salt
1/4 tsp. garlic powder
1/4 tsp. pepper
2 celery stalks, chopped
1 16-oz. can kidney beans, undrained

1/2 med. head cabbage, chopped
1 28-oz. can tomatoes, chopped
1 tomato can water
4 beef bouillon cubes

In a dutch oven, brown beef; add all remaining ingredients. Bring to a boil. Reduce heat and simmer, covered for 1 hour. Yield: 3 quarts. *Soup can be frozen to enjoy months later. I use 1-quart tomato juice plus some water instead of chopped tomatoes.*

Edna Hochstetler

CHEDDAR CHEESE SOUP

1 c. celery, chopped
1/4 c. onion, chopped
1/4 c. margarine
1/4 c. flour
3/4 tsp. dry mustard
2 tsp. Worcestershire sauce
2 c. chicken broth

1 c. carrots, chopped
3 c. potatoes, cubed
2 c. milk
2 c. Cheddar cheese, shredded
1/2-1 lb. smoky links, sliced (opt.)
Salt and pepper

Saute onion and celery in butter. Add flour, dry mustard and Worcestershire sauce. Stir in broth, carrots and potatoes (and sausage, if desired). Bring to a boil; reduce heat until vegetables are tender. Add milk and cheese; heat through. Salt and pepper to taste. *I often use skim milk to lower the fat content. This is my family's favorite.*

Mafra Maust

COLORADO CHEESE SOUP

1 c. celery, chopped
1 lg. onion, chopped
1 c. carrots, chopped
2 1/2 c. potatoes, chopped
4 chicken bouillon cubes
4 c. water

10-oz. bag frozen California Blend Vegetables
2 cans cream of chicken soup
1/2 c. water
1-lb. Velveeta cheese, diced

Simmer celery, onion, carrots and potatoes in 4 cups water with chicken bouillon cubes until soft. Add remaining ingredients. Works nice in crock pot.

Marilyn Miller (Willie)

The man who walks with God always gets to his destination!

WISCONSIN POTATO CHEESE SOUP

2 T. butter or margarine
1/3 c. celery, chopped
1/3 c. onion, chopped
4 c. peeled potatoes, diced
3 c. chicken broth
2 c. milk
1 1/2 tsp. salt

1/4 tsp. pepper
Dash of paprika
2 c. (8-oz.) Cheddar cheese,
  shredded
Croutons
Fresh parsley, chopped

In a large saucepan, melt butter over medium-high heat. Saute celery and onion until tender. Add potatoes and broth. Cover and simmer until potatoes are tender, about 12 minutes. In batches, puree potato mixture in a blender or food processor. Return to saucepan. Stir in milk and seasonings. Add cheese and heat only until melted. Garnish with croutons and parsley. Makes 8 servings. *I sometimes leave potatoes diced rather than pureeing them.*

Gloria Yoder

CALIFORNIA WHITE CHILI

4 split chicken breasts, cooked
  and cut into pieces
1-qt. jar Great Northern Beans
2 c. chicken broth
1 onion, chopped

1/2 tsp. cilantro
1/2 tsp. cumin
1/2 tsp. red pepper
Garlic salt
Water (to taste)

Combine all ingredients and heat through. Low in fat content.

Mike Metzler

EASY CHILI SOUP

1-lb. ground beef
1 sm. onion
1 can tomato paste
1 can tomato soup

2 15-oz. cans chili beans
2-3 soup cans of water
Salt and pepper (to taste)

Brown ground beef with chopped onion. Add remaining ingredients. Simmer for at least 1 hour before serving.

Tami Martin

EASY CHILI SOUP

1 26-oz. can tomato soup
1/4 c. onion
1/2 tsp. chili powder

1-lb. hamburger
1 15.5-oz. can kidney beans

Fry hamburger with onion; drain. Add tomato soup with 3/4 can water. Add drained kidney beans and chili powder. Bring to a boil and serve.

Delora Reinhardt

MIDWESTERN BUTTER BEAN CHILI

1-lb. hamburger or pork
1 c. onion, chopped
2 cloves garlic, minced
1 16-oz. can butter beans
1 8-oz. can tomato sauce
2 4-oz. cans green chili peppers,
   rinsed, seeded and chopped
1 T. chili powder

1/2 tsp. sugar
1/2 tsp. salt
1/2 tsp. dried basil, crushed
1/4 tsp. ground allspice
1/4 tsp. black pepper
1/8 tsp. ground red pepper
1 16-oz. can tomatoes, cut up

In a large skillet, cook meat, onion and garlic until meat is brown and onion is tender; drain off fat. Stir in undrained tomatoes, drained butter beans, tomato sauce and remaining ingredients. Bring to a boil. Reduce heat, cover and simmer for 30 minutes. Serve with corn chips, shredded cheese, rice or crackers.

Evelyn Troyer

SWICK'S FAVORITE CHILI

1-lb. hamburger
2 16-oz. cans tomatoes
1 16-oz. can kidney beans
1 med. onion, finely chopped
1 green pepper, finely chopped

1 lg. carrot, grated
1 box prepared macaroni and
   cheese mix
Salt, pepper and chili powder
   (to taste)

Brown hamburger, onions, peppers and carrots; drain any grease. Add remaining ingredients; simmer for 30 minutes. *You may use a crock pot to simmer the chili in. Optional: You may substitute ground turkey meat for the hamburger. This meat dish is high in Vitamins A and C.*

Jane Swick

CORN CHOWDER

5 slices bacon
1 med. onion, chopped
2 med. potatoes, peeled
   and diced (1 1/2 c.)
1/2 c. water

1 17-oz. can corn
2 c. milk
1 tsp. salt
Dash of pepper

In a large pan, cook bacon until crisp. Remove bacon, crumble and set aside. Drain all but 3 tablespoons drippings from pan; add onion and cook until tender. Add potatoes and water; cook until tender. Add corn, milk, salt and pepper. Cook until heated. Pour in warm bowls and top with crumbled bacon.

Merianne Shaffer

"Beloved, let us love one another; for love is of God."
1 John 4:7a

CREAM OF SOUP SUBSTITUTE

2 c. instant non-fat milk crystals
3/4 c. cornstarch
1/4 c. instant chicken bouillon
2 T. dried onion flakes
1/2 tsp. pepper
1 tsp. thyme (opt.-I use less by half)

Combine and mix all ingredients well. Store in airtight container. Makes 3 cups mix equivalent to 9-10 cans of soup. To Make: Combine 1/3 cup mix with 1 1/4 cup water in saucepan. Stir over low heat until warm and thickened. You can add mushrooms, cooked celery or dried herbs. This is equal to 1 1/2 cups of sauce.

Nelda Nussbaum

HAM, CORN AND TOMATO CHOWDER

2 lg. fresh tomatoes, chopped
1/2 c. onion, chopped
1/2 c. green pepper, chopped
2 T. regular oil
1 can chicken broth (or 2 c. water with 2 chicken bouillon cubes)
1 c. frozen corn
1 tsp. basil
1/2 tsp. salt
1/8 tsp. black pepper
3/4 c. cooked ham, cubed

Saute tomatoes, onion and peppers in oil. Add remaining ingredients and ham. Cook 15-20 minutes.

Margaret Hartzler

OYSTER STEW

1/2-pt. fresh oysters
3 c. milk
1/2 tsp. salt
Dash of pepper
Dash of seasoned salt
1/2 T. butter

Cut each oyster into 2-3 pieces. Place in a saucepan with the oyster liquid and a little water. Cook over medium heat just until the edges curl (less than 5 minutes). Add milk, seasonings and butter. Heat until butter melts and it is hot. Do not boil. Cool and refrigerate. *I make this in the morning to serve that evening, but the stew really tastes best 24 hours after it's made. The milk develops a good oyster flavor.* Makes 4 servings.

Merianne Shaffer

God, give me the ability to see good things in unexpected places and talents in unexpected people. Give me the grace to tell them so.

SALMON-ASPARAGUS SOUP

Chicken broth
Potatoes, cooked
Green beans
Several salmon patties, **baked**

Tarragon, minced
Asparagus powdered soup base
Onion, minced

This creation began with the thought, "Gee, I have nothing for lunch." In a few minutes, God gave me this recipe and it was delicious. I used chicken broth as my base (vegetable or beef would be okay, too). I added leftover potatoes along with these other ingredients. The asparagus powdered soup base made the soup thicken. This is just one of my soup "stories" that I find recorded throughout my cookbook journal. I'm happy to share it with my sisters at Yellow Creek Mennonite Church.

Lois (Metzler) Ramer

SPLIT PEA OR LENTIL SOUP

1/2-lb. (1 c.) green or yellow split peas or lentils
4 c. water
1 smoked ham hock
1 bay leaf

1/3 c. onion, chopped
1/3 c. celery, chopped
1/3 c. carrots, chopped
1/2 tsp. salt
1 sm. garlic clove (opt.)

Wash and drain split peas. Combine all ingredients in kettle with tight-fitting lid. Bring to a boil. Reduce heat and simmer, covered, for 2 hours, stirring occasionally. Remove ham hock and cut meat off the bone. Dice and add back to soup. Remove bay leaf before serving. *Note: Split peas require no soaking. Split pea soups are very thick and may need thinning. Can thin with water, stock or milk.* Makes 4-5 servings.

Merianne Shaffer

TORTELLINI-KALE SOUP

6 c. reduced sodium chicken broth
1 c. firmly packed kale, coarsely chopped
2 cloves garlic, minced (or 1/4 tsp. garlic powder)

8-oz. tortellini (any flavor*)
1/4 c. green onions, sliced (include tops)
1/2 c. Parmesan cheese

In a medium saucepan, bring chicken broth, kale and garlic to boiling. Add tortellini and cook according to package directions or until tortellini is tender, but firm. During last 2 minutes of cooking time, stir in green onions. Serve with Parmesan cheese. *Tortellini is stuffed pasta available in such combinations as meat, meat-cheese and cheese. Look for it in the freezer or refrigerated section of the supermarket. Per serving: 150 cal., 5 g. fat (3 g. sat.), 1152 mg. sodium.* Makes 5 servings.

Merianne Shaffer

Vegetables

VEGETABLES

BARLEY CASSEROLE

4 T. butter
1 med. onion, finely chopped
1/2-lb. mushrooms, thinly sliced

2 chicken bouillon cubes
1-qt. water
1 c. pearled med.-size barley

Melt butter in skillet over moderately-low heat. Add onion and mushrooms. Stir often until wilted. Bring water to boil in a saucepan; add bouillon and dissolve. Into a round ungreased 2-quart casserole (about 8 x 2 3/4-inches), turn barley, onion-mushrooms and hot bouillon. Bake, uncovered, at 350 degrees, stirring several times for 1 hour. Cover tightly. Continue baking until liquid is absorbed and barley is tender, but chewy (30 minutes longer). Serve hot. Makes 8 servings.

Merianne Shaffer

HARVARD BEETS

3 c. cooked beets, diced
1/2 c. sugar
1 T. cornstarch
1 tsp. salt

1/4 c. vinegar
1/4 c. water
2 T. butter

Mix sugar, cornstarch and salt; add vinegar and water and stir until smooth. Cook for 5 minutes. Add beets to the hot sauce and let stand for 30 minutes. Just before serving, bring to a boil and add butter. Serves 6.

Edna Hochstetler

BROCCOLI CASSEROLE

2 pkgs. frozen broccoli
1 can cream of mushroom soup
1 1/2 T. French dressing
1 T. lemon juice
3/4-1 c. Cheddar cheese, grated
(or Velveeta cheese cubes)

1 (2-oz.) jar pimento, chopped
1/2 c. almonds, slivered or sliced
1-1 1/4 c. cheese crackers,
crushed

Preheat oven to 375 degrees. Grease a 9 x 9-inch greased baking dish. Place frozen broccoli in baking dish. Heat mushroom soup; add cheese and heat, stirring often until cheese is melted. Add French dressing and lemon juice to soup mixture; mix well. Pour soup/cheese mixture over broccoli. Sprinkle pimento and almonds on top. Bake at 375 degrees for 45 minutes or until thoroughly heated. Sprinkle crushed cheese crackers over top and return to oven for 5 minutes or until crackers are slightly browned. Serves 6-8. Preparation time: 45 minutes or until thoroughly heated.

Joan Rhoade

CALIFORNIA CASSEROLE

1 20-oz. bag California Mix
   Vegetables
1 c. mushroom soup
1 egg, beaten

1/3 c. Miracle Whip
1/3 c. milk
2/3 c. sharp cheese, grated
Cornflake crumbs, buttered

Place raw vegetables in casserole. Mix remaining ingredients, except crumbs; pour over vegetables. Top with buttered cornflake crumbs. Bake at 375 degrees for 45 minutes.

Grace Weldy

LOUISIANA PUDDING

2 lg. eggs
2 c. long-grain rice, cooked
1/4-lb. Cheddar cheese, grated
   (1 c.)

17-oz. can cream style corn
1 sm. onion, minced (1/4 c.)
1 1/2 tsp. salt
1/8 tsp. pepper

Beat eggs until foamy; stir in rice, cheese, corn, onion, salt and pepper. Turn into a buttered 1 1/2-quart baking dish (10 x 6 x 1 3/4-inches). Bake at 350 degrees until golden brown around edges and set, about 45 minutes. (A metal knife inserted in center will not come out clean.) Let stand 10 minutes before serving. Makes 6 servings. *Gerry really likes this recipe.*

Merianne Shaffer

SCALLOPED CORN

2 cans cream style corn
1 can regular corn, with liquid
8-oz. lite sour cream

1 pkg. Jiffy corn muffin mix
1 egg

Mix together ingredients. Bake at 350 degrees for 35-45; minutes.

Katie Ann Schumm

SCALLOPED CORN

1 can creamed corn
1 can whole kernel corn
1 stick butter or margarine
1 box Jiffy corn bread mix

2 eggs, beaten
1 c. sour cream
Swiss cheese, grated

Mix together all ingredients, except cheese; put in greased 3-quart casserole. Add grated Swiss cheese on top. Bake at 350 degrees for 45 minutes or in a crock pot.

Connie Davidhizar

He who is faithful in a very little thing is faithful also in much.
Luke 16:10

LIMA BEAN CASSEROLE

2 bxs. frozen lima beans	1/2-lb. raw bacon
1/2 c. broth	1 can tomato soup
1 1/4 c. brown sugar	3 tsp. mustard
1 lg. onion, chopped	1 tsp. salt
1 green pepper, chopped	

Boil lima beans; drain. Mix all ingredients together. Bake at 350 degrees for 1 hour.

Beverly Coblentz

SWEETENED RED KIDNEY BEANS

6 slices bacon	2 cans kidney beans, drained
1 c. brown sugar	Salt and pepper (to taste)
1 c. catsup	

Dice bacon and fry until brown. Remove some of the grease. Add sugar and catsup; let come to a boil. Simmer 10 minutes. Add beans and heat through. Add salt and pepper to taste. Serves 6.

Rosalind Slabaugh

BAKED ONIONS

4 red or yellow onions	1/4 c. balsamic vinegar
Fresh ground pepper	1/4 c. olive oil
1/4 c. Worcestershire sauce	1/4 c. soy sauce

Peel onions and place in baking dish with lid. Mix ingredients and pour over onions. Cover. Marinate onions for 1 hour at room temperature. Bake at 375 degrees for 1 hour. Serve hot.

Christy Risser

GRILLED VIDALIA ONIONS

1 med.-lg. vidalia onion	Aluminum foil
2 T. beef stock base (to taste)	

Peel and score onion most of the way through. Wrap foil around onion, but do not close completely. Add beef stock base. Start with 2 tablespoons, but adjust amount of stock to taste. Close foil tightly and put on grill on medium-low flame. Allow to cook for approximately 1 hour. Eat while hot. *(They go great with burgers or steak!)*

Christy Risser

MAKE AHEAD MASHED POTATOES

10-12 potatoes	1 stick butter or margarine
8-oz. cream cheese	Milk

Peel and boil potatoes; put in electric mixer. Add some milk, but don't make too thin. Add margarine and cream cheese; beat. Put in casserole and cover with foil. Next day, bake at 350 degrees for about 1 hour. *Very good.*

Anabel Hartman

MASHED POTATO CAKES

Leftover mashed potatoes   **Onion, chopped (opt.)**
1 egg, beaten

Mix beaten egg and onion into mashed potatoes. The mixture should be stiff enough to be formed into patties. Coat patties with flour. Fry in a skillet with some oil until browned on both sides. This can be messy, but the egg helps hold the potatoes together. The mixture can be spooned directly into the skillet, but tastes better when coated with flour.

Merianne Shaffer

OVEN FRIED POTATOES

4 lg. baking potatoes, unpeeled   **1/4 tsp. garlic powder**
1/4 c. oil   **1/4 tsp. paprika**
1-2 T. Parmesan cheese   **1/8 tsp. pepper**
1/2 tsp. salt

Wash unpeeled potatoes and cut lengthwise into 4 wedges. Place skin side down in 9 x 13-inch pan. Combine remaining ingredients; brush over potatoes. Bake at 375 degrees for 1 hour, brushing with oil/cheese mixture at 15 minute intervals. Turn potatoes over last 15 minutes. Makes 4 servings. *These are wonderful with any roasted meat or use as a snack.*

Phyllis Kehr

PARMESAN CHEESE POTATOES

8-10 potatoes   **1 tsp. salt**
1/2 c. flour   **1/8 tsp. pepper**
1/2 c. Parmesan cheese   **1/2 c. margarine**

Cube potatoes. Keep in water until ready to use. Mix next 4 ingredients and coat potatoes. Pour melted margarine into a 9 x 13-inch baking pan. Put potatoes on top. Sprinkle remaining dry mixture over potatoes. Bake at 375 degrees for 1 1/2 hours, turning potatoes occasionally.

Lisa Heinz

POTATO CASSEROLE

5 med. potatoes   **1/4 c. margarine, melted**
1/2 can cream of chicken soup   **1 T. onion, diced**
1 c. sour cream   **Salt and pepper**
1/2 c. Cheddar cheese, grated   **Cracker crumbs**

Cook potatoes in skins the day before; cool. Grate potatoes. Mix cheese, margarine, soup, sour cream and onion. Mix in potatoes. Top with cracker crumbs or any other crumbs. Bake at 350 degrees for 1 hour.

Phyllis Garber

POTATO FILLING

6 med. potatoes
1/2 c. warm milk
1 onion, chopped
4 T. celery, chopped

1 c. bread, cubed
1 T. parsley, chopped
1 egg, well beaten
Salt and pepper (to taste)

Cook and mash potatoes. Add remaining ingredients. Put in greased casserole. Bake at 350 degrees for 45 minutes if prepared ahead.

Lou Thomas

POTATOES ROMANOFF

2 1/2-lbs. potatoes
1 lg. (1-lb., 8-oz.) container
  cottage cheese
1 16-oz. container sour cream

1-2 c. Cheddar cheese
Chives, onion, garlic salt
  and pepper (to taste)

Cook potatoes; cool and cube. Combine remaining ingredients, except cheese, and mix with potatoes. Sprinkle cheese over casserole. Bake at 350 degrees for 45 minutes.

Rosalind Slabaugh

STUFFED BAKED POTATO

8 baking potatoes
Vegetable oil
1/3 c. butter
1/4 c. fresh chives, chopped
  (or 2 T. dried chives)

Paprika
1 tsp. salt
1/4 tsp. pepper
1/3-1/2 c. evaporated milk

Rub the potato skins with oil; prick with a fork. Bake at 400 degrees for 1 hour or until tender. Allow potatoes to cool. Slice a small portion off the top of each potato. Scoop out pulp, leaving a thin shell. In a large bowl, mash pulp with butter, chives, salt, pepper and enough milk to obtain desired consistency. Stuff shells; sprinkle with paprika. Place on ungreased baking dish. Bake at 325 degrees until heated. Potatoes may be stuffed ahead and refrigerated or frozen. Makes 8 servings.

Gloria Landes

BUTTERNUT SQUASH

4 c. squash, chunked
2 apples, sliced
Sauce:
1/2 c. brown sugar

1/4 c. margarine
1 T. flour
1 tsp. salt
1/2 tsp. cinnamon

Put squash and apples in a 9-inch square pan. Heat and stir sauce ingredients until margarine melts. Pour over squash and apples. Bake at 350 degrees for 50-60 minutes.

Kathy Stoltzfus

ACORN CABBAGE BAKE

2 lg. acorn squash
1 med. onion, chopped
2 c. cabbage, shredded
3/4 tsp. salt
1/4 tsp. thyme
1/2-lb. sausage

1 sm. apple, peeled and
 chopped
2 T. slivered almonds
1/4 tsp. pepper
1/2 tsp. sage, crumbled

Cut squash in half lengthwise. Place in baking pan, cut side down; add 1/2-inch water. Bake at 400 degrees for 20 minutes. Cook sausage in skillet until brown. Drain off fat; add onion, cabbage, apple and almonds. Cook until vegetables are tender; add seasonings and mix well. Fill squash with cabbage mixture. Bake 30 minutes longer.

Bea Yoder

STIR-FRY VEGETABLES

Any vegetables you like,
 such as:
Carrots
Cabbage

Green beans
Broccoli
Green peppers

Chop vegetables in bite-size or slice. Place all vegetables in frying pan. Pour small amount of oil on top; stir through. Begin with high heat until quite hot, then reduce to medium or low heat. Cover and cook 3-5 minutes, stirring several times. Vegetables are crisp and gently cooked. Serve immediately. Pan of prepared vegetables can wait before cooking process. To serve, you can sprinkle with peanuts on the serving dish or from a separate dish.

Lois Leuz

SWEET POTATO CASSEROLE

4 c. canned sweet potatoes,
 drained
1/2 c. sugar
1/2 c. egg scramblers
1 tsp. vanilla

1/3 c. skim milk
1/4 c. margarine, softened
1/3 c. brown sugar
1/3 c. pecans, chopped

Combine and mix first 6 ingredients in mixing bowl until potatoes are mashed. Spray an 8 x 12-inch baking dish with non-stick cooking spray. Pour mixture into baking dish and sprinkle with brown sugar and chopped pecans. Bake at 350 degrees for 45 minutes. Serves 12.

Ruth Metzler

Knowing the Scripture is one thing;
knowing the Author is another.

SWEET POTATO BALLS

6 med. sweet potatoes	1 c. pecans or walnuts, chopped
1/2 c. margarine	12 lg. marshmallows
1 c. brown sugar	2 c. cornflakes, crushed

Cook, peel and mash potatoes. Mix with margarine, sugar and nuts. Form a ball around 1 marshmallow; roll in crushed cornflakes. Just before serving, warm balls in a 350 degree oven for 15 minutes or until marshmallows are softened or melted. Balls may be made ahead of time and refrigerated or frozen for later.

Florence Hershberger

PERFECT POTATO PANCAKES

4 lg. potatoes	1 tsp. salt
2 eggs	1/2 tsp. pepper
1/2 c. onion, finely diced	1/3 c. salad oil
1/2 c. flour	

Peel and shred potatoes; place in cold water. Drain potatoes well, squeezing out all water. Beat eggs and mix all together. Heat salad oil in skillet until hot. Drop potato mixture, 1/4 cup at a time, into hot oil about 3-inches apart. Flatten to make a 4-inch pancake. Cook until golden brown; turn to other side (about 4 minutes total). Place on paper towel to drain. Top with maple syrup or applesauce.

Phyllis Kehr

SWEET POTATO PUDDING

2 c. sweet potatoes, mashed	1/4 tsp. nutmeg
1/2 c. brown sugar	1/4 tsp. cloves
3 T. margarine, melted	2 T. sugar
2 eggs, separated	Dash of salt
3/4 c. orange juice	

Combine potatoes, brown sugar, margarine and egg yolk; stir well. Gradually add orange juice, nutmeg and cloves; set aside. Beat egg whites, gradually adding sugar. Fold into potatoes. Pour into baking dish and set in pan of water to bake at 350 degrees for 1 hour.

Phyllis Garber

SWEET POTATO SOUFFLE

1 lg. can sweet potatoes	1 tsp. vanilla
1 c. sugar	Topping:
2 eggs	1 c. brown sugar
1/2 c. milk	1/2 c. flour
1/2 tsp. salt	1/3 c. butter, melted
1/3 stick margarine	1 c. pecans

Drain and mash sweet potatoes. Add remaining ingredients and mix well. Pour into buttered pan. Crumble topping ingredients over potato mixture. Bake, uncovered, at 350 degrees for 35-45 minutes.

Annabelle Snyder

ZUCCHINI SQUASH CASSEROLE

1 1/2-lbs. zucchini squash,
  peeled and cubed
1 med. onion, chopped
1 carrot, grated
3/4 c. sour cream
1 can cream of chicken soup
1/2 stick margarine
1/2 pkg. Pepperidge Farm Herb
  Stuffing

Cook squash until partially done; put in a greased 1 1/2-quart casserole. Stir together onion, carrot, soup and sour cream. Mix with squash. Melt margarine and stir into stuffing. Put on top of squash mixture. Bake at 350 degrees for 45 minutes.

Lou Thomas

ZUCCHINI PATTIES

1/3 c. Bisquick mix
1/3 c. Parmesan cheese
1/8 tsp. pepper
2 eggs
2 c. zucchini, shredded

Mix first 4 ingredients well; add zucchini. (I squeeze the juice out of the zucchini.) Stir just to moisten. Fry in a skillet with melted butter until done. Salt each patty while frying.

Phyllis Stauffer

ZUCCHINI PIZZA

1/2 c. onion, chopped
5 c. zucchini, sliced
1 c. Bisquick
1/2 tsp. salt
1 clove garlic
2 2.5-oz. pkgs. shaved ham,
  cut up
1/4 c. oil
4 eggs
1/2 c. Parmesan cheese
2 tsp. dried parsley
1/2 tsp. oregano
Mozzarella cheese, shredded

Mix all ingredients, except mozzarella cheese, well. Spread in a 9 x 13-inch pan. Top with shredded mozzarella cheese. Bake at 350 degrees for 25 minutes. Slice into small squares when cooled.

Phyllis Kehr

---

*God grant me the serenity to accept
the things I cannot change;
the courage to change the things I can;
and the wisdom to know the difference.*

Cakes, Cookies, & Icings

CAKES, COOKIES & ICINGS

Cakes & Frostings

ALASKA SHEET CAKE

1 c. butter
1 c. water
2 c. sugar
2 c. + 2 T. flour
1 tsp. salt
3 eggs
1/2 c. buttermilk
1 1/2 tsp. soda

1 tsp. vanilla
Frosting:
1/2 c. butter
5 T. milk
1 tsp. vanilla or almond extract
1 c. nuts, chopped
1-lb. box powdered sugar

Bring butter and water to boil; add sugar, flour and salt. Set aside. In a small bowl, beat eggs, buttermilk, soda and vanilla. Add to first mixture. Put in greased jelly roll pan. Bake at 400 degrees for 20 minutes.

For frosting: Boil butter and milk lightly. Remove from heat and add remaining ingredients. Frost cake while warm.

Dawn West

FARM JOURNAL APPLESAUCE CAKE

2 c. flour, sifted
2 tsp. baking soda
1 tsp. cinnamon
1/4 tsp. nutmeg
1/4 tsp. cloves
1 T. cocoa
1/2 c. salad oil

1 c. sugar
1 1/2 c. unsweetened
   applesauce, heated
1/4 c. raisins (opt.)
1/4 c. walnuts, chopped
Caramel Frosting (recipe follows)

Sift together flour, soda, spices and cocoa. Combine oil and sugar; beat until well blended. Stir in hot applesauce, blending thoroughly. Add dry ingredients, blending well. Stir in raisins and walnuts. Pour into a well-greased and floured 9-inch square pan (spread batter into the corners as this cake tends to peak in the center like a nut bread). Bake at 400 degrees for 20 minutes, then reduce temperature to 375 degrees and bake 20 minutes longer. You can double this recipe and bake in a 13 x 9-inch pan. The hint of cocoa gives a distinctive flavor. Makes 6 servings.

Merianne Shaffer

*When a cake, cookie or muffin recipe asks for oil,
try substituting applesauce for part or all of the oil
to cut down on your fats. --Esther Martin*

CARAMEL FROSTING FOR APPLESAUCE CAKE

6 T. butter
3/4 c. brown sugar

3 T. milk
1 1/2 c. powdered sugar

Melt butter in saucepan over low heat. Stir in brown sugar. Bring to a boil over medium heat; boil hard for 2 minutes, stirring constantly. Remove from heat. Stir in milk. Return pan to heat and bring to a full boil. Remove from heat and cool to lukewarm. Stir in powdered sugar and beat until smooth. If frosting is too thick, beat in a little milk.

Merianne Shaffer

RAW APPLE CAKE

2 eggs
4 c. apples, diced
1/2 c. cooking oil
2 c. sugar
1/2 tsp. salt
2 tsp. baking soda
2 tsp. cinnamon
2 tsp. vanilla

2 c. flour
2 c. nuts (large pieces)
Frosting:
4 T. margarine or butter
8-oz. pkg. cream cheese
2 tsp. vanilla
1 1/2 c. powdered sugar

Combine all cake ingredients and mix well. Spoon into lightly greased 9 x 13-inch baking pan. Bake at 350 degrees for 1 hour; cool.

To prepare frosting: Cream together all ingredients. Frost cake after it has cooled.

Florence Nussbaum

BUTTERSCOTCH CAKE

1 yellow cake mix
1 can butterscotch pie filling
2 eggs
1/2 c. pecans, chopped
6-oz. butterscotch chips
2 T. brown sugar

Frosting:
1/2 c. butter
1 8-oz. pkg. cream cheese
3 1/2 c. powdered sugar
1 tsp. vanilla

Mix pie filling and eggs together; add cake mix. Pour into a 9 x 13-inch greased pan. Sprinkle butterscotch chips, brown sugar and pecans on top. Bake at 350 degrees for 40-45 minutes.

For frosting: Beat butter with cream cheese; add powdered sugar and vanilla. Frost cake when cooled.

Arlene Wenger

EASY CHERRY-CHOCOLATE CAKE

3 eggs
1 chocolate cake mix
1 can cherry pie filling

1/3 c. vegetable oil
1 pkg. chocolate instant
   pudding and pie filling

Beat eggs in large bowl. Stir in dry cake mix, cherry pie filling and oil until blended. Bake at 350 degrees for 35-40 minutes. Prepare pudding as directed on package for pie. Spread over cooled cake. You can use Cool Whip instead of chocolate pudding.

Beverly Coblentz

CARROT CAKE

2 c. white sugar
2 c. flour
2 tsp. soda
2 tsp. cinnamon
1 tsp. salt
1 1/2 c. cooking oil
4 eggs
3 c. carrots, grated

3 tsp. vanilla
Icing:
6 T. margarine or butter
1 8-oz. pkg. cream cheese
3 1/2 c. powdered sugar
2 tsp. vanilla
1 c. pecans, chopped

Mix first 5 cake ingredients together. Add oil, eggs and vanilla; beat 2 minutes. Add carrots and beat 1 minute. This makes 3 layers. Bake at 350 degrees for 30-35 minutes.

For icing: Cream margarine and cream cheese together. Add powdered sugar and vanilla; beat well. Add pecans. Frost cake when cool.

Gloria Tyson

FAVORITE CARROT CAKE

2 c. flour
2 tsp. baking soda
2 tsp. ground cinnamon
1/2 tsp. salt
3/4 c. oil
3/4 c. buttermilk
3 eggs
2 c. sugar
2 c. carrots, shredded
1 8-oz. can crushed pineapple, drained

1 1/3 c. flake coconut
1 c. walnuts, chopped
Glaze:
3/4 c. sugar
1/3 c. buttermilk
Frosting:
1/4 c. butter
1 8-oz. pkg. cream cheese
1 tsp. vanilla
1-lb. powdered sugar

For cake: Heat oven to 350 degrees. Mix flour, baking soda, cinnamon and salt; set aside. Whisk oil, buttermilk and eggs in a large bowl until well blended. Add sugar, carrots, pineapple, coconut, walnuts and flour mixture; mix well. Pour into greased and floured 13 x 9-inch baking pan. Bake 40-45 minutes.

For glaze: Heat sugar and buttermilk in saucepan over low heat until sugar is dissolved. Pour over hot cake; cool.

For frosting: Beat cream cheese and butter at medium speed with electric mixer until light and fluffy. Blend in vanilla. Gradually add powdered sugar, beating until blended. Frost glazed cake; refrigerate.

Renita Graber

If you dip the knife in hot water, then wipe dry, you can avoid the crumbling.

BIBLE FRUITCAKE

1 c. Psalm 55:21 (use either or both)
2 c. Jeremiah 6:20 (last part of verse)
6 Job 39:14
3 T. I Samuel 14:25
1/2 c. Judges 4:19 (first sentence)
4 1/2 c. I Kings 4:22

2 tsp. Leviticus 2:13
2 tsp. Amos 4:5
1/2 tsp. II Chronicles 9:9
2 c. Numbers 17:8
2 c. of both items in I Samuel 30:12, chopped to make 4 cups in all

Mix in a large bowl in order given. The third item should be carefully and thoroughly beaten in. The last 2 items should be added by hand, possibly following Solomon's advice for making a good boy (Proverbs 23:14). If you follow that, you will have a good cake. Bake at 250 degrees for 2 1/2 hours in four small oiled pans. You may line the pans with oiled brown paper. Allow to cool in the pans on sides or on racks. Then run a knife around edges and turn out. This is good eaten at once, but it gets better if wrapped in cheese cloth and soaked in fruit juice and keep in a cool place.

Dove Leinbach (via her sister in PA)

CHOCOLATE TURTLE CHEESECAKE

2 c. vanilla wafer crumbs
6 T. butter, melted
1 c. pecans, chopped
1 14-oz. bag Kraft caramels
1 5-oz. can evaporated milk

2 8-oz. pkgs. cream cheese
1/2 c. sugar
1 tsp. vanilla
2 eggs
1/2 c. chocolate chips, melted

Combine wafer crumbs and butter; press into bottom and sides of 9-inch spring form pan. Bake at 350 degrees for 10 minutes. Spread chopped pecans on cookie sheet. Toast in oven while crust is baking. Melt caramels with milk over low heat until smooth. Pour over crust. Top with pecans. Combine cream cheese, sugar and vanilla; mix at medium speed on electric mixer. Add eggs, 1 at a time, mixing well after each addition. Blend in chocolate, being sure mixture is completely blended. Pour over pecans. Bake at 350 degrees for 40 minutes. (Place a cookie sheet under pan while baking to catch butter that may leak out.) Loosen cake from rim of pan. Chill. Garnish with whipped cream, additional chopped pecans and maraschino cherries, if desired. Makes 10-12 servings.

Sherry Kehr

Cast all your anxieties on him, for he cares about you. 1 Peter 5:7

CHOCOLATE UPSIDE DOWN CAKE

1 1/4 c. flour
3/4 c. sugar
2 tsp. baking powder
1/4 tsp. salt
3 T. cocoa with more milk or
  1-oz. unsweetened chocolate
2 T. butter
1/2 c. milk
1 tsp. vanilla
1/2 c. nuts, chopped
2 T. cocoa
1/2 c. brown sugar
1/2 c. white sugar
1 1/4 c. boiling water

Mix first 9 ingredients together and pour into a 9 x 9-inch baking dish. Mix together cocoa, brown sugar and white sugar; sprinkle on top. Pour boiling water over top and bake at 350 degrees for 1 hour.

Nina Weaver

CRUMB CAKE

2 c. flour
1 1/2 c. granulated sugar
1/2 c. margarine or shortening
1 c. sour milk
1 tsp. soda
1 egg
Cinnamon
Ginger
Nutmeg
Pinch of salt

Rub and mix flour, sugar and margarine. Save 1/2 cup crumbs. Add egg, salt, sprays of cinnamon, ginger and nutmeg, soda and sour milk; beat well. Put in 7 x 10-inch loaf pan. Sprinkle crumbs on top. Bake at 375 degrees for about 35 minutes.

Bertha Weaver

TOLL HOUSE CRUMB CAKE

Topping:
1 T. flour
1/2 c. brown sugar
2 T. butter, softened
1/2 c. nuts, chopped
12-oz. pkg. Nestle's Little Bits*
Cake:
2 c. flour
1 tsp. baking powder
1 tsp. baking soda
1/2 tsp. salt
1/2 c. butter, softened
1 c. sugar
1 tsp. vanilla
3 eggs
1 c. sour cream
1 1/2 c. chocolate chips

For topping: Combine flour, brown sugar, and butter; stir in nuts and 1/2 cup chocolate chips. Set aside.

For cake: Preheat oven to 350 degrees. Combine dry ingredients; set aside. Combine butter, sugar and vanilla; beat until creamy. Add eggs, 1 at a time. Gradually beat in flour alternating with sour cream. Fold in remaining chips. Spread into greased 13 x 9-inch pan. Sprinkle topping over batter. Bake at 350 degrees for 45-50 minutes.
*I use regular size chips and crush them in blender.

Verna Gongwer

GERMAN UPSIDE DOWN CAKE

8-oz. coconut (opt.)
1 c. pecans, chopped
1 stick margarine, melted
1 German chocolate cake mix
1 c. margarine (2 sticks), room temp.
8-oz. pkg. cream cheese, room temp.
1-lb. box powdered sugar

Grease sides and bottom of 9 x 13-inch baking pan. Mix coconut, pecans and melted margarine together; pour in bottom of 9 x 13-inch pan. Mix cake mix per package directions; pour over mixture. Mix together 1 cup margarine, cream cheese and powdered sugar. Spoon on top of cake. Bake at 350 degrees for 45-55 minutes.

Barb Croyle

GINGERBREAD WITH LEMON SAUCE

2 1/4 c. flour
3/4 c. sugar
2 tsp. ginger
1 tsp. cinnamon
1 tsp. baking soda
1/2 tsp. baking powder
1/4 tsp. cloves
3/4 c. Shedd's Spread Country Crock, softened
3/4 c. water
1/2 c. molasses
Lemon Sauce:
1/3 c. sugar
2 T. cornstarch
1 1/3 c. water
3 T. Shedd's Spread Country Crock
2 tsp. grated lemon peel
2 T. lemon juice

Combine dry ingredients in a large bowl. Stir in Country Crock, water and molasses until well blended. Pour into a greased 9 x 9 x 2-inch pan. Bake at 350 degrees 40-50 minutes. Serve warm with Lemon Sauce. Makes 9-12 servings.

For Lemon Sauce: In a 2-quart saucepan, combine sugar and cornstarch. Gradually stir in water until smooth. Stirring constantly, bring to a boil over medium heat; boil 1 minute. Remove from heat. Stir in Country Crock, lemon peel and lemon juice until well blended. Pour into serving bowl; cover with waxed paper or plastic wrap. Cool slightly. Serve warm on gingerbread. Makes 2 cups.

Merianne Shaffer

LEMON POUND CAKE

1 pkg. lemon cake mix
1 sm. pkg. lemon instant pudding mix
1/2 c. oil
1 c. water
4 eggs
Glaze:
2 c. powdered sugar
Yellow food coloring
Lemon juice

Blend cake ingredients together. Bake in a greased and floured bundt pan. Bake at 350 degrees for 45 minutes. Cool right side up for 25 minutes, then invert onto serving plate. For glaze: Mix powdered sugar, yellow food coloring and lemon juice. Drizzle over cake.

Brenda Gongwer

HOT FUDGE PUDDING CAKE

1 1/4 c. sugar, divided	1/2 c. milk
1 c. flour	1/3 c. butter, melted
7 T. cocoa, divided	1 1/2 tsp. vanilla
2 tsp. baking powder	1/2 c. brown sugar, packed
1/4 tsp. salt	1 1/4 c. hot water

Heat oven to 350 degrees. In medium bowl, combine 3/4 cup sugar, flour, 3 tablespoons cocoa, baking powder and salt. Blend in milk, melted butter and vanilla; beat until smooth. Pour batter into square 8 x 8 x 2-inch pan. In small bowl, combine remaining 1/2 cup sugar, brown sugar and remaining 4 tablespoons cocoa. Sprinkle mixture evenly over batter, without stirring. Pour hot water over top. Do not stir. Bake 40 minutes or until center is almost set; let stand 15 minutes. Cake forms on top with chocolate pudding on bottom.

Deb Krawiec

ITALIAN CREAM CAKE

1/2 c. margarine	1 c. nuts, chopped
1/2 c. shortening	1 c. coconut
2 c. sugar	Dash of salt
5 eggs, beaten	Icing:
1 c. buttermilk	1 8-oz. pkg. cream cheese
2 c. flour	1/2 c. margarine
1 tsp. baking soda	1-lb. powdered sugar
1 tsp. vanilla	1 tsp. vanilla

Cream together margarine, shortening and sugar. Add eggs, buttermilk, flour, soda, vanilla, nuts, coconut and salt. Mix well and pour into 3 greased and floured round cake pans. Bake at 350 degrees for 20 minutes.

For icing: Beat together ingredients until creamy.

Jan Ramer (Brian)

LIME JELLO CAKE

1 box (2 layer) white cake mix	1 3-oz. box vanilla instant
1 3-oz. box lime jello	pudding mix
1 c. boiling water	1 1/2 c. milk
1/2 c. cold water	1 8-oz. carton Cool Whip
	topping

Prepare cake mix as directed on package. Bake in greased 9 x 13-inch (or larger) pan at 350 degrees for 30 minutes. Cool in pan 15 minutes; poke with fork at 1/2-inch intervals. Dissolve jello in boiling water; add cold water and pour mixture over cake in pan. Chill 3-4 hours. Whip pudding mix and milk until it begins to set. Immediately fold in Cool Whip and spread on cake. Makes a generous amount.

Mary Martin

NO FROST OATMEAL CAKE

1 1/2 c. boiling water
1 c. oatmeal
1 c. brown sugar
1 c. white sugar
1/2 c. shortening
2 eggs

1 tsp. soda
1 T. cocoa
1 c. chocolate chips
1/2 tsp. salt
1 1/2 c. flour
1/2 c. nuts

Mix together oatmeal and water; let stand 10 minutes. Cream together sugars and shortening; add to oatmeal mixture. Add eggs and beat again. Sift together dry ingredients; add to oatmeal mixture beating until moist. Stir in 1/2 cup chocolate chips and pour into greased 9 x 13-inch pan. Sprinkle on remaining 1/2 cup chocolate chips and nuts. Bake at 350 degrees for 30-35 minutes.

Shirleen Weaver

HUMMINGBIRD CAKE

3 c. all-purpose flour, sifted
2 c. sugar
1 tsp. salt
1 tsp. soda
1 tsp. cinnamon
1 1/2 c. oil

3 eggs, beaten
1 1/2 tsp. vanilla
1 1/2 c. crushed pineapple
1 1/2 c. bananas, mashed
1 c. pecans, chopped

With a large spoon, mix flour, sugar, salt, soda and cinnamon. Mix eggs and oil; stir into dry ingredients well by hand--do not use mixer. Add vanilla, pineapple, bananas and nuts. Pour into ungreased oblong 10 x 14-inch pan. Bake at 350 degrees for 30-40 minutes. Good without icing. Or bake in three layer cake pans for 30 minutes at 350 degrees. Cool on wire racks before icing.

Cream Cheese Frosting:
1 8-oz. pkg. cream cheese
1/2 stick margarine

1-lb. box powdered sugar
Milk

Have all ingredients at room temperature. Cream margarine and cream cheese thoroughly. Add powdered sugar, small amounts at a time, blending well between additions. Thin to desired spreading consistency with small amounts of milk. Spread between layers, on top and sides of cake.

Shirley Albrecht

If I have wounded a soul today.
If I have caused one foot to go astray.
If I have walked in my own willful way.
Dear Lord, forgive.

OUT-OF-THIS-WORLD CAKE

2 c. sugar
1/2-lb. butter or margarine, softened
4 eggs
1 c. milk
2 tsp. baking powder
3 1/3 c. graham cracker crumbs
1 c. coconut
1 c. nuts

1 20-oz. can crushed pineapple, drained

Topping:
1/4 c. butter or margarine, softened
2/3 c. brown sugar
1/4 c. milk
1 c. coconut
1 c. pecans, chopped

Beat first 6 ingredients together well. Fold in coconut, nuts and pineapple. Pour into greased 9 x 13-inch baking pan. Bake at 350 degrees for 1 hour.

For topping: Mix together ingredients and spread on cake. Return cake to oven and bake 5 minutes or until topping bubbles and is slightly browned.

Shirley Albrecht

PINEAPPLE CAKE

2 c. flour
2 c. sugar
1 #2 can crushed pineapple (with juice)
2 tsp. soda
2 eggs

Frosting:
1 8-oz. pkg. cream cheese
1 tsp. vanilla
1/2 stick butter, softened
1 c. powdered sugar

Mix cake ingredients and pour into a 13 x 9-inch pan. Bake at 350 degrees for 35-40 minutes.

For frosting: Beat together ingredients and frost cooled cake.

Beverly Coblentz

2 X 2 PINEAPPLE CAKE

1 20-oz. can crushed pineapple (with juice)
2 c. flour
2 c. sugar
2 tsp. baking soda
2 eggs

1 c. walnuts, chopped
Frosting:
2 c. powdered sugar
1 8-oz. pkg. cream cheese (fat-free works)
1 stick margarine (1/2 c.)

Preheat oven to 350 degrees. Mix cake ingredients well. Spread into a greased 9 x 13-inch pan. Bake 40-45 minutes.

For frosting: Blend ingredients until smooth. Frost while cake is still hot.

Deb Krawiec

*The most desirable time to read
the Bible is as often as possible.*

PUNCH BOWL CAKE

2 pkgs. cake mix (1 chocolate
  and 1 white)
1 lg. pkg. vanilla pudding mix,
  prepared
1 lg. Cool Whip

1 can pie filling (any kind)
Bananas
Fudge topping
Nuts, chopped

Bake cakes as directed on package; let cool. Layer as follows:
1st layer - chocolate cake in bite size pieces
2nd layer - cherry pie filling
3rd layer - Cool Whip to cover
4th layer - white cake in bite size pieces
5th layer - bananas
6th layer - vanilla pudding to cover
7th layer - Cool Whip to cover
8th layer - chocolate cake in bite size pieces
9th layer - chocolate fudge topping
10th layer - Cool Whip to cover
Sprinkle with nuts.

Bev Coblentz

WHOLE WHEAT PINEAPPLE CAKE

1 c. flour
1 c. whole wheat flour
2 tsp. soda
18-oz. can crushed pineapple
  (with juice)

1 1/2 c. sugar
2 eggs
Topping:
3/4 c. brown sugar
3/4 c. nuts

Mix cake ingredients well and pour into a greased pan. Add topping. Bake at 350 degrees for 35-45 minutes.

Phyllis Kehr

FLUFFY PUMPKIN ANGEL TORTE

1 pkg. angel food cake mix
1/2 c. canned pumpkin
2 tsp. ground cinnamon
1 tsp. ground ginger

1/2 tsp. ground cloves
1-pt. heavy cream, whipped
1/4 c. pumpkin

Heat oven to 350 degrees. Prepare cake mix as directed, except remove 1 cup of batter. Fold 1/2 c. pumpkin and spices into 1 cup of batter. Bake in ungreased tube pan; cool. Whip heavy cream. Fold 1/4 cup pumpkin into whipped cream. Split cake to make 3 layers. Fill layers with whipped cream mix (about 1 cup each). Frost cake with remaining whipped cream. Refrigerate torte.

Beth Fervida

*The greatest love mankind will ever experience
is God's eternal love.*

RICE CAKE

2 c. regular rice
3 c. water
1 c. oil
3 eggs
1 c. milk

1 c. sugar
1 c. flour
2 tsp. baking powder
1/4 tsp. salt

Soak rice and water overnight; drain. Mix rice, oil, eggs, milk, sugar, flour, salt and baking powder in blender. Bake in greased and floured tube pan at 375 degrees for 30 minutes.

Otis & Betty Hochstetler-Brazil

SHOO-FLY CAKE (Crustless)

4 c. flour
2 c. brown sugar
1 c. butter or margarine

1 c. dark Karo syrup
2 tsp. baking soda
2 c. boiling water

Combine flour, brown sugar and butter to make crumbs. Reserve 1 1/2 cups for topping. Mix together syrup, baking soda and boiling water. Add to crumb mixture. Mix well (batter will be thin). Pour into a greased and floured 8 x 12-inch pan. Sprinkle with remaining crumbs. Bake at 350 degrees for 45 minutes.

Rosemary Martin

SNACK CAKE

1 cake mix (white or yellow)
1 can pie filling (your choice)

1/3 c. brown sugar
1/2 c. nuts

Prepare cake mix as directed on package and pour into cake pan(s). Spoon pie filling over top of cake, just so fairly evenly distributed. Sprinkle brown sugar and nuts over filling. *With cherry filling, I use slivered almonds and omit brown sugar. After baking I dribble powdered sugar icing lightly over cake. Using peach or apple pie filling, I use walnuts or pecans with the brown sugar and omit icing. Takes 15-20 minutes longer to bake than as directed on package in a 350 degree oven.*

Florence Hershberger

"WAR CAKE"

2 c. sugar
1 c. margarine or butter
2 T. vanilla
2 tsp. baking powder
3 c. flour

1 c. milk
1/2 c. cocoa
1/2 c. warm water
No eggs

Mix sugar and butter until smooth. Add vanilla to batter. Slowly stir in flour, baking powder and cocoa to mix. Add milk and warm water. Bake at 325 degrees for 40 minutes.

Anita Thomas

TEXAS VANILLA SHEET CAKE

2 2/3 c. flour
2 c. sugar
1/2 c. margarine, divided
1/2 c. vegetable oil
1 c. water
2 eggs
2 tsp. vanilla, divided
1 tsp. cinnamon
1 1/2 tsp. soda

2/3 c. buttermilk
1 8-oz. pkg. cream cheese
1-lb. powdered sugar, sifted
Icing:
1/2 c. margarine
1 tsp. vanilla
Cream cheese
Powdered sugar

For cake: Mix together flour and sugar. In saucepan, combine margarine, oil and water. Bring to a boil. Pour over flour mixture and beat thoroughly. Beat in eggs, vanilla, cinnamon, soda and buttermilk. Pour into a greased 10 x 15-inch pan. Bake at 350 degrees for 20 minutes.

For icing: Mix margarine, vanilla and cream cheese. Mix in powdered sugar, beating until light and fluffy. Spread over warm cake. Add nuts, if desired.

Gloria Yoder

CHRISTMAS TREE (Edible Centerpiece)

16 cupcakes (white cake with
   green food coloring added to
   batter)
Maraschino cherries

1 sugar cone (ice cream cone)
White icing
Decorations

Take paper off cupcakes. Place one in center of plate and surround by 6 more. Pile 5 cupcakes on top, then 3, then 1. Ice the top cupcake and top with cone placed upside down. Place a cherry on each cupcake. Thin white frosting and drizzle down over cone (should run down all cupcakes). Decorate with sprinkles, silver balls, etc., as desired. Place a cherry on top of cone.

Dove Leinbach

CHOCOLATE BUTTERCREAM FROSTING

1 6-oz. pkg. Nestle's Toll House
   semisweet chocolate chips
1/2 c. butter, softened

2 c. powdered sugar
5 T. milk
1/2 tsp. vanilla

Melt chocolate chips in microwave or over hot water; stir until smooth. Set aside; cool 15 minutes. In large bowl, beat butter until creamy. Gradually add powdered sugar alternately with milk. Add melted chocolate and vanilla; beat until smooth. Makes 2 1/3 cups.

Let not your heart be troubled,
the Lord will see you through.

CREAMY FROSTING (For Cookies)

1 c. powdered sugar	1/4 tsp. salt
1/2 tsp. vanilla	1-2 T. milk

Mix sugar, vanilla and salt. Stir in milk until frosting is smooth and of spreading consistency.

WHITE FROSTING

3/4 c. Crisco	Pinch of salt
1-lb. powdered sugar	Vanilla
1/4 c. milk	1 egg white

Cream Crisco; add powdered sugar and milk alternately. Add salt, vanilla and egg white.

Betty Leinbach

Cookies

AMISH COOKIES

2 c. brown sugar	2 eggs, beaten
1 c. shortening (1/2 c. margarine + 1/2 c. solid shortening)	1 c. seedless raisins
	3 1/2 c. flour
1/2 c. hot water	4 tsp. baking powder (in flour)
1/2 c. coffee	1 tsp. vanilla
1 tsp. soda (in coffee)	

Mix sugar and shortening until creamy. Add water, coffee, eggs, raisins and vanilla. Combine dry ingredients; add to sugar mixture. Put in refrigerator for a few hours. Drop on cookie sheet. Bake at 375 degrees for 10 minutes.

Rosalind Slabaugh

FROSTED CASHEW COOKIE

1/2 c. butter	3/4 tsp. baking powder
1 c. brown sugar	3/4 tsp. soda
1 egg	1/4 tsp. salt
1/2 tsp. vanilla	1/3 c. sour cream
2 c. flour	1 3/4 c. cashews, chopped

Cream butter and sugar; add egg and vanilla and beat. Add sifted dry ingredients alternately with sour cream. Drop on cookie sheet. Bake at 400 degrees for 10 minutes. Frost with powdered sugar icing. *This recipe received 2nd place in State Archway Cookie Contest - 1989.*

Pat Stahly

Jesus said to him, "I am the way, and the truth, and the life, no one comes to the Father, but by me." John 14:6

CHOCOLATE CHIP COOKIES

1 1/2 c. margarine
1 1/2 c. white sugar
1 1/2 c. brown sugar
3 eggs
1 T. vanilla
3 T. hot water
5 c. flour
1 1/2 tsp. soda
1 tsp. salt
1 12-oz. pkg. chocolate chips
1 c. pecans, chopped

Soften margarine. Add white sugar and brown sugar; mix well. Add eggs, 1 at a time, beating well. Add vanilla and hot water; beat again. Sift flour, soda and salt together. Add to mixture. Add chocolate chips and nuts. Dough handles better if put in refrigerator overnight. Drop by spoonfuls onto cookie sheet. Bake at 375 degrees until brown. Makes about 6 dozen.

Esther Hostetler

CHOCOLATE CHIP COOKIES

1 c. butter flavored Crisco
1/3 c. margarine
1 c. sugar
1 c. brown sugar
2 eggs
2 tsp. vanilla
3 1/2 c. flour
1 tsp. soda
2 c. chocolate chips
1 sm. pkg. (3.4-oz.) instant
    vanilla pudding

Cream Crisco, margarine and sugars. Beat in eggs and vanilla. Sift flour, soda and pudding together. Stir into mixture. Add chocolate chips. Drop onto greased cookie sheet. Bake at 375 degrees for 8-10 minutes. Makes 5-6 dozen cookies.

Merianne Shaffer

SOFT MINI CHIP COOKIES

2 1/4 c. flour
1 tsp. baking soda
1/2 c. Crisco oil
1/2 c. margarine (stick)
1/3 c. brown sugar
2/3 c. white sugar
1 tsp. vanilla
1 pkg. (4 serving) instant Jell-O
    vanilla pudding (dry)
2 eggs
4-oz. Nestle's mini chocolate
    chips
1/2 tsp. baking powder

Mix flour, soda, oil, margarine, sugars, vanilla, baking powder and pudding; beat until smooth. Beat in eggs. Stir in chips. Drop by spoonfuls or roll in small balls and flatten. Bake at 350 degrees for 10 minutes. Yields 30 cookies.

Jane Schrock

Chilled cookie dough often crumbles when slicing.

CHOCOLATE-COVERED CHERRY COOKIES

1 1/2 c. flour
1/2 c. cocoa
1/4 tsp. salt
1/4 tsp. baking powder
1/4 tsp. baking soda
1/2 c. butter
1 c. sugar

1 egg
1 1/2 tsp. vanilla
1 c. chocolate chips
1/2 c. sweetened condensed
  milk
Maraschino cherries (with juice)

Mix dry ingredients; set aside. Cream butter, sugar, egg and vanilla. Add dry ingredients. Shape into 1-inch balls on ungreased cookie sheet. Press down center of dough with your thumb and put a maraschino cherry in center (I use 1/2 cherry). Melt chocolate chips and add condensed milk. Thin with 4 teaspoons cherry juice. Spoon about 1 teaspoon frosting over each cherry. Bake at 350 degrees for 10 minutes. *Makes a wonderful holiday cookie!*

Pat Stahly
Mafra Maust

CHRISTMAS BUTTER COOKIES

1 c. butter
1 c. sugar
1 egg
1 T. milk

1 tsp. vanilla
2 1/2 c. flour
1 tsp. baking powder
1/4 tsp. salt

Cream butter. Gradually add sugar; beat until light and fluffy. Add egg, milk and vanilla; beat thoroughly. Sift together flour, baking powder and salt. Gradually add to creamed mixture. Shape into 2 rolls; wrap in waxed paper. Chill. Slice into thin cookies. Bake at 350 degrees for 10-12 minutes. Don't overbake. Frost with powdered sugar frosting.

Diane Miller

CHRISTMAS COOKIES

1 c. shortening
2 c. sugar
3 eggs
1 tsp. salt
4 1/2 c. flour

1 1/2 tsp. vanilla
3/4 tsp. lemon or almond
  extract
1 tsp. soda

Beat all ingredients together, except flour. Stir in flour, using more flour to roll out dough. Bake at 375 degrees for 8-10 minutes.

Sandy Owen

The word is a lamp to my feet and a light to my path.
Psalm 119:105

COFFEE DROP COOKIES

2 c. brown sugar	1 heaping tsp. instant coffee
1 c. shortening	1/2 c. hot water
2 eggs	1 tsp. baking soda
4 c. flour	2 tsp. vanilla
3 tsp. baking powder	1 c. raisins
1/2 c. water	

Cream sugar, shortening and eggs together. Add water. Dissolve instant coffee in hot water; add soda to hot coffee. Sift flour with baking powder. Add flour and coffee alternately to creamed mixture. Add vanilla and raisins. Drop by teaspoonfuls. Bake at 350 degrees until lightly browned. Walnuts may be added and cookies frosted, if desired.

Gloria Tyson

CREAM WAFERS

1 c. butter or margarine	3/4 c. powdered sugar
1/3 c. cream	1 egg yolk
2 c. flour	1 tsp. vanilla
Frosting:	Food coloring, as desired
1/4 c. soft butter	in cookie or filling

For cookies: Mix butter, cream and flour well. roll out to 1/8-inch thick on floured board. Cut out small rounds 2-inches in diameter. Sugar dough rounds on both sides. Place on ungreased cookie sheet and prick each cookie with fork 4-5 times. Bake at 375 degrees for 7-9 minutes.

For frosting: Cream together ingredients. Frost bottom side of cookies making sandwiches.

Karen Graybill

GINGER COOKIES

1 c. brown sugar	2 eggs
1 c. shortening	1 tsp. soda
1 c. Brer Rabbit molasses	1 tsp. baking powder
1/2 c. hot water	1 tsp. ginger
4 c. flour	1 lg. tsp. cinnamon

Dissolve soda in hot water. Let batter set in refrigerator overnight. Roll out in thickness and as large as you like.

Bertha Weaver

Lord, you know how busy I will be today.
If I forget you, please do not forget me.

GINGER SNAPS

1 1/2 c. shortening
2 c. sugar
2 eggs
1/2 c. molasses
4 c. flour

2 tsp. soda
1 1/2 tsp. ginger
1 1/2 tsp. cinnamon
1 1/2 tsp. cloves

Cream shortening and sugar. Beat in eggs; add molasses and dry ingredients. Roll into 1-inch balls. Dip in sugar. Place on baking sheet 2-inches apart. Bake in moderate oven (375 degrees) for 15-18 minutes. Makes 5 dozen. *John David's favorite cookies.*

Ruth Zehr

KEEFLIES

2 c. sour cream
2-lb. butter (not margarine)
6-8 c. flour
12 egg yolks
Pinch of salt

Filling:
12 egg whites
2-lb. powdered sugar
1/2 tsp. lemon juice
3-lb. walnuts or pecans
2 tsp. vanilla

Combine egg yolks, butter, sour cream; mix well. Gradually add flour until dough is slightly stiff. Make balls the size of a walnut and place on waxed paper. Chill 2-3 hours or overnight. When ready to fill, roll out into small circles (very thin); fill with filling.

For filling: Beat egg whites until stiff. The rolled dough is to be filled with 1 teaspoon of filling and the dough is to be paper thin. Fold dough circle over so it is in a crescent shape and pinch ends. Bake at 375 degrees for 12 minutes or until straw colored. After baked, place on lightly powdered sugar table. Shake powdered sugar over warm Keeflies. Store only after completely cooled.

Ruby Panyako

NO PEEK COOKIES

2 egg whites
2/3 c. white sugar
1 tsp. vanilla

Dash of salt
1/2 c. chocolate chips
1/2 c. nuts, chopped

Preheat oven to 350 degrees. Beat egg whites until stiff. Gradually add sugar, vanilla and salt. Beat at High speed to a stiff meringue. Stir in nuts and chocolate chips. Drop by teaspoonfuls onto cookie sheet that has been covered with foil. Turn off oven and don't peek. Leave overnight or several hours until oven is cold.

Marge Detweiler

Daily prayers lessen daily cares.

COWBOY COOKIES

1 c. shortening	1 tsp. soda
1 c. white sugar	1/2 tsp. baking powder
1 c. brownsugar	1/2 tsp. salt
2 eggs	1 tsp. vanilla
2 c. flour	2 c. oatmeal

Cream shortening, sugars and eggs together. Add dry ingredients; mix well. Roll into nut sized balls; flatten with fork. Bake at 350 degrees for 10-12 minutes. For variation: nuts, coconut or raisins may be added.

Lawrence Troyer

GRANDPA'S OATMEAL DROP COOKIES

1 c. shortening	1 tsp. nutmeg
1 1/2 c. sugar	1 tsp. cinnamon
2 eggs	1 tsp. cloves
2 c. flour	1/2 c. nut meats (opt.)
2 tsp. baking powder	1 tsp. salt
1/2 c. milk	1 sm. jar plum baby food
1 tsp. soda	1/2-1 c. raisins
2 c. quick oats	

Bring raisins to boil (covered in water); set aside. Mix shortening, sugar and eggs together. Add remaining ingredients, adding oatmeal last. Blend just until mixed. Add drained raisins. Bake at 350 degrees for 8-10 minutes. Makes 6 dozen cookies. *These are very moist cookies. Store in container between waxed paper.*

Sarah Fervida

OATMEAL COOKIES

1 c. brown sugar	1 tsp. baking powder
1 c. sugar	3/4 tsp. salt
1 c. shortening	4 c. oatmeal
2 extra lg. eggs	1 tsp. vanilla
2 1/2 c. flour	Nuts (opt.)
1 tsp. soda	Chocolate chips (opt.)

Cream shortening and sugars; beat in eggs. Sift flour, baking powder, soda and salt; add to mixture. Stir in oatmeal. Make balls (size of walnuts) and flatten with glass bottom dipped in water and then sugar. Bake at 375 degrees for 10-12 minutes. *My grandchildren's favorite.*

Anabel Hartman

*Lo, I am with you always,
even unto the end of the world.
Matthew 28:20*

OATMEAL COOKIES

1 c. vegetable shortening	1 1/2 c. flour
1 c. brown sugar	1 tsp. soda
1 c. white sugar	1 tsp. salt
2 eggs	3 c. oatmeal
1 tsp. vanilla	

Cream together shortening, sugars, eggs and vanilla. Add flour, soda and salt; mix. Add oatmeal and work together. Form into rolls and chill. Slice and bake at 400 degrees for 8-10 minutes. *These can be dropped if you wish.*

Alice Newcomer

OATMEAL COOKIES

1 1/2 c. white sugar	2 tsp. baking soda
2 c. brown sugar	5 1/2 c. quick oatmeal
2 c. oil	3 c. flour
4 eggs	1 1/2 c. chocolate chips
1 tsp. salt	

Mix the first 6 ingredients until well blended. Add oatmeal and flour; stir in chocolate chips. Can be rolled out and cut into simple shapes or made into balls and pushed to 1/2-inch thickness. Bake at 350 degrees for 10 minutes. We blend old fashioned oats if we don't have quick oats almost like oat flour--just be sure to use the preblended measurement.

Jenae Rupp

OATMEAL-MOLASSES COOKIES

2 c. brown sugar	1 3/4 c. flour (part may be
1 c. shortening	whole wheat)
1/2 c. buttermilk (milk + 1	1 tsp. baking soda
tsp. vinegar)	2 T. molasses
1 tsp. vanilla	1/2-3/4 c. raisins
4 c. oatmeal	

Heat oven to 375 degrees. Mix sugar, shortening, buttermilk, molasses and vanilla. Stir in remaining ingredients. Shape into 1-inch balls. Place about 3-inches apart onto ungreased cookie sheet. Flatten cookies with bottom of glass dipped in water. Bake 8-10 minutes. Immediately remove from cookie sheet. Makes 7 dozen cookies.

Chris & Lois Leuz - Taiwan

If God is going to do something wonderful,
He starts with a problem.
If God is going to do something spectacular,
He starts with an impossibility.

PEANUT BUTTER CRINKLES

1 c. margarine
1 c. peanut butter
1 c. sugar
1 c. brown sugar
2 eggs
1 tsp. vanilla
2 1/2 c. flour
1 tsp. baking powder
1 tsp. baking soda
1 tsp. salt
Sugar
Nuts, chocolate kisses, jam or
    jelly

With mixer, beat first 6 ingredients until fluffy. At low speed, beat in next 4 ingredients. Shape into 1-inch balls; roll in sugar. Place 2-inches apart onto an ungreased cookie sheet. Bake at 350 degrees for 12-15 minutes or until browned. After removing from the oven, immediately press nuts, candy or jams into the centers of cookies. Makes 6 dozen cookies.

Tami Martin

MAGIC PEANUT BUTTER MIDDLES

1 1/2 c. flour
1/2 c. cocoa (Bakers)
1/2 tsp. baking soda
1/2 c. sugar
1/2 c. brown sugar, firmly packed
1/2 c. margarine
1/4 c. peanut butter
1 tsp. vanilla
1 egg
3/4 c. peanut butter
3/4 c. powdered sugar

In small bowl, combine flour, cocoa and baking soda; blend well. In large bowl, beat sugar, margarine and 1/4 cup peanut butter until light and fluffy. Add vanilla and egg; beat well. Stir in flour mixture; blend and set aside. In a small bowl, combine 3/4 cup peanut butter and powdered sugar. Roll into 1-inch balls (30). For each cookie, with floured hands, shape 1 tablespoon cookie dough around 1 ball, covering completely. Place onto greased cookie sheets. Flatten with bottom of glass dipped in sugar. Bake at 375 degrees for 7-9 minutes.

Lawrence Troyer

PEANUT BUTTER TEMPTATIONS

1/2 c. butter
1/2 c. peanut butter
1/2 c. sugar
1/2 c. brown sugar
1 egg
1/2 tsp. vanilla
1 1/4 c. flour
3/4 tsp. soda
1/2 tsp. salt
48 miniature Reese's cups

Cream together butter, peanut butter, sugars, egg and vanilla. Stir in dry ingredients until blended. Roll dough into 1-inch balls. Press into small muffin tins. Bake at 350 degrees for 9-10 minutes. Remove from oven and immediately press 1 miniature Reese's cup into crust. Cool and remove.

Shirley Albrecht

PEPPERNUTS

3/4 c. white sugar
3/4 c. brown sugar
2 T. Karo syrup
1/4 c. butter
1 egg, beaten
1/4 c. water
1/4 tsp. cloves
1/4 tsp. cinnamon
1/4-1/2 tsp. anise extract
1/4 c. nuts
1/4 tsp. ginger
1/4 tsp. baking powder
2 1/2 c. flour

Heat sugars, syrup, butter and water together until butter melts. Beat in egg. Add remaining ingredients. Let dough set several hours at room temperature. Roll into ropes which are 3/4-inch in diameter. Place on lightly greased cookie sheets and cut into 1/2-inch pieces, moving the ropes after each cut so the pieces are separate. Bake at 375 degrees for 8 minutes. They will be lightly browned. This is a tiny, crunchy, lower-fat cookie. Makes 7 cups.

Merianne Shaffer

SNICKER COOKIES

1/2 c. sugar
1/2 c. brown sugar
1/2 c. peanut butter
1 tsp. vanilla
1 egg
1/2 c. Crisco
1 1/2 c. flour
1/2 tsp. soda
1/2 tsp. baking powder
1/4 tsp. salt
Bite size Snicker candy bars

Mix egg, Crisco, sugar, brown sugar, peanut butter and vanilla. Add dry ingredients. Make dough in a ball the size of a walnut. Wrap around bite size candy. Bake at 350 degrees until brown.

Beverly Coblentz

SNICKERDOODLES

1 c. shortening (part butter
   or margarine)
1 1/2 c. sugar
2 eggs
2 3/4 c. flour
2 tsp. cream of tartar
1 tsp. soda
2 T. sugar
2 tsp. cinnamon

Heat oven to 400 degrees. Mix shortening, 1 1/2 cups sugar and eggs thoroughly. Sift flour, cream of tartar and soda together; stir in. Shape dough into 1-inch balls. Roll balls in mixture of 2 tablespoons sugar and cinnamon. Place 2-inches apart onto ungreased baking sheet. Bake 8-10 minutes. Cookies will puff up at first, then flatten out. Makes 6 dozen.

Merianne Shaffer

"Take delight in the Lord, and He will give you the desires of your heart."
Psalm 37:4

127

HOLIDAY FROSTED SUGAR COOKIES

2 c. sugar
1 c. Crisco
3 eggs
5-6 c. flour
3 tsp. baking powder
1 c. sour milk
1 tsp. soda

1 tsp. vanilla
Frosting:
1-lb. powdered sugar
1/2 c. butter (not margarine)
1/8 tsp. salt
1 tsp. vanilla
3-4 T. milk

Mix sugar, Crisco and eggs. Add flour, baking powder and soda along with milk and vanilla. Start adding enough of last cup of flour (6th cup) to prevent cookie dough from sticking to fingers. Roll and cut. Bake at 375 degrees for about 5 minutes (depending on thickness of cookies).

For frosting: Mix ingredients in order. Divide frosting up in small containers. Add different food coloring to each. Frost cookies and add sprinkles.

Delora Reinhardt

SUGAR KISSES COOKIES

1 1/2 c. flour
1 pinch salt
1/3 c. margarine or shortening
3/4 c. sugar
1 T. milk

1 pkg. Hershey Kisses
1 1/2 tsp. baking powder
1 egg
1 tsp. vanilla

Stir together flour, baking powder and salt. Beat margarine and sugar together. Add eggs, milk and vanilla; beat well. Add dry ingredients. Roll into balls. Flatten and place Hershey Kiss in middle; sprinkle with sugar. Bake at 375 degrees for 8-10 minutes.

Alpha Mae Mumaw

MARY'S SUGAR COOKIES

1 1/2 c. powdered sugar, sifted
1 c. butter or margarine
1 egg
1 tsp. vanilla

1/2 tsp. almond flavoring extract
2 1/2 c. flour
1 tsp. soda
1 tsp. cream of tartar

Mix sugar and butter. Add egg and flavorings; mix thoroughly. Sift dry ingredients together and blend in. Refrigerate 2-3 hours. Roll dough 3/16-inch thick on lightly floured surface. Cut with cookie cutter. Place on greased cookie sheet and bake at 375 degrees for 7-8 minutes. When cookies are cool, frost thinly with a powdered sugar-water glaze. Use just enough so that colored sugar will stick when sprinkled on. Or sprinkle sugar on cookies before baking. Can also be frosted. Makes 5 dozen 2-2 1/2-inch cookies.

Merianne Shaffer

SOFT SUGAR COOKIE

2 c. sugar
3 eggs
1 c. shortening
4 1/2 c. flour
1 tsp. salt

1 tsp. soda
1 tsp. baking powder
1 tsp. vanilla
1 c. sour cream

Cream sugar and shortening; add eggs and beat. Add dry ingredients, vanilla and sour cream; stir. Refrigerate overnight. Drop on greased and floured cookie sheet. Dip a greased tumbler in sugar and lightly press each cookie. Bake at 350 degrees for 10-12 minutes. Don't overbake. Good frosted too!

Pat Stahly

DATE-APRICOT BARS

3/4 c. part butter and shortening
1 c. brown sugar
1 3/4 c. flour
1/2 tsp. baking soda
1 tsp. salt

1 1/2 c. oatmeal
1 c. dates, diced
1/2 c. sugar
2 c. dried apricots
Water

Mix shortening and brown sugar; stir in flour, soda, salt and oatmeal. Place half of crumb mixture in greased 13 x 9-inch pan; press and flatten. Combine dates, sugar, apricots and water to cover in saucepan; cook until soft. Cool. Spread cooled filling over crust in pan; cover with remaining crumb mixture patting lightly. Bake at 350 degrees until browned lightly, approximately 30 minutes. Cut into bars and serve. *A favorite for the holidays.*

Carolyn F. Yoder

GOOEY BLONDIES

1/2 c. butter
1 16-oz. box dark brown sugar
2 eggs
1 tsp. vanilla

1 c. flour
1/2 tsp. salt
1 c. walnuts, coarsely chopped

Combine butter and brown sugar in saucepan. Cook over medium heat, stirring constantly, until bubbly. Let cool. Transfer cooled mixture to a mixing bowl; beat in eggs and vanilla. Quickly stir in flour, salt and walnuts. Pour batter into greased 13 x 9-inch pan. Bake at 325 degrees for 35 minutes. Let cool before cutting.

Jill Erb

*Every sunrise is a new message from God
and every sunset his signature.*

BROWNIES

1 c. fine graham crumbs
(24 crackers)
1/2 c. walnuts, chopped
8-oz. semisweet chocolate
pieces
2 tsp. artificial sweetener
(equal to 1/3 c. sugar)
1/4 tsp. salt
1 c. skim milk

Preheat oven to 350 degrees. Place all ingredients in bowl and stir until blended. Turn into lightly greased 8 x 8-inch pan. Bake 30 minutes. Cut into 16 2-inch squares while warm. 1 brownie = 1 fruit and 1 fat

Melba Martin

CHEWY BROWNIES

1/2 c. cocoa
1 c. butter
2 c. white sugar
4 eggs
2 tsp. vanilla
1 c. flour
1/2 c. walnuts, chopped
12-oz. pkg. chocolate chips

Cream cocoa, sugar, eggs and butter. Add flour and vanilla. Stir in 1/4 cup walnuts and half of chocolate chips. Bake in a 13 x 9-inch pan at 350 degrees for 25 minutes. Top immediately with other half of chocolate chips and chopped walnuts. Do not overbake.

Deb Krawiec

CHOCOLATE BROWNIES

1 1/2 c. flour
2 c. sugar
1/2 c. cocoa
1/4 tsp. salt
4 eggs
1 c. oil
2 tsp. vanilla
1 c. nuts (opt.)

Place all ingredients in mixer bowl. Beat at medium speed for 3 minutes. Place in greased 9 x 13-inch pan. Bake at 350 degrees for about 30 minutes. For Christmas - roll in powdered sugar after cutting into bars.

Chris & Lois Leuz - Taiwan

GRAHAM CRACKER DELIGHT BARS

8-10 graham crackers
2 sticks margarine
1/4 c. brown sugar
1/4 c. white sugar
1/2 c. pecans, chopped

Line a 9 x 13-inch cookie sheet with foil, dull side up. Lay graham crackers flat side down on top of foil. Mix together margarine, brown sugar and white sugar; bring to rolling boil. Boil 2 minutes. Pour over crackers; sprinkle with pecans. Bake at 350 degrees for 12 minutes. Cool and break into pieces.

Clare & Katie Ann Schumm

CREAM CHEESE BROWNIES

1 pkg. Betty Crocker Super Moist German Chocolate Cake Mix
1 8-oz. pkg. cream cheese, softened
1 egg
1/2 c. sugar
1/2 c. milk chocolate chips

Heat oven to 350 degrees. Grease and flour a jelly roll pan. Prepare cake mix as directed on package. Pour batter into pan. Mix remaining ingredients. Drop by tablespoonfuls onto batter. Cut through batter with knife or metal spatula several times for marbled effect. Sprinkle with additional chocolate chips or chopped nuts, if desired. Bake until cake springs back when touched lightly in center or when wooden toothpick inserted in center comes out clean, about 25-30 minutes.

Mike Metzler

DELUXE CHOCOLATE MARSHMALLOW BARS

3/4 c. butter
1 1/2 c. sugar
3 eggs
1 tsp. vanilla
1 1/3 c. flour
1/2 tsp. salt
1/2 tsp. baking powder
3 T. baking cocoa
1/2 c. nuts, chopped
Topping:
1 1/3 c. chocolate chips
3 T. butter
1 c. peanut butter
2 c. rice crisp cereal

In mixing bowl, cream butter and sugar; add eggs and vanilla. Beat until fluffy. Combine flour, baking powder, salt and cocoa. Add to creamed mixture. Stir in nuts and spread in a jelly roll pan. Bake at 350 degrees for 15-18 minutes. Sprinkle marshmallows evenly over cake. Cool.

For topping: Combine chocolate chips, butter and peanut butter in a small saucepan. Cook over low heat, stirring constantly, until melted and well blended. Remove from heat; stir in cereal. Spread over bars. Chill. Makes 3 dozen.

LEMON FILLED BARS

1 c. flour
1/2 c. butter
1/4 c. powdered sugar
2 eggs, beaten
2 T. lemon juice
1 c. sugar
2 T. flour
1/2 tsp. baking powder

Mix 1 cup flour, butter and powdered sugar; pat into an 8 x 8-inch pan. Bake at 350 degrees for 20 minutes. Mix together eggs, lemon juice, sugar, 2 tablespoons flour and baking powder. Pour on top of first mixture. Bake at 350 degrees for 25 minutes. Cool and cut into squares. Refrigerate.

Dawn West

LEMONY BARS

Base:
1 c. flour*
3/4 c. sugar
1/2 tsp. baking powder
1/4 tsp. salt
2 c. Rice Chex, crushed to 1/2 c.
1/2 c. butter or margarine

Topping:
2 eggs, beaten
3/4 c. sugar
2 T. flour
1/4 tsp. baking powder
4 tsp. lemon juice
1 tsp. grated lemon peel
Powdered sugar

Preheat oven to 350 degrees. Grease a 9-inch square pan. To prepare base: Combine flour, sugar, baking powder and salt. Stir in Chex crumbs. Cut in butter until very fine crumbs. Press mixture firmly into bottom of pan. Bake 12 minutes.

For topping: Combine all ingredients, except powdered sugar. Mix until well blended. Pour over hot base. Return to oven for an addition 15-20 minutes or until top is set but not browned. Cool. Sprinkle with powdered sugar. Cut into bars. *Stir flour; then spoon into measuring cup. Makes 24 bars. *Delicious!*

Eric Martin

PEANUT BUTTER BARS

1 c. creamy peanut butter
6 T. butter
1 1/4 c. sugar
3 eggs
1 tsp. vanilla
1 c. flour
1/4 tsp. salt
1 12-oz. pkg. peanut butter chips
1 12-oz. pkg. chocolate chips

Preheat oven to 350 degrees. In mixing bowl, combine peanut butter and butter; beat until smooth. Add sugar, eggs and vanilla; beat until creamy. Blend in flour and salt. Stir in peanut butter chips. Spread in greased 9 x 13-inch pan. Bake for 25-30 minutes or until edges turn brown. Sprinkle with chocolate chips. Return to oven just long enough to soften. Spread evenly over top. Cool completely.

Karen Leinbach

PECAN BARS

3 c. flour
1/2 c. sugar
1 c. butter, softened
1/2 tsp. salt
4 eggs
1 1/2 c. Karo syrup
1 1/2 c. sugar
3 T. butter, melted
1 1/2 tsp. vanilla
2 1/2 c. pecans, chopped

To make crust, blend together flour, 1/2 cup sugar, 1 cup butter and salt to coarse crumbs. Press firmly and evenly into greased 15 x 10 x 1-inch baking pan. Bake at 350 degrees for 20 minutes. In a large bowl, combine eggs, syrup, 1 1/2 cups sugar, 3 tablespoons melted butter and vanilla. Stir in pecans. Spread evenly over crust and bake at 350 degrees for another 25 minutes or until set. Cool; cut into small bars.

Phyllis Weaver

PEANUT BUTTER OATMEAL BARS

1/2 c. margarine
1/2 c. sugar
1/2 c. brown sugar
1 egg
1/3 c. peanut butter
1/2 tsp. soda
1/4 tsp. salt

1/2 tsp. vanilla
1 c. flour
1 c. quick oatmeal
1 6-oz. pkg. chocolate chips
1/2 c. powdered sugar
1/4 c. peanut butter
3 T. milk

Cream together margarine and sugars. Blend in brown sugar, egg, 1/3 cup peanut butter, soda, salt, vanilla, flour and oatmeal. Spread in 13 x 9-inch pan. Bake at 350 degrees for 20 minutes. Sprinkle chocolate chips on top. Return to oven for about 1 minute. Spread chips smooth. Cream powdered sugar, 1/4 cup peanut butter and milk. Drizzle on top.

Marge Detweiler

FESTAL PUMPKIN BARS

4 eggs
1 c. salad oil
2 c. sugar
1 16-oz. can pumpkin
2 c. flour
2 tsp. baking powder

1 tsp. soda
1/2 tsp. cloves
1/2 tsp. salt
2 tsp. cinnamon
1/2 tsp. ginger
1/2 tsp. nutmeg

Mix eggs, sugar, oil and pumpkin in a large bowl; beat well. Add dry ingredients; mix well. Bake at 350 degrees for 25-30 minutes.
Frosting:
6-oz. cream cheese
3/4 stick butter or margarine
1 T. milk

1 tsp. vanilla
4 c. powdered sugar

Beat cheese, butter, vanilla and milk together until soft. Add powdered sugar until correct consistency to spread. Cut into 2 x 3-inch bars. Makes 36 bars.

Shirleen Weaver

PUMPKIN SQUARES

1 1-lb. can (2 c.) pumpkin
1 c. sugar
1 tsp. salt
1/2 tsp. ginger
1 tsp. cinnamon

1/2 tsp. ground nutmeg
1 c. pecans, chopped
1/2-gal. vanilla ice cream
36 ginger snaps or ginger wafers

Combine pumpkin, sugar, salt and spices. In a chilled bowl, fold pumpkin mixture into ice cream. Add chopped pecans. Line bottom of a 9 x 13 x 2-inch pan with half of the ginger snaps; top with half of ice cream mixture. Cover with another layer of ginger snaps and remaining ice cream mixture. Freeze; cut into squares. Makes 18 generous servings.

Shirley Albrecht & Kathy Stoltzfus

PUMPKIN PIE SQUARES

1 c. flour	1/2 tsp. salt
1/2 c. quick rolled oats	1 tsp. cinnamon
1/2 c. brown sugar	1/2 tsp. ginger
1/2 c. butter	1/4 tsp. cloves
2 c. pumpkin (1-lb. can)	1/2 c. brown sugar
1 13 1/2-oz. can evaporated milk	2 T. butter
2 eggs	1/2 c. pecans, chopped (opt.)
3/4 c. sugar	

Combine flour, oats, 1/2 cup brown sugar and 1/2 cup butter in mixing bowl. Mix until crumbly, using electric mixer on low speed. Press into ungreased 13 x 9-inch pan. Bake at 350 degrees for 15 minutes. Combine pumpkin, evaporated milk, eggs, sugar, salt and spices in mixing bowl; beat well. Pour onto crust. Bake at 350 degrees for 20 minutes. Combine 1/2 cup brown sugar, 2 tablespoons butter and pecans; sprinkle over pumpkin filling. Return to oven and bake 15-20 minutes or until filling is set. Cool in pan and cut into 2-inch squares. Makes 2 dozen.

Marla Reinhardt
Lou Thomas

RECIPE FOR A HAPPY DAY

Mix together the following ingredients: One full measure of chirping, trilling, birdsong, four quick sprites of gentle, soft spring mist, the sparkling glow in a loved one's look, the enjoyment of a friend's visit. Add the softness of a cuddly, drowsy kitten, the trust and devotion in a puppy's eyes, the festive twinkling of Christmas lights, the whisper of the leaves in a gentle breeze, the bubbling, gurgling murmur of gently flowing water. Fold in five large white, billowy clouds that have been thoroughly laced with early June sunshine. Sprinkle liberally with joyous children's laughter. Bake in the cozy warmth of a snowy, blowy winter evening's kitchen, surrounded by your dear ones.

Desserts

DESSERTS

ANGEL FOOD DESSERT

1 angel food cake, cut in pieces
1 can peach pie filling
8-oz. cream cheese
1 c. powdered sugar
1 c. Cool Whip

Mix cream cheese and powdered sugar; fold in Cool Whip. Layer angel food cake pieces, cream cheese mixture, then pie filling. Continue several times. *Delicious with fresh peach pie filling.*

Beverly Coblentz

ANGEL FOOD CAKE DESSERT

1 13-oz. angel food cake
2 sm. (or 1 lg.) box strawberry jello
2 c. boiling water
2-qts. strawberry ice cream

Let ice cream soften. Break up cake in 9 x 12-inch pan. Dissolve jello in boiling water. Add ice cream to jello and pour over cake. Cover. Let set in refrigerator overnight.

Ira Hoover

BAKED APPLES

8 baking apples
3/4 c. brown sugar
2 T. minute tapioca
1 c. hot water
1/4 c. red hot cinnamon candies

Peel, core and cut apples into halves. Arrange core side up in a shallow baking dish. Sprinkle brown sugar and tapioca pudding on top. Cover with hot water. Sprinkle apples with candies. Bake at 350 degrees for 30-40 minutes. Apple should be soft and firm, but not mushy. Turn apples over once during baking. Sprinkle more red hots over top while hot and top with a little whipped cream to serve.

Phyllis Weaver

STUFFED BAKED APPLES

4 med. apples
1/4 c. raisins
1/4 tsp. ground cinnamon
3/4 c. water
1 tsp. lemon juice

Core apples through center. Peel the top 1/3 of each apple; place in an 8-inch square dish. Place 1 tablespoon of raisins in each cavity and sprinkle evenly with cinnamon. Combine water and lemon juice; pour over apples. Cover and bake at 375 degrees for 45 minutes. Makes 4 servings.

Linda Hartman

BAKED APPLES

8 apples, peeled, cored
  and halved
Dough:
2 c. flour
2 1/2 tsp. baking powder
1/2 tsp. salt
2/3 c. shortening

1/2 c. milk
Sauce:
2 c. brown sugar
2 c. water
1/4 c. butter
1/4 tsp. cinnamon

Mix above dough ingredients. Roll out and cut into 8 parts. Between the two halves of the apples place a dab of butter, 1/2 teaspoon brown sugar and cinnamon. Wrap the apple in the dough and place in a deep baking dish. Make sauce and boil for 5 minutes. Pour sauce over apples. Bake at 350 degrees for 40 minutes. *This is likely to run over, so use a deep baking dish.*

Marilyn (G. Keith) Miller

APPLE CRISP

4 c. cooking apples, peeled and
  sliced
1 T. lemon juice
1/3 c. flour
1 c. oats, uncooked

1/2 c. brown sugar, firmly packed
1/2 tsp. salt
1 tsp. cinnamon
1/3 c. butter or margarine,
  melted

Place apples in shallow baking dish. Sprinkle with lemon juice. Combine dry ingredients; add melted butter, mixing until crumbly. Sprinkle crumb mixture over apples. Bake in preheated moderate oven (375 degrees) for 30 minutes or until apples are tender. Makes 6 servings.

Kris Skyrm

APPLE DESSERT

4 c. flour
2 c. sugar
1 1/2 c. margarine
2 eggs, beaten

5 c. apples, cut up
1/2 c. sugar
1 tsp. cinnamon

Mix flour, 2 cups sugar and margarine thoroughly; add eggs. Press half of mixture in a 10 x 15-inch pan. Top with apples, 1/2 cup sugar and cinnamon. Put remaining dough on top. Bake at 350 degrees for 45 minutes.

Marlene Sutter

Store unused whipping cream in freezer by putting in 1-ounce paper cups. Cover cups and place in freezer bags. Thaw and use as needed.

APPLE DESSERT WITH CARAMEL TOPPING

1 c. white sugar	1/2 tsp. cinnamon
1 c. brown sugar	4 c. apples, chopped
1/2 c. butter	1/2 c. nuts, chopped
2 eggs, beaten	Topping:
2 c. flour	1 1/4 c. brown sugar
2 tsp. soda	1 c. light Karo syrup
1/2 tsp. salt	1/4 c. butter
1/2 tsp. nutmeg	1 c. whipping cream

Cream sugars and butter. Stir in remaining ingredients. Bake in greased 9 x 13-inch pan at 350 degrees for 45 minutes.

For topping: Boil brown sugar, syrup and butter for 5 minutes, stirring constantly. Remove from heat and add whipping cream. Return to a rolling boil. Serve dessert warm with topping and Cool Whip.

Jan Ramer (Brian)

APPLE SLICES

2 1/2 c. flour	Milk
1 T. sugar	2/3 c. cornflakes, crushed
1 tsp. salt	5 c. apples, sliced
1 c. Crisco	1 1/2 c. sugar
1 egg	

Mix together flour, 1 tablespoon sugar, salt and Crisco. Put egg into measuring cup; add milk to make 2/3 cup. Add to Crisco mixture and mix. Roll out half of dough into 15 x 11-inch on baking sheet. Cover with cornflakes and then apple slices. Sprinkle 1 1/2 cups sugar over apples. Roll out remaining dough for top crust. Pinch edges. Bake at 350 degrees for 45 minutes or until dough browns. While hot, drizzle powdered sugar glaze over top.

Beverly Coblentz

BANANA SPLIT CAKE

2 pkgs. graham crackers, crushed	3-4 bananas, sliced
	1 lg. can crushed pineapple, well drained
1/2 c. butter	
1-lb. box powdered sugar	1-qt. fresh strawberries, sliced
1/2 c. butter	Cool Whip
2 eggs	

Melt 1/2 cup butter; add cracker crumbs and press in bottom of 13 x 9-inch pan. Bake at 350 degrees for 10 minutes. Beat powdered sugar, 1/2 cup butter and eggs until fluffy. Spread over cooled crust. Layer bananas, pineapple and strawberries. Top with Cool Whip. Chill until serving time.

Phyllis Weaver

137

BANANA TORTE

3 T. margarine
3 egg yolks
3 T. sugar
2 c. flour
4 bananas
1 can Eagle Brand milk

Mix margarine, eggs, sugar and flour; press into a greased 7 x 12-inch pan. Slice bananas over crumbs. Pour milk over bananas. Bake at 375 degrees for 45 minutes.

Otis & Betty Hochstetler-Brazil

CHOCOLATE CAKE DESSERT

1 18.25-oz. box chocolate cake mix
1 14-oz. can sweetened condensed milk
1 jar caramel ice cream topping
1 8-oz. Cool Whip, thawed
1 chocolate bar, grated (or 1 c. walnuts or pecans)

Bake cake according to package directions in a 13 x 9-inch pan. Remove from oven and poke holes all over cake top with a toothpick or fork. Pour combined condensed milk and caramel topping over cake; cool completely. Spread whipped topping over top of cake and sprinkle with grated chocolate. Refrigerate until ready to serve. Serves 12-15.

Carolyn Graber
Patty Bontrager

BAKED CUSTARD

4 eggs
1/2 c. sugar
1/2 tsp. salt
4 c. milk
1 tsp. vanilla
Nutmeg (opt.)

Beat eggs slightly; add sugar, salt and vanilla. Scald milk and pour slowly over egg mixture. Stir until thoroughly mixed. Pour into custard cups, filling 2/3 full (or use a 1 1/2-quart shallow baking dish). Sprinkle with nutmeg. Set cups or baking dish into a larger pan and pour hot water around them until it comes to the level of the custard. Bake at 325 degrees for approximately 40 minutes or until a silver knife comes out clean when inserted in the center of the custard. Makes 8 servings.

Mary Martin

QUICK CHERRY CRUNCH

1 box white cake mix
1 can cherry pie filling
1 stick butter (1/2 c.)
3/4 c. walnuts or pecans, chopped

Spread pie filling on bottom of an 8-inch square pan. Sprinkle with dry cake mix. Melt butter and drizzle over cake mix. Sprinkle with chopped nuts. Bake at 350 degrees for 45 minutes or until browned. Cool and serve with ice cream or whipped topping.

Sherry Kehr

BLUEBERRY CHEESECAKE DESSERT

16 graham crackers
3/4 c. sugar
1/4 c. butter, softened
1 tsp. vanilla

1 c. sugar
1 8-oz. pkg. cream cheese
2 c. blueberry pie filling (or cherry pie filling)

Crush graham crackers; mix with 3/4 cup sugar and butter. Press into a 9 x 13-inch tupperware cake pan. Mix vanilla, 1 cup sugar and cream cheese together; put on top of crust layer. Put pie filling on top of cream cheese mixture.

Sandy Owen

FAST AND EASY FRUIT COBBLER

1 c. self-rising flour
1 c. sugar
1 c. milk

1 stick margarine
1 can pie filling

Mix flour, sugar, milk and softened margarine with electric mixer until margarine is mixed in thoroughly (small clumps will remain in batter). Pour batter into ungreased glass baking dish. Spread pie filling evenly over batter. Bake at 350 degrees for approximately 1 hour or until pie is set in center.

Kathy Kulp
Sue Klaassen

PEACH COBBLER

3 c. Bisquick
3 c. sugar
2 1/4 c. milk or cream

3 tsp. vanilla
1/2-lb. butter
4 1-lb. cans peach slices

Drain peaches; reserve 1/2 of juice. Combine dry ingredients. Melt butter; pour into dry ingredients. Add vanilla, milk or cream and peach juice; mix. Pour peaches into a large greased baking dish. Pour batter over peaches. Bake at 350 degrees for 1-1 1/2 hours.

Amy Martin

PEACH COBBLER

3/4 c. milk
1 c. sugar
3/4 stick margarine
2 tsp. baking powder

3/4 c. flour
Pinch of salt
2 c. peach slices

Combine flour, sugar, baking powder, salt and milk into a batter. Melt margarine in 9 x 9-inch baking dish. Pour batter in middle of melted margarine. Pour peaches in middle of batter. Do not stir. Bake at 350 degrees for 1 hour.

Rosalind Slabaugh

PEACH COBBLER

3 c. fresh peaches, sliced
1 T. lemon juice
1/4 tsp. almond extract
1 c. flour, sifted

1 c. sugar
1/2 tsp. salt
1 egg, beaten
6 T. margarine, melted

Preheat oven to 375 degrees. Butter a 10 x 6-inch baking dish. Place peaches on bottom. Sprinkle with lemon juice and extract. Sift together dry ingredients. Add egg and mix with fork until crumbly. Sprinkle over peaches. Drizzle with margarine. Bake for 35-40 minutes.

Evelyn Stichter

GLAZED FRUIT DESSERT

1 3.4-oz. pkg. instant vanilla
pudding
1 20-oz. can chunk pineapple
(in natural juice)

1 11-oz. can mandarin oranges
2 bananas

Drain juice from pineapple and reserve. Drain juice from oranges. Mix pineapple and pudding mix; stir until thick. Fold in fruits. Refrigerate until serving time.

Jeffery Weaver

ORANGE DESSERT

1 1/2 c. orange juice
2 3-oz. pkgs. orange jello
1 c. vanilla ice cream

2 c. whipping cream
1 or 2 cans mandarin oranges,
drained

Dissolve jello in hot orange juice. Add ice cream; stir to melt. Whip cream and add to above mixture. (I substitute a small container of Cool Whip for 1 cup of cream.) Stir in drained oranges; put mixture in 9 x 13-inch pan. Refrigerate.

PAVLOVA (Australian Dessert)

6 egg whites (at room temp.)
1/2 tsp. cream of tartar
1/2 tsp. salt
1 1/2 c. sugar
1 tsp. vanilla

Whipped cream
Ice cream (opt.)
Bananas, sliced
Strawberries

In a large bowl, beat egg whites, cream of tartar and salt until soft peaks form. Gradually add sugar, 2 tablespoons at a time, beating constantly until dissolved. Beat in vanilla until firm and glossy. Spread 1/3 of meringue in 2 circles of 8-inch diameter on baking sheet covered with waxed paper. Using remaining meringue, build up sides to make rims about 1 1/2-inches high. Bake in preheated 250 degrees oven for 1 1/2 hours. Turn oven off; leave to cool with door closed for 1 hour. Before serving, fill with cream, ice cream, bananas, strawberries (or other favorite fruit).

Dwight & Margaret Hartzler

PEANUT BUTTER DESSERT

Crust:
1 1/4 c. chocolate wafers,
  crushed
1/3 c. butter, melted
Cream filling:
1 8-oz. pkg. cream cheese

1 1/2 c. powdered sugar
1/2 c. milk
12-oz. chunky peanut butter
  (or smooth)
2 9-oz. cartons Cool Whip

Press crust into a 9 x 13-inch pan. Mix cream cheese, powdered sugar, milk and peanut butter. Add Cool Whip. Pour filling over crust. Top with shaved chocolate. Freeze. *(Can use 1 box of Nabisco Chocolate Wafers with 1 stick butter.)*

Martha Ramer

PISTACHIO ICE CREAM DESSERT

1/2-gal. vanilla ice cream
2 bxs. instant pistachio pudding
1 1/3 c. milk

72 Ritz crackers
1 stick butter
8-oz. Cool Whip

Crush Ritz crackers; mix with melted butter. Spread evenly on bottom of 9 x 13 x 2-inch baking dish. Mix ice cream, pudding and milk; pour over cracker mix and freeze for 1 hour. Spread Cool Whip on top. May garnish with a few crushed Ritz crackers. (For a smaller amount, cut all ingredients in half.)

Ron Huber

BAKED RICE PUDDING (From Taiwan)

1/3 c. rice
4 c. milk
1/3 c. sugar

1 T. margarine
Few grains of salt
1 tsp. vanilla

Heat all ingredients on stove top until very hot, stirring often. Pour into baking dish. Bake at 325 degrees for 1 hour or until top is nicely browned.

Lois & Chris Leuz

BRAZILIAN PUDDING

1/3 c. sugar
1 T. water
1 can Eagle Brand Milk

2 c. milk
3 eggs, beaten
1 tsp. vanilla

Heat sugar in saucepan until liquid and golden. Add water and pour into pudding mold or tube cake pan. Mix Eagle Brand Milk, eggs and vanilla. Pour over caramelized sugar. Set pan in a pan with water to bake. Bake at 350 degrees for 45 minutes or until fork comes out clean. Cool slightly and invert. Serve cold. Makes 6 servings.

Otis & Betty Hochstetler-Brazil

BUTTERSCOTCH PUDDING

1/4 c. butter
3 c. milk
2/3 c. flour

2 c. brown sugar
2 eggs
1 c. milk

Brown butter; add 3 cups milk and heat. Mix other ingredients and add to hot milk, stirring constantly. Cool.

Marilyn (G. Keith) Miller

CHOCOLATE TRIFLE

1 pkg. chocolate fudge cake
mix
1 6-oz. box instant chocolate
pudding mix

2 c. heavy cream, whipped
6 Heath bars, crushed

Bake cake according to package directions; cool. Prepare pudding according to package directions; set aside. Crumble cake, reserving 1/2 cup. Place half of remaining cake crumbs in bottom of a 5-quart decorative glass bowl. Layer with half of pudding, half of whipped cream and half of crushed candy bars. Repeat layers. Combine remaining cake crumbs with remaining candy bars; sprinkle over top. Refrigerate 4-5 hours before serving. Yield: 8-10 servings.

Beth Fervida

DELICIOUS DESSERT

1 c. butter flavored Crisco
3/4 c. brown sugar
3/4 c. white sugar
2 eggs
2 tsp. vanilla
2 c. flour
1 tsp. baking soda
1 12-oz. pkg. milk chocolate
chips

1 pkg. walnut pieces
1 bag miniature marshmallows
Frosting:
1/2 c. margarine, melted
1-lb. powdered sugar
3 T. cocoa
Milk

Beat together Crisco, sugars, eggs and vanilla. Add flour, baking soda, chocolate chips and nuts; mix well. Spread in an 11 x 15-inch pan. Bake at 375 degrees for 20 minutes. Remove from oven and spread miniature marshmallows over top. Return to oven for 5-8 minutes. Mix frosting ingredients and add enough milk to make a spreadable mixture. Frost while hot. Cut into squares and serve.

Lou Thomas

Freeze cranberries, then grind. They won't splatter juice all over kitchen.

BROWN SUGAR PUDDING

Pudding:
3/4 c. brown sugar
1 egg
2 T. margarine
1 1/2 c. flour
1/2 c. boiling water
3/4 tsp. baking soda
Salt

1 tsp. baking powder
Sauce:
3 eggs, beaten
1 1/2 c. powdered sugar
1/2 c. butter, melted until boiling hot
1 tsp. vanilla

Mix first 3 ingredients. Add flour, baking powder and salt. Add baking soda dissolved in boiling water. Put batter into a bundt pan and set in a large kettle of boiling water. (Make sure water doesn't run into pan of batter. If pan touches bottom of kettle, put shallow pan in bottom of kettle upside down for pan to rest on.) Cover and steam for 1-1 1/2 hours. Don't uncover. Serve hot. Place on plate and cut. Pour sauce over pudding.

For sauce: Add powdered sugar to eggs and beat in melted butter and vanilla.

Rheta Mae Wiebe

DIRT PUDDING

Gummy worms
20-oz. pkg. Oreo cookies, crushed
2 8-oz. pkgs. cream cheese, softened

16-oz. Cool Whip
2 c. powdered sugar
2 lg. or 3 sm. any flavor instant pudding
4 c. cold milk

Beat cream cheese; add sugar. Fold in Cool Whip. Mix pudding and milk until it starts to set. Fold into cream cheese mixture. Layer with Oreos in flower pot ending with pudding. Save crumbs for the top. Refrigerate. To serve, push worms into pudding. Top with crumbs. Serve with trowel.

Jan Ramer (Brian)
Dianne Hartman

OREO DESSERT

1 1-1 1/2-lb. pkg. Oreo cookies
2 8-oz. pkgs. cream cheese
2 sm. bxs. instant vanilla pudding mix

2 envs. Dream Whip (or 4 c. Cool Whip)

Crush cookies slightly. Mix pudding as directed; blend in cream cheese and Cool Whip. *(Soften cream cheese in microwave for better blending.)* Fold together cookies and pudding mixture. *(I usually wait until shortly before serving.)* Serve immediately or refrigerate until serving time.

Ethel Hoffman

GRAPE NUT PUDDING

1 lg. box instant vanilla pudding
Milk
8-oz. whipped topping

1 c. Grape Nuts cereal
1 banana, sliced (opt.)

Mix pudding according to package directions. Fold in whipping topping; add Grape Nuts. Chill 1 hour before serving. Add sliced banana just before serving; fold in. *A very quick and easy dessert and delicious!*

Esther Martin

GRAPE NUT PUDDING

2 eggs, separated
1 c. milk
4 T. Grape Nuts cereal
2 T. flour

2 T. lemon juice
3/4 c. sugar
4 T. butter
Grated rind of 1 lemon

Cream butter. Add lemon rind and sugar; blend well. Add egg yolks and beat thoroughly. Add lemon juice. Blend in flour, Grape Nuts and milk, mixing well. Beat egg whites to stiff peaks. Fold into butter mixture. Turn into greased baking dish; place in pan of hot water. Bake in slow oven (325 degrees) for about 1 hour. Pudding will have a crust on top and jelly below.

Mildred Lehman

HEAVENLY DESSERT

2 tubes or 72 Ritz crackers
1 stick margarine, melted
1 c. pecans, chopped
Filling:
1 pkg. instant vanilla pudding

1 pkg. instant coconut cream
   pudding (or any favorite
   flavor)
1 1/2 c. milk
1-qt. vanilla ice cream, softened
1-qt. Cool Whip

Mix crackers, margarine and pecans; spread 2/3 of mixture in the bottom of a 13 x 9-inch pan. Mix milk with dry pudding mix. Blend in softened ice cream and Cool Whip. Pour over cracker mixture. Top with remaining crumbs. Freeze. Set out to thaw slightly before serving. *(Add sliced bananas with banana pudding or shaved chocolate with chocolate pudding.)*

Barb Croyle

MEDIUM TAPIOCA PUDDING

5 c. water
3/4 tsp. salt
1/2 c. baby pearl tapioca

1/2 c. sugar
1 3-oz. pkg. jello
1 c. whipped cream

Bring water and salt to boil. Add tapioca, stirring constantly, until it boils again. Cover and simmer for 15 minutes. Stir in sugar and jello. Let cool and refrigerate until set. Add your favorite fruit and fold in whipped cream. *This recipe is not for large pearl or minute tapioca.*

Edna Hochstetler

144

ROBERT REDFORD DESSERT

1 c. flour
1/4-lb. margarine, melted
1 c. nuts, chopped
1 16-oz. carton Cool Whip
1 8-oz. pkg. cream cheese
1/2 c. sugar

1 pkg. instant vanilla pudding
1 pkg. instant chocolate
    pudding
3 c. milk
2 tsp. vanilla

Layer 1: Mix flour, margarine and 3/4 cup nuts; spread into a 9 x 13-inch pan. Bake at 325 degrees for 25 minutes.

Layer 2: Mix 3/4 carton of Cool Whip, cream cheese and sugar; spread on cooled first layer.

Layer 3: Mix puddings and milk together. Add vanilla. Spread on top of second layer.

Layer 4: Spread remaining Cool Whip on top. Sprinkle with remaining 1/4 cup nuts.

Marilyn Stauffer

S'MORE PUDDIN' DESSERT

9 Keebler Honey Graham
    crackers
2 3/4 c. milk
1 pkg. (5 1/4-oz.) vanilla
    pudding and pie filling (not
    instant)

3 1.65-oz. plain milk chocolate
    candy bars
2 1/2 c. miniature marshmallows

Line bottom of an 8 x 6 x 2-inch glass or metal baking dish with 3 graham crackers. In a medium saucepan, combine milk and pudding mix. Cook over low heat until mixture comes to a full boil. Cool 5 minutes. Spread half of pudding over crackers; top with second layer of crackers. Place candy bars on crackers. Spread remaining pudding over candy bars. Top with a third layer of crackers. Sprinkle with marshmallows. Broil until golden brown. Serve warm or chill in refrigerator.

Phyllis Stauffer

STRAWBERRY DESSERT

1 3-oz. pkg. strawberry gelatin
1/4 c. sugar
1 1/2 c. boiling water

1-lb. frozen strawberries, cut up
2 c. whipped topping, thawed

In a large bowl, dissolve gelatin and sugar in boiling water; add strawberries and stir until berries separate. Refrigerate mixture until slightly thick. Fold in whipped topping. Refrigerate until set.

Ruth Bauman

It is impossible to have the feeling of peace and serenity without being at rest with God.

MILE HIGH STRAWBERRY DESSERT

2 egg whites
1 c. frozen strawberries, drained
1 tsp. lemon juice
1 c. sugar
Pinch of salt
1 tsp. vanilla
1 sm. container whipped
  topping
Crust:
1 c. graham cracker crumbs
3 T. brown sugar
1/4 c. butter, melted

For crust: Add sugar to graham cracker crumbs; mix and add melted butter, mixing thoroughly. Press firmly into a 9-inch pie pan. Bake at 375 degrees for 5-8 minutes. Cool. (Reserve 2 tablespoons cracker crumbs for top.)

For topping: Place all ingredients, except whipped topping, in a large mixer bowl; beat 20 minutes at High speed. Gently fold in whipped topping and pile high in graham cracker crust. Freeze. Makes 1 real high pie or may be divided into 2 pans.

Rosemary Maust

PUMPKIN DESSERT

1 spice cake mix, prepared
1 sm. can pumpkin filling
2 sm. bxs. vanilla instant
  pudding
2 sm. bxs. butterscotch instant
  pudding
1/2 tsp. cinnamon
1/2 tsp. allspice
1/2 tsp. nutmeg
2 1/2 c. milk
1 lg. container Cool Whip
Cherries

Combine pumpkin, dry pudding, spices and milk in a large bowl; mix. Alternate 3 layers of crumbled spice cake, filling and Cool Whip. Top with a little cake and cherries.

Martha Ramer

YUM YUM DESSERT

1 c. dates, chopped
1 1/2 c. boiling water
1 tsp. baking soda
1 c. sugar
3/4 c. margarine
2 eggs
1 1/2 c. flour
1/4 tsp. salt
1 tsp. vanilla
1/4 tsp. baking soda
1 6-oz. pkg. chocolate chips
1/2 c. nuts, chopped
1/4 c. sugar

Combine dates, boiling water and 1 teaspoon baking soda; let stand to cool. Cream 1 cup sugar, margarine and eggs. Add date mixture to creamed mixture. Add vanilla. Add flour, salt and 1/2 teaspoon baking soda. (This is very runny.) Place in a greased 9 x 15-inch pan. Sprinkle chocolate chips, nuts and 1/4 cup sugar, 1 at a time, on top. Bake at 350 degrees for 30-35 minutes.

Kari Leinbach

Pastries & Pies

PASTRIES & PIES

Pastries

PIE HINTS
- Bake pies on the lowest oven shelf setting.
- If baking in a disposable aluminum pan, place a cookie sheet under the pie pan so it will heat better.
- Brush raw egg white inside the bottom crust before pouring in the filling. This will help prevent a soggy crust.
- Brush raw egg white on the top crust and sprinkle with sugar before baking for an attractive glisten.
- To thicken pie fillings, substitute Clear Jel, Perma Flo or cornstarch at half the amount of flour in the recipe (2 tablespoons Clear Jel equals 1/4 cup flour). The filling will be clear instead of cloudy.

Merianne Shaffer

BEST PIE CRUST

2 c. New Rinkle pastry flour	1 egg, beaten
1/2 tsp. salt (opt.)	2 tsp. vinegar
3/4 c. butter flavored Crisco	1-2 T. ice water

Cut Crisco into flour and salt. Combine egg, vinegar and 1 tablespoon ice water. Sprinkle over crumbs and toss until dough forms. Add remaining tablespoon of ice water if dough is crumbly. This recipe makes 1 double crust 9-inch pie or 2 single crusts. *New Rinkle pastry flour will make a much flakier crust than regular flour. I buy a 10-pound sack and use it only for pie crusts. It's available at Everett's & Family Fare supermarkets. The pie crust will be even better if the flour and Crisco are mixed together and then chilled in the refrigerator several hours before adding the liquid ingredients. It will absorb less flour when rolled out and will be very flaky.*

Merianne Shaffer

FAVORITE PIE CRUST

3/4 c. barley flour	4 T. ice water
3/4 c. all-purpose flour	3/4 tsp. salt
1/3 c. oil	

Mix ice water into oil and pour into flour mixture. Stir with a fork until it forms a ball. Pat into a 9-inch pie pan. Bake as for any pie crust or pie. *Sometimes I use oat flour instead of all-purpose flour.*

Florence Hershberger

*To keep pecan pies from becoming too sweet,
add 1 teaspoon vinegar.*

NEVER FAIL PIE CRUST

2 c. flour   1 c. shortening
1 tsp. salt   1 T. vinegar
1/3 c. milk

Mix flour, salt and shortening. Pour vinegar into milk and stir. Add milk mixture to flour mixture and stir with fork.

Dorcas Snyder

NEVER FAIL PIE CRUST

3 c. flour   1 1/2 c. Crisco
5 T. cold water   1 tsp. vinegar
1 egg

Mix flour and shortening until crumbly. Add remaining ingredients until well blended. Roll out onto a floured surface. Makes 3 9-inch pie crusts.

Rosemary Martin

Pies

APPLE PIE WITHOUT APPLES

15 soda crackers   Butter
1 c. water   Cinnamon
1 1/2 c. sugar   Nutmeg
1 1/2 tsp. cream of tartar

Line an 8-inch tin with pie crust. Break soda crackers into quarters (being sure not to crush them); arrange inside pie crust. Boil together remaining ingredients. Pour hot mixture over crackers. Add dots of butter and sprinkle with cinnamon and nutmeg. Put a top crust on and bake at 425 degrees for 10 minutes; turn oven down to 325 degrees and bake 20 minutes longer or until brown. *It really looks and tastes like apple pie. Ritz crackers can be used in place of soda crackers.*

Ruth Metzler

APPLE PIE

3/4 c. sugar   1/4 tsp. cinnamon
1 T. flour   4-5 apples (4 c. sliced apples)
1/2 tsp. salt   5 pats of butter or margarine

Combine sugar, flour, salt and cinnamon; mix with apples. Put into a **deep 9-inch pastry** lined pie pan. Dot with butter. Cover with top crust, lapping upper crust over bottom crust. Press together firmly. Flute edges. Bake at 425 degrees for 40 minutes. Be sure apples are tender when pricked with fork. *I use 1/4 cup of sugar for the pie. I also use red delicious apples.*

For Apple Cheese Pie: Add 1/4 cup Cheddar cheese onto top of crust after pie is baked. Put in oven to melt cheese.

Rosemary Martin

APPLE CREAM PIE

1 c. sugar
1 T. flour
Cream or milk

Apples, sliced
Cinnamon

Make a sauce by adding cream or milk to the mixture of sugar and flour. Fill a 9-inch unbaked pie crust with sliced apples. Pour sauce over apples. Sprinkle cinnamon on top. Bake at 450 degrees for 10 minutes; then bake at 325 degrees for 35 minutes.

Rosemary Martin

APPLE & CREAM PIE

3/4 c. walnuts, chopped
4 med. cooking apples, sliced
1 c. whipping cream
1 c. sugar
1 egg

3 T. flour
1 tsp. cinnamon
1 tsp. vanilla
1/4 tsp. nutmeg
1/8 tsp. salt

Make your favorite pie crust in a 9-inch pie plate. Layer apple slices over crust. Mix together whipping cream, sugar, egg, flour and seasonings. Pour over apple slices. Sprinkle walnuts on top. Bake at 450 degrees for 10 minutes; then reduce heat to 350 degrees and bake until apples are tender, 35-40 minutes.

Sherry Kehr

GLAZED MAPLE APPLE PIE

5 c. apples, sliced
1 T. lemon juice
1/4 c. maple syrup
3 T. whipping cream
1/4 c. cornstarch
3/4 c. sugar
1/2 tsp. cinnamon

1/2 tsp. salt
Topping:
2 T. butter
1/4 c. brown sugar
1 T. cream
1/2 c. nuts, chopped

Toss apples, lemon juice, maple syrup and cream. Mix in cornstarch, sugar, cinnamon and salt. Put into pie shell. Bake at 400 degrees for 50 minutes. After 50 minutes, add topping. Put back into oven for 2 minutes or until bubbly.

For topping: Cook first 3 ingredients just until bubbly. Add nuts. *This was the first place pie at Octoberfest Mens' Fellowship Supper in 1994.*

Pat Stahly

APPLE BUTTER PIE

1 T. apple butter
1 T. flour
2 T. sugar

1 egg
1-pt. sweet milk

Mix and pour into an unbaked pie shell.

Bertha Weaver

149

SOUR CREAM APPLE PIE

2 T. flour
1/8 tsp. salt
3/4 c. sugar
1 egg, unbeaten
Pastry for 9-in. pie
1 c. sour cream
1 tsp. vanilla

1/4 tsp. nutmeg
2 c. apples, finely diced
Spicy topping:
1/3 c. sugar
1/3 c. flour
1/4 c. margarine
1 tsp. cinnamon

Sift together flour, salt, and sugar. Add egg, sour cream, vanilla and nutmeg. Beat to a smooth, thin batter. Stir in apples. Pour into pastry lined pan. Bake at 400 degrees for 15 minutes; then at 350 degrees for 30 minutes. Remove from oven and top with spicy topping mixture. Return to 400 degree oven for 10 minutes.

Florence Nussbaum

APRICOT PIE

15 dried apricot halves
1 15-oz. can apricots
3/4 c. sugar

2 T. cornstarch
1 T. tapioca

Cook dried apricots in water until plump; drain off any excess water. Add can of apricots, sugar, cornstarch and tapioca. Put into unbaked pie shell and top with upper crust. Bake at 425 degrees for 10 minutes; then lower heat to 350 degrees for 20-30 minutes.

Pat Stahly

APRICOT PIE

17-oz. can apricots
1/2 c. dried apricots (20 halves)
1/2-3/4 c. sugar
1 T. tapioca

2 T. Clear Jel
1 T. lemon juice
1/4 tsp. almond flavoring
2 T. butter

Drain juice from canned apricots; add tapioca to the juice and let soak 30 minutes. Meanwhile, cut dried apricots into pieces. Cover with water and simmer until soft and water is absorbed. Mix sugar and Clear Jel. Add both kinds of apricots, the juice and tapioca, lemon juice and almond flavoring. Pour into crust. Dot with butter. Top with crust. Bake at 425 degrees for 15 minutes; then bake at 375 degrees for 45 minutes more. *Do not use lite canned apricots as the flavor is not as good. Cornstarch can be substituted for Clear Jel, but the Clear Jel gives a nicer consistency and does not separate and become watery when refrigerated.*

Merianne Shaffer

*Butter knife before cutting meringue pie
to get a clean cut without damage.*

BOB ANDY PIE

1 c. sugar
3 T. flour
1 tsp. cinnamon
1/2 tsp. cloves

1 T. butter
3 egg yolks, beaten
2 c. milk
3 egg whites

Mix dry ingredients together. Add butter, yolks and milk; mix together. Beat egg whites (not too stiff) and mix with other ingredients. Bake in **one 9-inch unbaked pie shell** at 350 degrees until done.

Roy Ramer

CHERRY PIE USING PIE FILLING

1/2- 3/4 c. sugar
2 T. cornstarch
1 T. tapioca
1 21-oz. can cherry pie filling

1 capful almond flavoring
Red cake coloring
1 1/2 c. water for a 10-in. pie
(or 1 c. water for a 9-in. pie)

Mix together water, sugar, cornstarch, tapioca in saucepan and cook until thickened. Add pie filling, red cake coloring and almond flavoring. Pour into **unbaked pie shell**; add top crust. Bake at 425 degrees for 10 minutes; then at 325 degrees for 40-50 minutes.

Donnabelle Hoover

COCONUT CRUNCH PIE

3 eggs, separated
1 1/4 c. sugar
1 tsp. salt
1/2 c. milk
2 T. butter

1/2 tsp. almond extract
1/4 tsp. lemon extract
1 c. coconut
1 unbaked pie crust

Combine egg yolks, sugar and salt. Add milk, butter, almond extract and lemon extract. Fold in coconut. Beat egg whites until stiff and fold into mixture. Pour into unbaked pie shell. Bake at 350 degrees for 35-40 minutes or until brown.

Alice Newcomer

OLD FASHIONED CREAM PIE

1/2 c. brown sugar
1/2 c. white sugar
3 T. flour

1-pt. real whipping cream
Pinch of salt
Nutmeg

Mix together sugars, flour and salt. Add cream and mix. Pour into a **9-inch unbaked pie shell**. Sprinkle with nutmeg. Bake at 350 degrees for 1 hour. *Note: For a thick 10-inch pie, I double this recipe.*

Amy Martin

When making juicy berry pie, sprinkle bottom of crust lightly with sugar and flour mixed in equal portions. This keeps bottom crust from becoming soggy.

FRENCH SILK PIE

1 c. butter, softened
2 c. powdered sugar
3 eggs
1 tsp. vanilla
1 1/2 c. walnuts
3 squares semisweet chocolate,
   softened

Crust:
1 1/4 c. fine graham cracker
   crumbs
1/4 c. sugar
6 T. butter or margarine, melted

Cream together butter and powdered sugar. Add eggs, 1 at a time. Add remaining ingredients. Pour into crust.

For crust: Combine crumbs, sugar and butter. Press firmly into a 9-inch pie pan. Bake at 375 degrees for 6-8 minutes or until edges are browned; cool. For unbaked crust, chill 45 minutes.

Esther Martin

FUNNY CAKE (Pies)

1 c. sugar
1/2 c. cocoa
3/4 c. hot water
1 tsp. vanilla
2 9-in. pie crusts
2 c. sugar

1 tsp. shortening
2 eggs
1 tsp. vanilla
2 c. flour
2 tsp. baking powder
1 c. milk

Mix 1 cup sugar, cocoa, water and vanilla; set aside to cool. Mix shortening in sugar; then add eggs and mix. Add flour, baking powder, vanilla and milk. Pour bottom part (chocolate mixture) into pie shells. Carefully pour top part on top of chocolate. *(I pour it in a circular way starting from the outside and working towards the center.)* Bake at 400 degrees for 30-40 minutes or until done.

Dove Leinbach

LEMON CAKE PIE

1 c. white sugar
2 T. butter
3 T. flour

2 eggs, separated
1 lg. lemon

Mix sugar, butter and flour. Add egg yolks, grated rind and juice of lemon; mix well. Beat egg whites; add to mixture. Pour into **unbaked pie crust**. Bake at 350 degrees for 30 minutes.

Grace Weldy

Make your own Pumpkin Pie Spice:
3/4 tsp. cinnamon
1/4 tsp. nutmeg
1/8 tsp. ginger
1/8 tsp. cloves

LEMON LUSCIOUS PIE

1 8-in. pie shell	3 egg yolks, unbeaten
1 c. sugar	1 c. milk
4 T. cornstarch (or Clear Jel)	1 c. sour cream
1/4 c. butter or margarine	Whipped cream
1 T. grated lemon rind	2 T. walnuts, chopped
1/4 c. lemon juice	

Combine sugar and cornstarch in saucepan. Add lemon rind, lemon juice, egg yolks and butter (butter does not need to be melted). Stir in milk. Cook over medium heat, stirring until thick; cool. Fold in sour cream. Spoon into baked shell. Chill at least 2 hours. Serve with whipped cream and chopped walnuts. *If you like lemon pie, this one will top the list of all the others you have ever eaten.*

Esther Martin

MALT BALL PIE

1-pt. vanilla ice cream	6-oz. malt balls, crushed
8-oz. Cool Whip	1 Oreo Cookie Pie Crust

Soften ice cream; mix in Cool Whip and crushed malt balls. Pour into pie crust and freeze. *Easy and delicious.*

Kathy Kulp

PARADISE PUMPKIN PIE

8-oz. fat free cream cheese	2 eggs, beaten
1/4 c. sugar	1 tsp. cinnamon
1/2 tsp. vanilla	1/4 tsp. ground ginger
1 egg	1/4 tsp. ground nutmeg
1 9-in. unbaked pastry crust	Dash of salt
1 1/4 c. pumpkin	Maple syrup
1 c. evaporated skim milk	Pecans
1/2 c. sugar	

Combine cream cheese, 1/4 cup sugar and vanilla at medium speed until well blended. Blend in egg. Spread onto bottom of pastry crust. Combine remaining ingredients, except syrup and nuts, and mix well. Pour over cream cheese layer. Bake at 350 degrees for 65 minutes; cool. Brush with maple syrup. Top with pecans.

Ruby Panyako

PUMPKIN ICE CREAM PIE

1 c. pumpkin	1/2 tsp. cinnamon
1/2 c. brown sugar	1/2 tsp. nutmeg
1/2 tsp. salt	1-qt. vanilla ice cream, softened

Mix all ingredients together. Put in graham cracker crust and freeze until firm.

Beverly Coblentz

PECAN PUMPKIN PIE

3 eggs
1 c. pumpkin
1/3 c. sugar
1 tsp. pumpkin pie spice
2/3 c. Karo corn syrup
1/2 c. sugar
3 T. butter, melted
1/2 tsp. vanilla
1 c. pecans, halved
1 9-in. unbaked pastry shell

Stir together 1 slightly beaten egg, pumpkin, 1/3 cup sugar and pie spice. Spread over bottom of pie shell. Combine 2 eggs, syrup, 1/2 cup sugar, butter and vanilla. Stir in nuts. Spoon over pumpkin mixture. Bake at 350 degrees for 50 minutes or until filling is set.

Marilyn Miller (Willie)
Becky (Stichter) Brenneman

RHUBARB PIE

3/4 c. evaporated skim milk
1 c. sugar
3 T. flour
2 T. margarine
3 c. rhubarb, chopped
Oil Crust:
1 1/4 c. flour
1/2 tsp. salt
1/2 c. oil
2 T. milk

Mix all rhubarb ingredients and pour into unbaked oil crust. Bake at 425 degrees for 10 minutes; then at 325 degrees to finish baking (approximately 25 minutes).

For crust: Mix ingredients together in a 9-inch pie pan. Press with fingers to form crust. *Oil crust is very good when used with any tart filling.*

Pat Stahly

RHUBARB PIE

3 c. rhubarb
1 1/3 c. sugar
2 1/2 T. flour
1 12-oz. can Carnation milk
Nutmeg

Cut rhubarb into 1/4-inch pieces. Mix together sugar and flour. Pour into rhubarb and stir. Add carnation milk; mix well. Pour into **10-inch unbaked pie shell**. Sprinkle with nutmeg. Bake at 350 degrees for 45-60 minutes.

Amy Martin

RHUBARB CUSTARD PIE

4 c. rhubarb, cut into 1/2-in. pieces
1 9-in. unbaked pastry shell
1 c. sugar
1 T. flour
1/4 tsp. ground nutmeg
3 eggs, slightly beaten

Place rhubarb in pastry shell. Combine sugar, flour and nutmeg. Add eggs; beat well. Pour egg mixture into pastry shell. Bake at 375 degrees for 45 minutes or until pie is nearly set. (Pie appears soft in center, but sets upon cooling.)

Vera Brubacher

RHUBARB CUSTARD PIE

3 eggs
3 T. milk
1 3/4 c. sugar
1/4 c. flour

1 T. nutmeg
4 c. rhubarb, cut up
2 T. butter

Slightly beat eggs; add milk. Mix together sugar, flour and nutmeg. Stir into milk-egg mixture. Mix in diced rhubarb and pour into a **9-inch pastry shell**. Dot with butter. Bake at 375 degrees for 50-60 minutes.

Grace Weldy

RASPBERRY CREAM PIE

Filling:
1/2 c. sugar
3 T. flour
3 T. cornstarch
2 c. milk
1/2 tsp. salt
1 egg, beaten
1 tsp. vanilla
1/2 c. Cool Whip
Glaze:
1/2 c. red raspberries

1/2 c. water
1/4 c. sugar
1 T. cornstarch
Cool Whip
Crust:
1 1/2 c. flour
1 tsp. salt
1 tsp. sugar
1/2 c. oil
2 T. milk

For filling: Mix together all ingredients, except Cool Whip. Cook until thickened, stirring constantly. Cool several hours; then whip with beater and fold in Cool Whip.

For glaze: Cook together ingredients, except Cool Whip, and cool. Put on top of pudding mixture. Top with desired amount of Cool Whip.

For crust: Mix crust ingredients together; pat into pie pan. Bake at 350 degrees for 20 minutes.

Carolyn Graber

SODA CRACKER PIE

3 egg whites, beaten
1 c. sugar
1 tsp. vanilla

1 c. walnuts or pecans, chopped
3/4 c. soda cracker crumbs
1 tsp. baking powder

Beat egg whites. Gradually add sugar and vanilla. Fold in chopped nuts. Mix together cracker crumbs and baking powder. Fold into first mixture. Bake in glass pie pan at 325 degrees for 30 minutes. This pie makes its own crust. *Delicious and crisp.*

Doris Schrock

To prevent soggy crust on one-crust pie, brush unbaked crust lightly with unbeaten egg white and let dry before filling.

RED RASPBERRY CREAM PIE

Filling:
1/2 c. sugar
3 T. flour
3 T. cornstarch
1/2 tsp. salt
1 egg, beaten
1 tsp. vanilla
2 c. milk
Glaze:
1 c. strawberries or red
  raspberries

1 c. water
1/2 c. sugar
2 T. cornstarch
Pie Crust:
1 1/2 c. flour
1 tsp. salt
1 tsp. sugar
1/2 c. oil
2 T. milk

For filling: Mix filling ingredients; cook until thickened. Cool. Make crust while filling is cooling.

For crust: Mix flour, salt and sugar. Beat milk into oil with fork; add to flour mixture. Press with hands into pie pan. Bake at 350 degrees for 20 minutes or until browned. Cool.

For glaze: Mix ingredients and cook until thickened. Cool. Add filling mixture and glaze to crust. Top with Cool Whip. Refrigerate until serving time. Note: One Box Red Raspberry Danish Junket made according to package directions can be substituted.

Carolyn F. Yoder

SQUASH PIE

1 c. cooked, mashed squash
2 eggs, separated
2 T. flour
3/4 tsp. salt

3/4 tsp. cinnamon
3/4 c. sugar
1 1/2 c. milk
Nutmeg

Combine squash, egg yolks, flour, salt, cinnamon, sugar and milk. Beat egg whites until stiff and fold into squash mixture. Pour into unbaked pie shell. Sprinkle with nutmeg. Let stand in refrigerator for several hours before baking. Remove from refrigerator; bake at 350 degrees for 1 hour.

Rosalind Slabaugh

STRAWBERRY PIE

1 3-oz. box vanilla pudding mix
  (not instant)
1 3-oz. box strawberry jello
2 c. water

1 T. lemon juice
Fresh strawberries
Baked pie shell

Cook pudding, jello, water and lemon juice until thickened. May be done in microwave. Add strawberries and pour in baked pie shell. *For diabetics, use sugar free pudding and jello. Substitute any fresh fruit and jello flavor.*

Carol Martin

AMISH VANILLA PIE

1 c. white sugar	1 c. brown sugar
4 T. flour	1 tsp. baking soda
1 egg, beaten	1 tsp. cream of tartar
1 c. molasses	1/4 c. margarine
2 c. water	1/4 c. shortening
1 tsp. vanilla	2 unbaked pie shells
2 c. flour	

In a large saucepan, combine white sugar, 4 tablespoons flour, egg, molasses, water and vanilla. Bring to a full rolling boil; set aside to cool. In a large bowl, combine 2 cups flour, brown sugar, baking soda, cream of tartar, margarine and shortening. Cut together to make crumbs. Pour 1/2 of cooked mixture into each pie shell. Cover each pie with crumbs. Bake at 350 degrees for 40-45 minutes.

Mafra Maust

VANILLA CRUMB PIE

Filling:	Crumbs:
2 c. sugar	2 c. flour
2 c. water	1/2 c. sugar
2 c. molasses	1/2 c. lard (not quite full)
2 eggs, well beaten	1 tsp. cream of tartar
2 heaping T. flour	1 tsp. baking soda
Vanilla	

For filling: Boil together ingredients; set aside to cool . Pour into **4 unbaked pie shells**.

For crumbs: Mix together ingredients; put on top of 4 pies with syrup in bottom.

Bertha Weaver

SHOO-FLY PIE

Bottom Part:	Top Part:
2 c. brown sugar	3 c. flour
2 eggs	1 c. brown sugar
1 c. dark Karo syrup	1/2 c. Crisco
2 c. water	Pinch of salt
1 tsp. baking soda	

For bottom part: Mix brown sugar and eggs together. Add syrup, water and baking soda.

For top part: Combine sugar, flour and Crisco to make crumbs. Pour liquid (bottom part) into **two 9-inch unbaked pie shells**; top with crumbs. Bake at 350 degrees for 50-55 minutes.

Rosemary Martin

FAVORITE RECIPES

Recipe Name   **Page #**

Candy, Snacks, & Applebutter

CANDY, SNACKS & APPLE BUTTER

ALMOND BALLS

12-oz. pkg. chocolate chips
6-oz. pkg. butterscotch chips
1 1/2 c. powdered sugar, sifted
1 c. sour cream
1 1/2 tsp. lemon peel

1/4 tsp. salt
3 1/2 c. vanilla wafer crumbs
(2 bxs.)
1 c. toasted almonds, chopped

Melt chips together; remove from heat. Add powdered sugar, sour cream, lemon peel and salt; mix well. Blend in crumbs. Chill 15-20 minutes. Shape into balls and roll in almonds. Keep in airtight container in refrigerator or freezer for up to 1 month.

Deb Krawiec

CARAMEL PECAN TURTLES

1/2 c. sugar
3/4 c. white Karo syrup
1/2 c. cream
1/4 c. butter

2 tsp. vanilla
3 6-oz. pkgs. chocolate chips
Pecans

Mix sugar, syrup, cream and butter. Cook over low heat, stirring constantly, to 236 degrees (soft ball stage). Remove from heat; add vanilla. Drop by spoonfuls onto pecans arranged on waxed paper. Cool for 15 minutes. Melt chocolate chips over hot water (not boiling). Spoon 1 teaspoonful onto each turtle. Set in a cool, dry place until firm.

Marilyn Miller (Willie)

CHOCONUT CARAMEL BARS

1 12-oz. pkg. (2 c.) Nestle's Milk
   Chocolate Morsels
2 T. shortening
30 vanilla caramels

3 T. butter
2 T. water
1 c. peanuts, coarsely chopped

Melt morsels and shortening over hot water. Stir until mixture is smooth. Pour 1/2 of melted chocolate into an 8-inch foil-lined square pan. Spread evenly. Refrigerate until firm (15 minutes). Combine caramels, butter and water over boiling water. Stir until melted and smooth. Stir in nuts. Pour into chocolate lined pan; spread evenly. Refrigerate until tacky (about 15 minutes). Top with remaining melted chocolate. Spread evenly to cover caramel filling. Chill until firm. Cut into squares. Refrigerate until ready to serve.

Martha Ramer

This is the day which the Lord has made;
We will be glad and rejoice in it.

NO POPCORN CARAMEL CORN

8 c. corn pops (found in chip isle)   1/4 c. light corn syrup
1 c. brown sugar, packed   1/2 tsp. baking soda
1/2 c. butter or margarine   1 tsp. vanilla

In a large saucepan, combine sugar, butter and corn syrup. Bring to a boil over medium heat, stirring constantly, for 2 minutes. Remove from heat. Stir in baking soda and vanilla. Pour over corn pops; stir well. Bake on cookie sheet at 250 degrees for 30 minutes, stirring every 10 minutes. *This is a terrific snack item.*

Barb Croyle
Sherry Kehr

DATE-NUT BALLS

1 stick margarine   2 c. Rice Krispies
1 c. sugar   1/2 c. nuts
2 T. water   1 tsp. vanilla
8-oz. dates, chopped   Coconut

Mix margarine, sugar, water and dates in a saucepan; boil 7 minutes, stirring constantly. Remove from heat. Add Rice Krispies, nuts and vanilla. Shape into balls and roll in coconut. *Good keepers. They also freeze well.*

Esther Hostetler

CHOCOLATE FUDGE (Super Creamy)

3 6-oz. pkgs. chocolate chips   1/4 tsp. cream of tartar
1/2-lb. butter, cut in pieces   2 tsp. vanilla
12-oz. can evaporated milk   1 c. walnuts, chopped (opt.)
4 1/2 c. sugar

Place chocolate chips and butter in a large dish that can withstand heat. Mix sugar, milk, cream of tartar and bring to a boil. Continue boiling for 6 minutes, stirring constantly. Pour over chips and butter; add vanilla and nuts, if desired. Stir until chips and butter are melted and mixture is smooth. Pour into a greased 9 x 13-inch pan. Let stand at room temperature for 1 hour; refrigerate 1 hour. Cut into pieces and remove from pan. Stores well in refrigerator. Makes 5 pounds.

Sherry Kehr

PEANUT BRITTLE

1 c. sugar   1/4-1/2 tsp. baking soda
1 c. roasted peanuts

Melt sugar in a heavy skillet. Have ready crushed peanuts; stir in baking soda. Add peanuts to melted sugar. Pour on oiled board and roll out thin as possible.

Lucille Christophel

160

NUTTY O'S

1/2 c. brown sugar
1/2 c. dark corn syrup
1/4 c. butter

6 c. Cheerios cereal
1 c. (or less) pecans, walnuts
or peanuts

Heat oven to 325 degrees. Butter a jelly roll pan. Heat sugar, syrup and butter in a 3-quart saucepan over medium heat, stirring for 5 minutes. Remove from heat; stir in cereal and nuts until well coated. Pour into pan and bake for 15 minutes. Cool; loosen with spatula. Put in container. Makes 8 cups.

Grace Weldy

PEANUT BUTTER FUDGE

1 1/2 sticks butter
2/3 c. evaporated milk
3 c. sugar

1/2 tsp. vanilla
1 c. peanut butter

Heat butter, evaporated milk and sugar in a large pan at medium heat, stirring continuously until it reaches the soft ball stage (350 degrees). Turn off heat; add peanut butter and vanilla. Stir vigorously until everything is mixed together. (Must hurry before the fudge sets.) Pour into a greased 9 x 13-inch glass pan. Let fudge set for several hours before cutting.

Karl Leinbach

PEANUT BUTTER SNACK

1/3 c. peanut butter
1/4 c. chocolate chips

1/2 c. oatmeal

Measure ingredients and stir together. Form into balls.

Jason Rupp

PEANUT BUTTER SQUARES

1/2 c. butter or margarine,
melted
1/2 c. peanut butter
1/2-lb. powdered sugar

1/2 pkg. graham crackers,
crushed (about 3/4 c.)
1 6-oz. pkg. chocolate chips
6-oz. butter, melted

Put first 4 ingredients in bowl and mix well. Spread in bottom of buttered 8 x 8-inch pan. Melt butter and chocolate chips; spread on top. Refrigerate until firm. *This is similar to Reese's Peanut Butter Cups.*

Grace Weldy

*The most difficult translation of the Bible is that
which must be translated into Christlike living.*

161

ROCKY ROAD CANDY

1 12-oz. pkg. semisweet
  chocolate morsels
1 14-oz. can sweetened
  condensed milk (not
  evaporated milk)

2 T. margarine or butter
2 c. dry roasted peanuts
1 10 1/2-oz. pkg. miniature
  marshmallows

In top of double boiler over boiling water, melt morsels with sweetened condensed milk and butter. Remove from heat. In a large bowl, combine nuts and marshmallows. Fold in chocolate mixture. Spread in waxed paper-lined 13 x 9-inch pan. Chill 2 hours or until firm. Remove from pan. Peel off waxed paper and cut into squares. Cover and store at room temperature. Makes about 40 squares.

Kris Skyrm

GRANDFATHER TAFFY CANDY

2 c. sugar
1 c. cream

1 c. white Karo syrup

Mix in a heavy bottom large kettle, cook ingredients to nearly hard ball stage or when testing in cold water, it forms a firm ball. Pour into 3 buttered pie pans. Let cool until able to handle. Pull with buttered hands until light colored, then pull in a long rope and clip with scissors into bite size pieces. To keep, if you can, put in jars with some powdered sugar and keep in refrigerator.

Bertha Weaver

TIGER BUTTER CANDY

2 c. almond bark (9 sqs.)
1 c. peanut butter

1 c. chocolate chips

Melt almond bark in microwave on Medium power for approximately 5 minutes, stirring after 2-3 minutes. Stir in peanut butter. Spread on waxed paper lined 11 x 15-inch cookie sheet. Swirl in melted chocolate chips. Chill. Break into pieces when solid.

Kathy Leinbach

Add to the pleasure of others;
Subtract from another's unhappiness;
Multiply the pleasure of others;
Divide the good things that come your way.

TOFFEE

1 c. white sugar
1 stick (1/4-lb.) margarine
1 stick (1/4-lb.) butter
3 T. water
1 tsp. vanilla
3 1.55-oz. Hershey bars
1/3 c. pecans, finely chopped

Place sugar, margarine, butter and water in a heavy saucepan on medium heat, stirring constantly until mixture boils. Continue cooking, stirring frequently, until mixture is the color of peanut brittle and a temperature of 290 degrees (this takes about 10 minutes). Remove from heat and add vanilla. Pour onto greased cookie sheet or pizza pan. Break Hershey bars into pieces over hot mixture. Spread with a knife when melted. Sprinkle nuts on top of melted chocolate. When cold, break into pieces.

Merianne Shaffer

WHITE CHOCOLATE PARTY MIX

1-lb. white chocolate
3 c. Rice Chex
3 c. Corn Chex
3 c. Cheerios
2 c. stick pretzels
2 c. dry roasted peanuts
1 12-oz. pkg. M&M's plain candy

Slowly melt white chocolate in top of double boiler over simmering water. Combine all other ingredients in a large bowl. Slowly pour chocolate over mixture and stir to coat evenly. Spread mixture on waxed paper and cool. Break into small pieces. Store in airtight container and refrigerate to keep fresh. Makes 12-14 cups.

Patty Bontrager

TRADITIONAL APPLE BUTTER (Crock Pot)

12-14 cooking apples (about
   16 c.)
2 c. cider
2 c. sugar
1 tsp. ground cinnamon
1/4 tsp. ground cloves

Core and chop apples (unpeeled). Combine apples and cider in slow cooking crock pot. Cover and cook on Low for 10-12 hours or until apples are mushy. Puree in food mill or sieve. Return pureed mixture to pot; add sugar, cinnamon and cloves. Cover and cook on Low for 1 hour. Will keep for several weeks in refrigerator or pour into hot sterilized jars and seal. Can also freeze. Makes about 8 cups.

Ruby Panyako

*There is no better excerise for strengthening the heart
than reaching down and lifting people up.*

FAVORITE RECIPES

Recipe Name   **Page #**

Old Time Favorites

OLD TIME FAVORITES

APPLE CRUNCH PIE

8 tart apples (approx.)	1/2 c. sugar
1/2 c. sugar	3/4 c. flour
1 tsp. cinnamon	1/3 c. butter

Arrange apple slices in a **9-inch pie crust**. Sprinkle with 1/2 cup sugar and cinnamon. Mix remaining ingredients until crumbly. Sprinkle over apples. Bake at 450 degrees for 10 minutes; then at 350 degrees for about 40 minutes longer or until apples are tender.

Ruby Panyako

APPLE DUMPLINGS

6 med. baking apples	Sauce:
2 c. flour	2 c. brown sugar
2 1/2 tsp. baking powder	2 c. water
1/2 tsp. salt	1/4 c. butter
2/3 c. shortening	1/2 tsp. cinnamon
1/2 c. milk	1/2 tsp. nutmeg

Pare and core apples. For pastry: Sift flour, baking powder and salt together. Cut in shortening until particles are size of small peas. Sprinkle milk over mixture and press together. Roll out crust and cut into 6 squares. Place 1 apple on each square. Sprinkle apple with cinnamon and brown sugar; wrap dough completely around apple. Place in pie pan. Mix sauce ingredients; pour over apples. Bake at 375 degrees for 35-40 minutes. Baste occasionally.

Deb Krawiec

ELEPHANT STEW

1 med. sized elephant	Brown gravy
2 rabbits (opt.)	Salt and pepper (to taste)

Cut elephant into bite size pieces. This will take about 2 months. Reserve the trunk, you will need something to store the pieces in. Add enough gravy to cover. Cook over a kerosene fire at 475 degrees for about 4 weeks. Serves 3,800. If more people are expected, add 2 rabbits, but only in extreme necessity. People don't like to find hare in their stew.

MINUTE PUDDING

Milk	Egg
Flour	

Put milk in pan; let come to a boil. Take 1 egg and flour and rivel together with a little milk. Put rivels in boiling milk; cook until thick as mush. Eat with sweet milk. *(Also called rivel soup.)*

Carl Ramer

GREAT GRANDMOTHER COOKIES

2-lbs. sugar
3/4-lb. butter
1-pt. sweet milk
6 eggs

Cinnamon and cloves (to taste)
1 T. baking soda
Flour

Cream butter and sugar until creamy. Add beaten eggs and milk. Sift baking soda in flour (enough flour for soft cookies to drop and more if you roll and cut).

Bertha Weaver

BANANA PUDDING

2 c. sugar
4 egg yolks
1/2 c. cornstarch
1 c. milk
5 c. milk
1 c. brown sugar

1 tsp. salt
4 T. butter
1/2 c. cold water
Graham crackers
Bananas
Whipped cream

Mix sugar, egg yolks, cornstarch and 1 cup milk. Mix and cook in 5 cups milk. Mix brown sugar, salt, butter and cold water; cook to hard boil. Mix the two together. Make layers of graham crackers, bananas, whipped cream and pudding.

Ruth Bauman

GRANDMA'S CHERRY PUDDING

1/2 c. sugar
1/2 c. milk
1 T. baking powder
Salt
2 T. butter

1 c. flour
1 c. sour cherries
1 c. hot water
1 c. sugar

Mix first 6 ingredients. Place in an 8 x 8-inch pan. Top with cherries, hot water and 1 cup sugar. Do not stir into batter. Bake in hot oven until brown. Use extra juice for extra sauce.

Grace Weldy

FRUIT PUNCH

4 c. sugar
6-qts. water
1 sm. can frozen lemonade

1 sm. can orange juice
1 lg. can pineapple juice
5 bananas

Boil sugar and water for 5 minutes; cool. Place last 4 ingredients in blender. After blended, add to sugar water and place in freezer. Allow to thaw to the point of being a slush before serving. *Note: The sugar water may be made the day before and cooled.*

Ruby Panyako

BAR B Q SAUCE

2 No. 10 (1-gal.) cans tomato
   puree
4 sm. bottles Tabasco sauce
2-qts. Worcestershire sauce
4 10-oz. bottles Heinz 57 Sauce
4 tsp. granulated garlic
13 T. salt
5 T. black pepper
5 lg. onions, chopped

2 46-oz. cans pineapple juice
2 46-oz. cans tomato juice
1-qt. lemon juice
2 1/2 c. sugar
1-qt. vinegar
2 1/2 c. mustard
4-oz. liquid smoke
2 1/2-lbs. margarine

Heat ingredients thoroughly; simmer while filling jars. Do not boil. Makes about 40 pint jars. Seal with lids and bands and store with canned goods.

Beulah West
Dawn West
Evelyn Troyer

EGG OMELET

2 eggs
Salt
6 T. flour

1 tsp. baking powder
2 c. milk

Preheat a 10-inch skillet. Pour ingredients into greased skillet. Cook until brown. Cut into pie shapes, turn and brown other side. Serve.

Vera Brubacher

BAKED OATMEAL

1 c. vegetable oil
1 1/2 c. brown sugar
4 lg. eggs
6 c. quick oatmeal

1 T. + 1 tsp. baking powder
1 tsp. salt
2 c. milk

Mix oil, sugar and eggs; beat with electric mixer on high speed until yellow and glossy. Add remaining ingredients and beat on medium speed until well blended. Bake in greased 9 x 13-inch pan at 400 degrees for 30-40 minutes. *May add 1 cup chopped apple plus 1 teaspoon cinnamon, or 1 cup raisins or 1/2 cup sunflower seeds.* Serves 12. *(May substitute granulated sugar for brown sugar.)*

Doris Schrock

SAUSAGE AND CABBAGE

1-lb. sausage
1/2 c. onion, chopped

1-qt. cabbage, chopped

In a 10-inch skillet, cook sausage and onion over medium heat, stirring occasionally, until lightly browned. Spread evenly in skillet; top with cabbage. Cover to steam. Serve when crunchy.

Vera Brubacher

OLD TIME BEEF STEW

2-lbs. beef chuck, cut in 1 1/2-   6 carrots
    inch cubes   1 T. salt
2 T. fat   1 tsp. sugar
4 c. boiling water   1/2 tsp. pepper
1 T. lemon juice   1/2 tsp. paprika
1 tsp. Worcestershire sauce   Dash of allspice (or cloves)
1 clove garlic   1-2 bay leaves
1 med. onion, sliced   1-lb. (6-8) sm. onions

Thoroughly brown meat on all sides in hot fat. Add water, lemon juice, Worcestershire sauce, garlic, sliced onion, bay leaves and seasonings. Cover and simmer for 2 hours, stirring occasionally to keep from sticking. Remove bay leaves and clove of garlic. Add carrots and onions. (Cubed potatoes may also be added.) Cover and cook 45 minutes or until vegetables are done. Remove meat and vegetables. Thicken liquid for gravy, if desired.

For gravy: Skim most of fat from the stew liquid. For 3 cups of liquid, put 1/2 cup water in shaker or screw-top jar. Add 1/4 cup enriched flour. Shake flour with water to mix. Add flour mixture slowly to meat stock, stirring constantly, until gravy bubbles all over. Cook about 5 minutes more, stirring often. Pour over meat and vegetables.

Mary Rhoade

*She measured out the butter
with a very solemn air,
The milk and sugar also, and
she took the greatest care,
To count the eggs correctly,
and to add a little bit,
Of baking powder, which you
know beginners oft omit.
Then she stirred it all together
and baked it for an hour,
But she never quite forgave herself
for leaving out the flour!*

Lo-Cal, Diabetic

LO-CAL, DIABETIC

BREAD: CHOLESTEROL FREE

2 pkgs. active dry yeast
2 T. Canola Oil
2 T. honey
2 tsp. salt

2 c. hot water (90-100 degrees)
3 c. whole wheat flour
3-4 c. white flour

Place first 5 ingredients into mixing bowl and let stand until yeast begins to bubble. Add whole wheat flour; mix well. Gradually add white flour. Knead until dough works freely, not sticky. Cover and let rise in bowl until double. Shape into pans; let rise. Bake at 375 degrees until crusty brown. Makes 2 loaves of bread.

Ruby Panyako

LO FAT CHOCOLATE CAKE

1 c. white sugar
4 T. cocoa
1 c. water
1 c. fat free Miracle Whip

2 tsp. baking soda
2 c. flour
2 tsp. vanilla

Combine sugar and cocoa; mix in remaining ingredients. Bake at 350 degrees for 35-40 minutes.

Lo Fat Chocolate Frosting:

8-oz. pkg. low or fat free
   cream cheese
3/4 c. cocoa

2 1/2 c. powdered sugar
1 T. vanilla

Mix well; spread on cooled cake.

Deb Krawiec

NATURALLY SWEET SOFT COOKIES

1/2 c. raisins
1/2 c. packed dates, chopped
1 med. ripe banana, sliced
1/3 c. creamy peanut butter
1/4 c. water

1 egg
1 tsp. vanilla
1 c. oatmeal
1/2 c. flour
1 tsp. baking soda

Combine raisins, dates, banana, peanut butter, water, egg and vanilla. Blend well. Add oatmeal, flour and baking soda. Mix to blend thoroughly. Drop by teaspoonfuls onto nonstick baking sheets or baking sheets coated with vegetable cooking spray. Flatten slightly. Bake at 350 degrees for about 15 minutes or until brown on bottom. Makes about 1 1/2 dozen (18) cookies. 1 cookie = 1 starch exchange, 90 calories, 17 gm. carbohydrate, 2 gm. protein, 2 gm. fat.

Melba Martin

SUGAR FREE COOKIES

1 c. raisins
1/2 c. dates
1 c. water
2 eggs
Nuts, chopped

1/2 c. margarine
1 tsp. vanilla
1/4 tsp. cinnamon
1 c. flour
1 tsp. baking soda

Combine raisins, dates and water in pan. Cook for 3-5 minutes. Cream together eggs, margarine and vanilla. Add cinnamon, flour, baking soda and nuts. Add fruit mixture and mix well. Drop by teaspoonfuls onto a lightly greased baking sheet. Bake at 375 degrees for 8-10 minutes. Don't overbake.

Ruth Tyson

SUGAR-FREE RAISIN BARS

1 c. raisins
1/2 c. water
1/4 c. margarine
1 tsp. cinnamon
1/4 tsp. nutmeg
1 c. flour

1 egg
3/4 c. unsweetened applesauce
1 T. sugar substitute
1 tsp. baking soda
1/4 tsp. vanilla

In a saucepan over medium heat, cook raisins, water and margarine. Add remaining ingredients. Spread into a greased 8-inch square pan. Bake at 350 degrees for 25-30 minutes. Yield: 16 servings.

Verna Gongwer

WHOLE WHEAT BUTTERMILK PANCAKES

1 c. buttermilk
2 T. oil
1 egg
1/2 c. whole wheat flour

1/2 c. white flour
1 tsp. baking powder
1/2 tsp. baking soda
1/2 tsp. salt

Combine buttermilk, oil and egg; mix with a fork. Mix in remaining ingredients only until moistened. Spray pan with Pam and fry in hot pan.

Ruby Panyako

APPLE PIE

1 (6-oz.) can frozen
  unsweetened apple juice
  concentrate, thawed

2 T. flour
1 tsp. cinnamon
6 c. apples, sliced

Mix apple juice, flour and cinnamon in a 3-quart saucepan until well blended. Cook over medium-high heat, stirring constantly, until mixture boils and thickens. Remove from heat. Add apples to hot mixture; stir until well coated. Pour into a 9-inch unbaked pie shell. Top with a top crust. Bake at 450 degrees for 15 minutes; then reduce heat to 350 degrees and bake 35 minutes longer or until apples are tender.

Rosemary Martin

FRESH APPLE CINNAMON ICE CREAM

2 T. margarine
3 lg. Red Delicious apples,
  peeled, cored and chopped

2-in. cinnamon stick
2-qts. vanilla ice cream

Melt margarine in a heavy skillet over medium heat. Add apples and cinnamon stick. Saute for 5 minutes. Remove from heat and cool completely. Soften ice cream in refrigerator until it can be whipped with an electric beater. Transfer ice cream to a large mixing bowl; whip on low until smooth. Remove cinnamon stick from apple mixture and fold into ice cream. Transfer to a covered freezer container. Freeze for several hours before serving. (If the ice cream becomes solid, soften slightly in the refrigerator before serving.) Makes 16 servings. Exchange (per serving): 110 calories, 1 bread, 1/4 fruit.

Lois Blosser

PEACH CRUMB BAKE

2 c. fresh peaches, sliced
Vegetable cooking spray
1/3 c. graham cracker crumbs
1/2 tsp. cinnamon

1/8 tsp. nutmeg
2 tsp. reduced-calorie
  margarine, melted

Layer sliced peaches in bottom of an 8-inch square baking dish coated with vegetable cooking spray. Combine graham cracker crumbs, cinnamon and nutmeg in a small bowl, stirring well. Add margarine and stir until well combined. Sprinkle graham cracker crumb mixture over peaches. Bake at 350 degrees for 30 minutes. Serve warm. Makes 4 (1/2-cup) servings. Exchange (per serving): 78 calories, 1 fruit, 1/2 fat.

Lois Blosser

SNOW PUDDING

1 T. granulated gelatin
1/2 c. cold water
1 T. grated lemon rind
1/4 c. fresh lemon juice
1 1/4 c. boiling water

Sugar substitute equivalent to
  1/2 c. sugar
2 med. egg whites
1/4 tsp. pure vanilla extract
1/4 tsp. pure lemon extract

Soak gelatin in cold water. Meanwhile, combine lemon rind, juice and boiling water in a saucepan; bring to a boil, then remove from heat. Add softened gelatin and sweetener; mix well to dissolve both. Chill until it is the consistency of unbeaten egg whites. Then add unbeaten egg whites, vanilla extract and lemon extract. Beat with a rotary beater until it is very fluffy and holds its shape. Pile into 6 serving dishes. Chill until firm. Makes 6 (1/2-cup) servings. Exchange (per serving): 19 calories; up to 1/2 cup may be considered "free"; 1 cup should be counted as 1/2 skim milk.

Lois Blosser

CRANBERRY PIE

1 vanilla wafer crumb crust
1 T. granulated gelatin
2 c. cold water
3 c. raw fresh or frozen
  cranberries
1/4 tsp. grated orange rind
1/4 tsp. pure orange extract
Sugar substitute equivalent to
  10 T. sugar
1 1/2 c. frozen whipped topping

Soak gelatin in 1/2 cup cold water; set aside. Pick over fresh or frozen cranberries, wash and measure; put in a deep, heavy saucepan with 1 1/2 cups water and orange rind. Cook over moderate heat until all cranberries pop, stirring occasionally. Remove from heat. Stir in gelatin, orange extract and sweetener; mix until gelatin is dissolved. Let cool for about 30 minutes, stirring occasionally. Taste to see if enough sweetener has been added because cranberries vary greatly in tartness. Spoon carefully and slowly into pie crust and smooth evenly with the back of spoon. Chill in refrigerator. When cool, spread whipped topping on pie, smoothing and swirling evenly. Chill in refrigerator for 3-4 hours before serving. Makes 8 servings. Exchange (per serving): 149 calories, 2 fat, 1 starch.

Lois Blosser

SUGAR-FREE LOW FAT BANANA NUT BREAD

5 med. ripe bananas
2 pkgs. artificial sweetener
1/2 c. egg substitute
1 3/4 c. cake flour
1/2 tsp. baking powder
3/4 c. pecans, chopped
1/2 tsp. lite salt

Sprinkle sugar substitute over bananas and stir until dissolved; blend in egg substitute. Stir together flour, baking powder and salt; blend into banana mixture. Add nuts. Pour into loaf pan sprayed with cooking spray. Bake at 350 degrees for 25 minutes. Reduce heat to 300 degrees and finish baking until done. A toothpick inserted in center will come out clean when done.

Roxane Ouimet

OATMEAL-BLUEBERRY MUFFINS

1 c. + 2 T. all-purpose flour
6-oz. uncooked regular oats
1 T. baking powder
Sugar substitute to equal
  2 T. sugar
1/2 tsp. salt
1 c. skim milk
1 egg
1/4 c. vegetable oil
1 c. fresh blueberries
Vegetable cooking spray
1 tsp. cinnamon

Combine flour, oats, baking powder, sugar substitute and salt in a medium bowl; make a well in center of mixture. Combine milk, egg and oil; add to dry ingredients, stirring just until moistened. Gently fold in blueberries. Spoon batter into muffin pans coated with cooking spray, filling 2/3 full. Sprinkle cinnamon over muffins. Bake at 425 degrees for 20-25 minutes or until lightly browned. Makes 12 muffins. Exchange (per muffin): 127 calories, 1 starch, 1 fat, 5 grams fat.

Lois Blosser

BLUEBERRY LOAF

1 c. all-purpose flour
3/4 c. whole wheat flour
1/2 c. shreds of wheat bran
  cereal
Brown sugar substitute to
  equal 1/3 c. brown sugar
2 tsp. baking powder
1/2 tsp. baking soda
1/2 tsp. salt
3/4 c. unsweetened orange juice
1 egg
1 T. vegetable oil
1 c. fresh blueberries
Vegetable cooking spray

Combine flours, cereal, brown sugar substitute, baking powder, soda and salt in a medium bowl, stirring until well combined. Set aside. Combine orange juice, egg and oil in a large bowl; beat at medium speed of an electric mixer until well blended. Gradually add flour mixture, stirring just until moistened. Gently fold in blueberries. Spoon batter into an 8 1/2 x 4 1/2 x 3-inch loaf pan coated with cooking spray. Bake at 350 degrees for 50 minutes or until a wooden toothpick inserted in center comes out clean. Cool in pan 10 minutes; remove from pan, and cool completely on a wire rack. Makes 16 slices. Exchange (per slice): 85 calories, 1 starch, 2 grams fat.

Lois Blosser

OAT BRAN BLUEBERRY MUFFINS

2 T. vegetable oil
1 c. skim milk
1 tsp. vanilla
1/4 c. dark molasses
2 egg whites
2 c. oat bran
1/2 c. brown sugar
1/2 c. flour
2 tsp. baking powder
1 tsp. baking soda
Salt
1 tsp. cinnamon
1 c. blueberries

Mix together oil, milk, vanilla, molasses and egg whites. Mix together oat bran, brown sugar, flour, baking powder, baking soda, salt and cinnamon. Mix the two mixtures together just until moistened. Stir in blueberries. Fill muffin pan 1/2 full. Bake at 375-400 degrees for 15 minutes.

Gloria Tyson

SUGARLESS FRUIT & NUT MUFFINS

1 c. dates, chopped
1/2 c. raisins
1/2 c. prunes, chopped
1 c. water
1/2 c. margarine, cut into pats
1/4 tsp. salt
2 eggs, beaten
1 tsp. vanilla
1 c. flour
1 tsp. baking soda
1/2 c. nuts

Combine dates, raisins, prunes and water; boil 5 minutes. Stir in margarine and salt; cool. Add remaining ingredients; stir. Put into muffin cups and bake at 350 degrees for 15 minutes. *Delicious!*

Phyllis Garber

CHINA TOWN SOUP

7-oz. ground turkey
1 sm. onion
1 sm. green pepper
1/4 tsp. lite salt
1/4 tsp. pepper

1 T. low sodium soy sauce
1 lg. can tomato juice
1 c. water chestnuts
1 c. Chinese vegetables

Brown and drain first 5 ingredients. Drain vegetables; add remaining ingredients to meat mixture. Add a little water, if desired.

Ruby Panyako

GARDEN SOUP

6 c. water
2 c. tomato juice
1 c. diced, peeled potato
1 c. chopped onion
1 c. whole kernel corn
1 c. lima beans, cooked and
drained

3/4 c. cooked chicken, chopped
1/2 c. carrots, sliced
1/2 c. celery, chopped
2 T. chicken flavored bouillon
granules
1 tsp. garlic powder
1 1/2 tsp. Worcestershire sauce

Combine all ingredients in a large Dutch oven. Cover and bring to a boil. Reduce heat and simmer 45 minutes to 1 hour. Serve hot. Makes 10 (1-cup) servings. Exchange (per serving): 84 calories, 1 starch, 1 gram fat.

Lois Blosser

TURKEY CHILI

1-lb. lean ground turkey
1 c. celery, chopped
1 16-oz. can tomatoes, cut up
1 16-oz. can red kidney beans,
drained
1 8-oz. can tomato sauce
1/2 c. water
1 6-oz. can vegetable juice
cocktail

1 bay leaf
2 T. dried minced onion
1 tsp. dried basil
1/2 tsp. instant beef bouillon
1/2 tsp. cumin
1/4 tsp. garlic powder
1/4 tsp. crushed red pepper

Brown turkey and celery in a large skillet. Transfer to a crock pot. Add remaining ingredients; stir. Cook on Low for 6 hours or High for 4 hours. 165 calories per serving, 0 fat.

Cheryl Bontreger

NON-FAT COTTAGE CHEESE SALAD

16-oz. non-fat cottage cheese
8-oz. non-fat Cool Whip

3-oz. sugar free lime jello (dry)
20-oz. sugar free crushed
pineapple, drained

Dump all ingredients into a bowl; mix and chill. Easy and ready to eat.

Roxane Ouimet

CHICKEN TACO SALAD

1-lb. ground white chicken
1/2 head lettuce
2 med. tomatoes
1 can kidney beans
1 pkg. taco seasoning

1/2 c. non fat Cheddar cheese, grated
1/2 bag Smart Temptation tortilla chips (baked, not fried)
1 bottle Kraft Fat Free Catalina Salad Dressing

Place chicken in a bowl; cover with waxed paper. Cook in microwave for about 5 minutes. Remove, drain chicken and remove any fat. Prepare taco mix as directed substituting chicken for beef. Place lettuce, tomatoes and chips in a large bowl. Add drained beans, grated cheese and salad dressing; mix well.

Joy VanDiepenbos

FREE BEAN SALAD

1 can green beans, drained
1 can French style green beans, drained
1 can yellow wax beans, drained
1 can carrots, drained
1 c. celery, diced
1 med. green pepper, diced

1/2 c. apple cider vinegar
Sweetener to equal 1/2 c. sugar
1/2 tsp. dry mustard
1/2 tsp. basil
1/2 tsp. oregano
2 tsp. parsley flakes

Combine all ingredients and marinate.

Ruby Panyako

RICHARD SIMMONS HOME ON THE RANGE TUNA SALAD

1 can tuna
2 c. low fat cottage cheese
2 hard cooked eggs, chopped
1/2 c. celery
1/2 c. green onion

2 T. parsley, chopped
1 tsp. lemon pepper seasoning
1/2 tsp. salt
1/2 c. fat free mayonnaise

Mix all together and use as a salad or in a sandwich.

Ruby Panyako

SALMON HASH

15 1/2-oz. can red salmon, drained
2 c. peeled potatoes, finely chopped

2 T. reduced-calorie margarine, melted
3 green onions, finely chopped
1/8 tsp. pepper

Remove and discard skin and bones from salmon; flake with a fork and set aside. Saute potatoes in margarine in a large skillet for 15 minutes or until tender. Remove from skillet and set aside. Add green onions to skillet and saute 2-3 minutes. Stir in pepper. Add potatoes and salmon. Cook over medium heat, without stirring, until thoroughly heated. Makes 6 (1/2-cup) servings. Exchange (per serving): 111 calories, 1 medium-fat meat, 1/2 starch.

Lois Blosser

STUFFED CABBAGE ROLLS

2 lg. cabbage leaves	Dash of salt
2-oz. ground veal	Dash of pepper
2-oz. ground lean beef	Dash of nutmeg
3 T. skim milk	1/2 c. beef broth
1 slice dry bread, crumbled	1 T. flour
1 tsp. onion, grated	

Cook cabbage leaves in boiling salted water until tender; drain. Combine ground veal, beef, skim milk, bread crumbs, onion, salt, pepper and nutmeg; mix thoroughly. Place half of meat mixture in a cabbage leaf and roll up, tucking ends in. Secure with toothpicks. Place in small baking dish. Repeat with remaining meat mixture and cabbage leaf. Blend beef broth and flour; pour over cabbage rolls. Bake at 350 degrees for 45-50 minutes. Makes 1 serving. Exchange: 396 calories, 4 medium-fat meat, 1 vegetable, 1 bread.

Lois Blosser

EASY FISH BAKE

1-lb. haddock	2 tsp. dried parsley
1 med. onion, chopped	2 T. lemon juice
1 can mushroom pieces	1 T. vegetable oil
1 tomato, chopped (fresh	1 bay leaf
or canned)	Pepper (opt.)

Place all ingredients, except fish, in a baking pan just large enough to hold fish and vegetables. Mix in pan. Cut fish into 4 pieces and arrange on vegetable mixture. Spoon half the vegetable mixture over fish. Cover tightly with aluminum foil. Bake at 350 degrees for 35 minutes or until fish is flaky. Do not overbake. Serve fish with vegetable sauce. Serves 4. 3 lean meat exchanges and 1 scant fat exchange = 225 calories.

Gloria Tyson

OVEN FRIES

3 med. unpeeled potatoes,	1/4 tsp. salt
cut for French fries	1/8 tsp. pepper
2 T. oil	Cooking spray

Scrub potatoes and cut for French fries. Place in bowl of cold water. Let stand 30 minutes; drain. Pat dry with paper towels. Combine oil, salt and pepper in a large bowl. Add potatoes and toss to coat. Put in pan coated with cooking spray. Bake at 475 degrees for 25 minutes or until done, turning every 10 minutes.

Grace Ramer

POTATO PUFFS

1/2 c. potatoes, cooked
   and mashed or whipped
1 c. flour
1 1/2 tsp. baking powder
1/2 tsp. salt
1 egg, well beaten
1/2 c. milk
Oil for deep-fat frying

With a fork, break up and mash enough potatoes to fill a small cup. Combine with remaining ingredients, except oil. Beat well. Heat oil to 375 degrees. From a tablespoon, drop a walnut-size piece of dough into hot fat. Remove when puff rises to the surface, about 2-3 minutes, and is golden brown. Repeat with remaining dough. Drain. Makes 24 puffs. Exchange (per 2 puffs): 160 calories, 1 bread, 1 1/2 fat.

Lois Blosser

ROASTED POTATOES

1-lb. (about 2 med.) potatoes
Boiling water
1 tsp. salt (for cooking water)
2 T. margarine, melted
1/2 tsp. salt
1/8 tsp. freshly ground pepper
1 T. fresh parsley, finely minced
   (or fresh dill)

Prepare a pie plate with vegetable pan-coating. Wash potatoes, boil in skins in enough salted boiling water to cover for 20-25 minutes or until tender when pierced with a fork. Preheat oven to 400 degrees. Drain potatoes and peel immediately. Cut each potato into 4 pieces and place on prepared pie plate. Baste each potato with melted margarine and sprinkle with salt, pepper and parsley. Roast in oven for 15 minutes or until potatoes are nicely browned. Makes 4 servings (2 pieces of potato each serving). Exchange (per serving): 124 calories, 1 starch, 1 fat.

Lois Blosser

WILD RICE CASSEROLE

10-oz. pkg. brown and wild
   rice mix
1 tsp. salt
1 med. onion, minced
1 med. size green pepper,
   chopped
2 T. reduced-calorie margarine,
   melted
1/2 10 3/4-oz. can cream of
   mushroom soup, undiluted
1/2 c. skim milk
4-oz. jar whole pimiento, drained
   and minced
Vegetable cooking spray

Cook rice according to package directions, using 1 teaspoon salt; set aside. Saute onion and green pepper in margarine until tender. Combine cooked rice, sauteed vegetables, soup, milk and pimiento, stirring well. Spoon into a 1 1/2-quart casserole dish coated with cooking spray. Bake at 350 degrees for 30 minutes. Makes 10 (1/2 cup) servings. Exchange (per serving): 135 calories, 1 1/2 starch, 2 grams fat.

Lois Blosser

PIZZA CASSEROLE

1-lb. ground turkey
1 c. V8 or tomato juice
1/2 c. mushrooms
1/2 c. onion

1/2 c. green pepper
6-8 slices low fat or fat free
cheese

Brown ground turkey; add onion, green pepper and mushrooms. Drain. Add V8 juice. Layer ingredients with cheese. Bake at 350 degrees for 30 minutes. Each serving contains 1 meat and 1 dairy serving.

Ruby Panyako

CHEESY ZUCCHINI WITH TOMATO

Vegetable cooking spray
1/2 c. onion, chopped
1 clove garlic, minced
1 lg. zucchini, sliced
1/2 c. (2-oz.) low fat process
  American cheese, shredded

3 sm. tomatoes, sliced
4 eggs
1/2 c. skim milk
1/4 tsp. dried whole oregano
1/4 tsp. dried whole basil
1 T. Parmesan cheese, grated

Coat a small skillet with cooking spray; place over medium heat until hot. Add onion and garlic; saute until tender. Remove form heat and set aside. Layer half of zucchini in a 2-quart shallow baking dish coated with cooking spray. Sprinkle with half each of shredded cheese and sauteed mixture. Repeat layers, with remaining zucchini, shredded cheese and sauteed mixture. Arrange sliced tomatoes around edge of dish. Combine eggs, milk and herbs, stirring until blended. Pour evenly over top of vegetables; sprinkle with Parmesan cheese. Bake, uncovered, at 350 degrees for 40 minutes. Makes 8 (1/2 cup) servings. Exchange (per serving): 116 calories, 1 medium-fat meat, 1 vegetable.

Lois Blosser

HOT CIDER

2 c. apple cider
2 3-in. cinnamon sticks
1/2 tsp. whole cloves

1/8 tsp. nutmeg
2 env. aspartame sweetener
2 tsp. rum flavoring

In a small saucepan, heat apple cider, cinnamon sticks, whole cloves and nutmeg until boiling. Reduce heat and simmer gently for 5-6 minutes. Remove from heat. Remove cinnamon sticks and whole cloves. Stir in aspartame sweetener and rum flavoring. Pour into 2 preheated cups or mugs. (To preheat mugs: Pour boiling or very hot water into mugs; allow to stand for 1-2 minutes, then pour out hot water and fill with drink.) Makes 2 servings. Exchange (per serving): 100 calories, 1 fruit.

Lois Blosser

Microwave

MICROWAVE

MICROWAVE CARAMEL CORN

1 c. brown sugar
1 stick margarine
1/4 c. white syrup

1/2 tsp. salt
1/2 tsp. baking soda
3 or 4-qts. popped corn

Combine all ingredients, except baking soda; bring to a boil and cook on HIGH power for 2 minutes. Remove and stir in baking soda. Put popcorn in a brown paper bag and shake. Put bag in microwave and cook on HIGH power for 1 1/2 minutes. Shake bag. Cook for 1 1/2 minutes more. Remove from microwave and shake.

Rosalind Slabaugh

CHEESY CHICKEN SANDWICHES

4-oz. (1 c.) mild Cheddar
  cheese, shredded
5-oz. can chunk chicken
  packed in water, drained

4-oz. can chopped green
  chilies, drained
3-oz. pkg. cream cheese,
  softened
6 English muffins or bagels, split

In a medium bowl, combine all ingredients, except English muffins; mix well. Spread about 2 tablespoons cheese mixture on each English muffin half. Place 2 sandwich halves at a time in microwave on double layer of microwave-safe paper towels. Microwave on HIGH for 30-60 seconds or until hot. (Cheese may not appear melted.) Repeat with remaining sandwich halves. Makes 6 servings.

Lois Blosser

CHICKEN CASSEROLE

1/2 pkg. frozen broccoli
1 can cream of chicken soup
1 c. Minute Rice
1 T. dried onion

1 c. cooked chicken, diced
1 c. milk
1/2 c. cheese, grated

Place frozen broccoli in microwave baking dish and cook on HIGH for 5 minutes (best to add 2 tablespoons water to broccoli). Remove from oven; add remaining ingredients and stir well. Microwave on HIGH for 6 minutes. Stir again and cover with extra cheese, if desired, and microwave 3 more minutes. Casserole dish needs to be covered with glass lid or plastic wrap.

Joy VanDiepenbos

God does not ask of us the perfection of tomorrow, nor even of tonight, but only of the present moment.

QUICK CHEESY POTATOES AND SAUSAGE

4-5 potatoes
1/2 c. cheese, cubed
1 can cream of mushroom soup
1/3 c. milk
Salt and pepper (to taste)

Garlic and onion powder
(to taste)
1-lb. smoked sausage, cut into
1-in. chunks

Cut washed potatoes in 1/2-inch cubes. Place in a 3-quart casserole with 2 tablespoons water. Cover and microwave on HIGH for 5-8 minutes. Stir half way through cooking time. Cook until partly tender. Add seasonings, soup, milk and cheese; mix. Cover and microwave until bubbly, about 4-5 minutes, on HIGH. Add sausage and microwave until meat is hot, about 3 minutes more. Serves 4. *Note: I have also used leftover ham.*

Kathy Stoltzfus

CRUSTLESS QUICHE LORRAINE

9-10 slices bacon, cooked and
crumbled
1 c. cheese, shredded
1/4 c. onion, chopped

4 eggs
1 c. evaporated milk
1/4 tsp. sugar
Dash of pepper

Sprinkle bacon, cheese and onion into a 9-inch glass pie pan. Beat eggs, milk, sugar and pepper until well blended. Pour over bacon mixture. Microwave on Level 8 (80%) for 9 1/2-11 minutes or until knife inserted near center comes out clean. Let stand 1 minute before serving. *Note: Onion is optional. Try adding cooked, crumbled sausage or 1 grated potato.*

Rita Rupp

MICROWAVE DANISH APPLE PIE

8 or 9 cooking apples, peeled,
cored and sliced (about 6 c.)
3/4 c. sugar
2 T. flour
1/8 tsp. salt
1 tsp. cinnamon

1 baked pie shell (deep dish or
9-in. pan)
2 T. butter
1/4 c. flour
1/4 c. brown sugar

Place apples in a large mixing bowl. Mix sugar, 2 tablespoons flour, salt and cinnamon. Add to apples and stir to coat. Pour apples evenly into pie shell. Mix together remaining 3 ingredients for topping and sprinkle over apples. Microwave on HIGH for 12-14 minutes or until apples are fork tender. Cool before serving.

Arlene Hartman

I can do all things in Him who strengthens me.
Phil. 4:13

MICROWAVE MEAT LOAF

1 1/2-lbs. ground beef
1/2 c. fine dry bread crumbs
1 egg, beaten
3/4 c. milk

1/4 c. onions, finely chopped
1 1/2 tsp. salt
1/4 tsp. pepper
1/2 c. catsup

Mix ground beef lightly with bread crumbs, egg, milk, onion, salt and pepper in a bowl. Pack mixture lightly into a 2-quart (9 x 5 x 3-inch) glass loaf dish. Cover with waxed paper. Microwave for 5 minutes on Roast. Top with catsup. Rotate dish 1/2 turn. Insert temperature probe at an angle near center of meat. Cook in microwave set at 170 degrees and Roast. Remove from oven, cover with aluminum foil and allow to stand for 5 minutes. Makes 6 servings.

Arlene Hartman

MEATZA PIE

1-lb. hamburger
1/2 c. cornflake crumbs
Dash of garlic powder
Dash of pepper
1/4 tsp. oregano (or poultry
  seasoning)

2/3 c. milk
1 can mushrooms, drained
1/3 c. catsup
2-3 slices American cheese
2 tsp. Parmesan cheese, grated

Press raw meat into a deep 9 or 10-inch pie pan. Cover with waxed paper. Microwave on HIGH for 3-4 minutes, stirring when half done. (Some meat will still be pink.) Stir in crumbs, garlic, pepper, oregano and milk; mix well with a fork. Press firmly in pie pan making it thicker at the edges and thinner in the center. Frost top with catsup and arrange mushrooms on top. Sprinkle with Parmesan cheese. Top with cheese slices. Microwave on HIGH 3-4 minutes, turning occasionally, until cheese melts and mixture bubbles and is hot. Let set 5 minutes before serving. *I use ground turkey instead of hamburger. This is a nice dish for summer as it doesn't heat the kitchen.*

Merianne Shaffer

MICROWAVE HINT

Use the waxed paper bags from cold cereal boxes to cover food being heated in the microwave. It is stronger than regular waxed paper and can be wiped off and reused many times. Cheerios and Rice Krispies bags work well; Cornflakes bags are too flimsy. I press them flat and use as a double layer.

Merianne Shaffer

TURKEY CHOW MEIN

2 turkey thighs (1 1/4-lbs. each), boned and cut into 1/2-in. cubes
2 T. cornstarch
1/4 c. water
2 tsp. instant chicken bouillon granules
2 T. soy sauce
1 c. celery, thinly sliced
1 med. onion, chopped
1 16-oz. can chow mein vegetables, drained
1 sm. can mushrooms
1/2 c. chow mein noodles

Place turkey pieces in a 3-quart casserole; cover. Microwave on HIGH for 5-6 minutes or until meat is no longer pink, stirring after half the time. Drain. Blend cornstarch and water. Add to casserole. Stir in all remaining ingredients, except noodles; cover. Microwave on HIGH for 10-12 minutes or until sauces thicken and vegetables are hot, stirring 2 or 3 times. Top with chow mein noodles. Serves 6. *Note: I have also replaced the turkey with chicken.*

Kathy Stoltzfus

TAKE TIME FOR 10 THINGS

1. Take time to work -- it is the price of success.
2. Take time to think -- it is the source of power.
3. Take time to play -- it is the secret of youth.
4. Take time to read -- it is the foundation of knowledge.
5. Take time to worship -- it is the highway of reverence and washes the dust of earth from our eyes.
6. Take time to help and enjoy friends -- it is the source of happiness.
7. Take time to love -- it is the one sacrament of life.
8. Take time to dream -- it hitches the soul to the stars.
9. Take time to laugh -- it is the singing that helps with life's loads.
10. Take time to plan -- it is the secret of being able to have time to take time for the first nine things.

Pickles,
Relishes,
& Misc.

PICKLES, RELISHES & MISC.

CHRISTMAS RECIPE

1 Mother Mary
1 Father Joseph
1 Star

1 Manger
1 Birth of Jesus

Mix well with Wise Men and Shepherds. Add a dash of Angels. Let it sit overnight for all to worship, then let it go until December 25th. Mix well with 1 cup of Wisdom, a box of smiles, and a bushel of Love. Serve to everyone all year long.

Beulah Ganger

EASY SWEET-DILL PICKLES

2 c. vinegar
2 c. water
3 c. sugar
2 T. salt

Garlic cloves
Dill
Small cucumbers

Place in pint jar: 2 garlic cloves, 1 head of dill (1/2 if they are large). Fill with small cucumbers or slices. Boil vinegar, water, sugar and salt for brine. Fill jars, leaving 1/2-inch space. Process in water bath canner for 5 minutes.

Mafra Maust

SUN DILLS

4 heads dill
4 or 5 cloves garlic
2/3 c. salt (or less)

1 c. vinegar
Cucumbers
Water

Put dill, garlic cloves, salt and vinegar in a glass gallon jar with lid. Fill with cucumbers. Add water to fill jar. Put lid on and shake well to mix salt. Set in sun for 2 days (more or less depending on how sour you like them). Store in refrigerator.

Esther Martin

EASY SWEET STICK PICKLES

3-pt. pickles
6 c. boiling water
2 1/3 c. vinegar
2 1/4 c. sugar

2 T. salt
1 tsp. celery seed
3 1/4 tsp. turmeric
3/4 tsp. mustard seed

Cut pickles in strips. Pour boiling water over pickles overnight; drain. Pack solid in jars. Combine remaining ingredients; boil 5 minutes. Pour hot liquid in jars and seal. Heat in jars 5 minutes to seal.

Vera Brubacher

Bury avocados in flour to hasten ripening.

SWEET DILL ZUCCHINI

1 c. distilled white vinegar	1/4 tsp. dry mustard
1/4 c. water	2 zucchini, thinly sliced (2 1/2 c.)
1/3 c. sugar	1/2 c. lg. red bell pepper, seeded
2 tsp. salt	and cut into small squares
1/2 tsp. mustard seed	5 dill sprigs (or 1 tsp. dry dill weed)

In a medium saucepan, combine vinegar, water, sugar, salt, mustard seed and dry mustard. Stir until sugar is dissolved; bring to a boil. Add zucchini and bell pepper. Simmer 2 or 3 minutes or until zucchini is barely tender. Place zucchini and red bell peppers in half pint jars, spacing the pepper pieces for color effect and adding a dill sprig to each. Pour in the syrup. Cover tightly. Let stand at room temperature overnight to blend flavors. Store in the refrigerator up to 3-4 months. Makes 5 half-pint jars, 5 servings per half-pint.

Thelma Mishler

SALSA

8 c. tomatoes	1 1/2 c. onion
1/2 c. banana pepper (or 3-4 jalapeno peppers)	3 tsp. salt
1 green pepper	6 garlic cloves
	3 c. vinegar

Peel and chop tomatoes. Seed and finely chop peppers (*I use jalapeno peppers and Roma tomatoes*). Chop onions and garlic cloves finely. Mix all ingredients and simmer for several hours. Can and process for 30 minutes in hot water bath. Let age several weeks before using.

Lou Thomas

SALSA

16-lbs. tomatoes, peeled	1 tsp. chili powder
2 4-oz. cans green chilies	4 tsp. garlic salt
6 med. onions	1 clove garlic
1 12-oz. jar jalapenos (including juice)	

Chop first 4 ingredients; add remaining ingredients. Simmer for 3 hours. Pour into hot jars and seal lids. Place in hot water bath for 15 minutes.

Rita Rupp

To remove the stain that often gets on your hands from vegetable canning season, rub hands with a slice of raw potato.

SPAGHETTI SAUCE (Fancheon Resler)

1-gal. thick tomato juice (reserve 1/2 c.)
4 med. onions
1/2 tsp. garlic powder
1/2 c. salad oil
1/2 c. sugar
2 T. parsley
2 T. oregano
2 T. salt
2 tsp. basil
1 tsp. pepper
2 bay leaves
4 T. cornstarch

Chop onions with a small amount of the juice in a blender. Put all ingredients, except cornstarch, in a large kettle and boil down one third. Use a metal ruler to measure before boiling and again to measure later. Mix cornstarch with reserved 1/2 cup juice and stir into boiling sauce. Stir until thick. Remove bay leaves; pour into hot sterilized jars. Process in a hot water bath for 10 minutes. Mixture can also be cooled and frozen in airtight containers. Makes 8 pints.

Merianne Shaffer

SPAGHETTI-PIZZA SAUCE

1-gal. thick tomato juice
4 med. onions
4 cloves garlic
1 T. oil
1 T. salt
1/2 c. sugar
2 bay leaves
2 T. parsley
2 T. oregano
2 T. basil
1 tsp. pepper
4 T. Perma Flo

Reserve 1/2 cup of the tomato juice; set aside. Chop onions and garlic with some of the juice in a blender. Pour the onion-garlic mixture along with tomato juice, oil, salt, sugar and bay leaves in a large kettle. Boil down one third (use a metal ruler to measure before boiling and again to measure later). Mix Perma Flo with reserved 1/2 cup juice. Stir into boiling sauce along with parsley, oregano, basil and pepper. Stir until thick. Place bay leaves in the bottom of 2 jars (or remove). Pour sauce into hot jars and process in canner at 5-pounds pressure for 10 minutes. Makes 5 pints. *I use fresh herbs (1 tablespoon fresh equals 1 teaspoon dried) but the amount given in this recipe is for dried. You can substitute cornstarch or Clear Jel for the Perma Flo but Perma Flo is better. When a recipe calls for catsup or tomato sauce, I use this.*

Merianne Shaffer

AMISH PEANUT BUTTER

1 1/4 c. corn syrup
1 c. peanut butter
1/2 c. marshmallow creme

Mix all ingredients together. If it is a little too stiff to spread, add a little bit of water.

Esther Martin

APPLE PIE FILLING

6-qts. apples, sliced or chopped
6 c. water
5 c. sugar
1 tsp. salt

7 tsp. cinnamon
2 c. water
1 1/2 c. Clear Gel (not instant) or
Perma Flo

Place apples in a large pan. Heat 6 cups water, sugar, salt and cinnamon. Add mixture of 2 cups water and Clear Gel (which has been mixed thoroughly) to the hot ingredients, stirring constantly until partially thick. Immediately stir into apples. Spoon into quart jars; seal. Process in pressure canner at 5-pounds pressure for 15 minutes.

Phyllis Kehr
Sherry Kehr

HOMEMADE PLAY DOUGH

1 c. flour
1/2 c. salt
2 tsp. cream of tartar

2 tsp. vegetable oil
1 c. water
Food coloring

Mix well and cook on medium heat until it forms a ball. Store in airtight containers.

Marilyn (G. Keith) Miller

GRAHAM CRACKERS

4 c. graham flour
2 c. white flour
2 c. brown sugar
Pinch of salt

1 c. lard
2/3 c. milk (or enough to make
dough right consistency)
2/3 tsp. baking soda

Mix all ingredients well. Roll out very thin and bake at 350-400 degrees. Cut in cracker size before baking.

MOCK MINCEMEAT

2 apples
2 green tomatoes
1 c. sugar
1/2 c. raisins
1 T. butter

1 tsp. cinnamon
1 tsp. nutmeg
1/2 tsp. cloves
Few grains of salt

Chop or grind apples, tomatoes and raisins. Mix with remaining ingredients. Boil 15 minutes. *I triple this recipe and freeze it. I serve it thawed as a dessert topped with ice cream or plain. Can be served hot or cold.* Makes 2-3 pints.

Grace Weldy

*Soften hard brown sugar with a soft slice of bread.
Or warm in microwave a couple of minutes.*

NOODLES

1 c. flour	1 egg
1 T. margarine	2 T. water
1/4 tsp. salt	

Beat ingredients together with a fork. Knead slightly. Use flour to roll out quite thin. Cut into diamond shapes. Boil for 15 minutes with beef and potatoes or chicken and potatoes in the broth. Cut thinner strips and use for soups. Longer, wider strips can be boiled in water for 15 minutes and used in lasagna dishes.

Chris & Lois Leuz-Taiwan

THE INCREDIBLE GRILLED SANDWICH

2 pieces bread, buttered	Smoked turkey
1 slice provolone cheese	Mayonnaise
1 egg	Tomato

Fry egg hard in a Pam coated skillet. Place egg, turkey and cheese between two pieces of bread. Grill in skillet. Add mayonnaise and tomato.

Wes Bontreger

ITALIAN BEEF SANDWICHES

1 lg. onion	3 c. water
1/2 c. vinegar	1 pkg. Italian dressing
3 cloves garlic	3-4 lb. rump roast
1 jar mild pepper rings	

Put all ingredients in a crock pot for 4 1/2 hours. *(After 2-3 hours, I slice the meat and continue cooking.)* Slice meat and put on French bread.

Brenda Gongwer

TURKEY, CHICKEN OR TUNA TURNOVERS

2 cans of 10 buttermilk biscuits	1 c. Cheddar cheese, shredded
Filling:	1 T. onion, finely chopped
1 c. cooked ground turkey,	Mayonnaise (to moisten)
cooked diced chicken or tuna	Salt and pepper

Combine filling ingredients in a mixing bowl. Roll 2 biscuits together into 1/4-inch thick rounds or squares. Place about 2 tablespoons filling on each, fold over and seal. Brush tops with melted margarine. Bake on ungreased baking sheet at 400 degrees for 10-13 minutes or until golden brown. Makes 10 turnovers.

Marla Reinhardt

Make extra-fine popcorn salt in your blender.
Use regular salt and blend on high speed.

CROCK POT OATMEAL

2 c. old-fashioned oatmeal
4 c. water
1 lg. apple, chopped

1 c. raisins
1 tsp. cinnamon
1-2 T. orange peel

Combine all ingredients in the crock pot. Turn on low setting before going to bed. In the morning, the oatmeal is ready to eat.

Beulah Ganger

PRETZELS

1 cake yeast
1 1/2 c. warm water
1 tsp. salt
1 T. sugar

4 c. flour
1 lg. egg, beaten
Coarse salt

Dissolve yeast in warm water. Add salt and sugar. Blend in flour and knead until smooth. Cut into small pieces and roll into ropes. Twist ropes into pretzel shapes and place on paper lined cookie sheets. Brush pretzels with beaten egg and sprinkle generously with course salt. Bake at 425 degrees for 12-15 minutes or until brown. For hard pretzels, decrease water to 1 1/4 cups and add 1/4 cup melted butter.

Ruby Panyako

PRETZEL (prétsel) n. A type of German biscuit. From the Latin word *pretiola,* meaning *a small reward.* First made by monks in Southern Europe as a reward for children who learned their prayers. It was shaped to represent the crossed arms of a child praying.

World Book Encyclopedia

SWEETENED CONDENSED MILK

1/3 c. water
2/3 c. sugar

3 T. margarine
1 c. powdered milk

In a two cup glass measure, put in the first 3 ingredients and microwave 1 1/2-2 minutes or until liquid boils, stirring every 30 seconds. Combine in blender with powdered milk; process until smooth. Refrigerate until needed. Cooling also helps to make it thicker.

Nelda Nussbaum

Make substitute for sour cream by blending
cottage cheese until smooth.

When cooking cauliflower, add 1/2 teaspoon sugar
to water to keep it white.

Add a bit of bleach with tap water to your
coffee or tea mugs to take the stains out.

Use a cabbage head as a dish and center
piece for your favorite dip, jello, potato salad, etc.

Clean the inside of your microwave by boiling
water inside. The steam softens dried splatters
and you can simply wipe them clean.

After shredding cheese, sprinkle it with
flour and toss. The cheese will not stick
together while stored.

COOKING FOR 100

Coffee .... 3 pounds
Cream .... 3 quarts
Sugar .... 3 pounds
Milk .... 6 gallons
Whipping Cream .... 4 pints
Juices .... 4 No. 10 cans
Soup .... 5 gallons
Weiners .... 25 pounds
Meat Loaf .... 24 pounds
Beef .... 40 pounds
Roast Pork .... 40 pounds
Ham .... 40 pounds
Ground Beef .... 30 to 35 pounds
Potatoes .... 35 pounds
Scalloped Potatoes .... 5 gallons
Vegetables .... 5 No. 10 cans
Baked Beans .... 4 gallons
Cabbage for Cole Slaw .... 20 pounds
Bread .... 10 loaves
Rolls .... 16 dozen
Butter .... 3 pounds
Potato Salad .... 4 gallons
Lettuce .... 20 heads
Pies 18
Cakes 8
Ice Cream .... 5 gallons
Cheese .... 3 pounds
Pickles .... 3 quarts
Nuts .... 3 pounds

CONTENTS

Can Size	Cups	Can Size	Cups
8-oz.	1 cup	No. 303	2 cups
No. 1	1 1/3 cups	No. 2	2 1/2 cups
Milk		No. 2 1/2	3 1/2 cups
Evaporated	1 1/2 cups	No. 3	4 cups
Condensed	1 1/3 cups	No. 10	13 cups
Sweetened	1 1/3 cups	No. 1 Tall	2 cups.

SUBSTITUTIONS

1 tsp. baking powder .... 1/4 tsp. baking soda plus
1/2 tsp. cream of tartar

1 c. cake flour, sifted .... 1 c. minus 2 T. all purpose flour

1 c. self-rising flour .... 1 c. all purpose flour plus
1/4 tsp. salt and 1 1/2 tsp. baking powder

1 T. flour, for thickening 1 1/2 tsp. cornstarch or 1 1/2 tsp. potato
starch, 1 1/2 tsp. rice starch and 2 tsp. quick cooking tapioca

1 medium onion, chopped .... 1 tsp. instant minced onion

1 c. sugar .... 1 c. maple syrup plus 1/4 c. corn syrup,
but reduce liquid in recipe by 1/4 c. or 1 c. honey,
but reduce liquid in recipe by 1/4 c.

1 sq. (1-oz.) unsweetened chocolate .... 3 T. cocoa, plus
1 T. butter or shortening

2 sq. (2-oz.) sweet chocolate .... 1/3 c. chocolate chips

1 T. prepared mustard .... 1 tsp. dry mustard plus
1 T. white wine or vinegar

1 c. sour milk or buttermilk .... 1 T. lemon juice or 1 T. vinegar
to make 1 cup milk. Stir and let stand 5 minutes

Whole milk .... 1 (14-oz.) can sweetened condensed milk
plus 2 5/8 c. water

1 cake yeast .... 1 (1/4-oz.) pkg. dry or 2 tsp. active dry yeast

3/4 c. cracker crumbs .... 1 c. bread crumbs

1 c. biscuit mix........................... 1 c. flour, 1 1/2 tsp. baking powder,
1/2 tsp. salt and 1 T. shortening

1 c. beef stock........ 1 tsp. beef flavored concentrate in 1 cup water
or beef bouillon cube dissolved in 1 cup water

1 c. whole milk, fresh ...... 1 c. reconstituted non-fat dry milk plus
2 tsp. butter or 1/2 c. evaporated milk plus 1/2 c. water

1 1/2 c. cream sauce .... 1 (10 1/2-oz.) can condensed cream of
mushroom or celery soup plus 1/4 c. milk

1 c. coffee cream .... 3 T. butter plus 7/8 c. milk

1 c. heavy cream .... 1/3 c. butter plus 3/4 c. milk

1 c. sour cream .... 1/3 c. butter plus 2/3 c. milk

1 c. shortening . 1 c. plus 2 tsp. butter or margarine, or 1 c. minus
2 T. lard or oil plus 1/4 tsp. salt

1 whole egg .... 2 egg yolks plus 1 T. water (in cookies, etc.)
2 egg yolks (in custards and such mixtures)

1 c. brown sugar, firmly packed .... 1 c. granulated sugar

1 T. prepared mustard .... 1 tsp. dry mustard

10 miniature marshmallows .... 1 lg. marshmallow

WEIGHTS AND MEASURES

Standard Abbreviations

tsp. - teaspoon
T. - tablespoon
c. - cup
f.g. - few grains
pt. - pint

qt. - quart
oz. - ounce
lb. - pound
pk. - peck
bu. - bushel

A Guide to Weights

1 teaspoon = 60 drops
3 teaspoons = 1 tablespoon
2 tablespoons = 1 fluid oz.
4 tablespoons = 1/4 cup
5 1/3 tablespoons = 1/3 cup
8 tablespoons = 1/2 cup
16 tablespoons = 1 cup

1 pound = 16 ounces
1 cup = 1/2 pint
2 cups = 1 pint
4 cups = 1 quart
4 quarts = 1 gallon
8 quarts = 1 peck
4 pecks = 1 bushel

Substitutions and Equivalents

2 tablespoon of fat .... 1 ounce

1 cup fat .... 1/2 pound

1 pound of butter .... 2 cups

1 cup of hydrogenated fat plus 1/2 tsp. salt .... 1 cup butter

2 cups of sugar .... 1 pound

2 1/2 cups packed brown sugar .... 1 pound

1 1/3 cups packed brown sugar .... 1 cup granulated sugar

3 1/2 cup powdered sugar .... 1 pound

4 cups sifted all purpose flour .... 1 pound

4 1/2 c. sifted cake flour .... 1 pound

1 ounce bitter chocolate .... 1 square

4 T. cocoa plus 2 tsp. butter .... 1 ounce bitter chocolate

1 c. egg whites.. 8 to 10 whites

1 c. egg yolks .... 12 to 14 yolks

16 marshmallows .... 1/4 pound

1 tablespoon cornstarch .... 2 tablespoons flour for thickening

1 T. vinegar or lemon juice plus 1 cup milk .... 1 cup sour milk

1 cup whipping cream .... 2 cups whipped

HELPFUL HINTS

1 pound nuts .... Serves 30
1 pound mints .... Serves 40
1 pound coffee .... Makes 80 cups
1 pint half and half .... Serves 100
1 gallon punch .... Serves 32

If lemons are warmed before you squeeze them, nearly double the quantity of juice can be extracted.

To crack nuts easily, soak in water overnight.

To prevent fish from sticking in a skillet, add a bit of vinegar in the fat.

Bread crumbs added to scrambled eggs not only improve the flavor, but make larger servings.

When baking potatoes, prick with fork before baking. They will be lighter and won't explode in the oven.

If you put potatoes in hot water 15 minutes before baking, it takes only half the time.

When shredded coconut is dry and hard, place in a small sieve and steam for a while.

To cut fresh bread or cake without crumbling, use a thin bladed knife heated in hot water, then dried.

To prevent nuts and raisins from sinking to the bottom of a cake, heat in oven, then rub with flour before adding to mixture.

Brush top of pie with sweet milk or white of egg before baking to give it that golden color.

Add a little vinegar to boiled icing; it will not crack and fall off.

EQUIVALENTS

3 teaspoons .... 1 tablespoon
4 tablespoons .... 1/4 cup
8 tablespoons .... 1/2 cup
12 tablespoons .... 3/4 cup
16 tablespoons .... 1 cup
2 cups .... 1 pint
2 pints .... 1 quart
4 quarts .... 1 gallon
16-oz. .... 1 pound
Dash .... 2 to 3 drops
Pinch .... that which can be taken between finger and thumb
1 pound butter .... 2 cups
1 large marshmallow .... 10 miniature marshmallows
3 to 4 slices bread .... 1 cup dried bread crumbs
1/4 pound cheese .... 1 cup shredded cheese
15 graham crackers .... 1 cup fine crumbs
22 soda crackers .... 1 cup fine crumbs
1 pound raisins .... 3 1/4 cup
1 pound dates .... 2 1/2 cups chopped
1 medium onion .... 1/2 cup chopped onion
1 cup broken, uncooked macaroni .... 2 2/3 cups cooked
1 cup broken, uncooked spaghetti .... 2 cups cooked
3 1/2 T. cocoa plus 1/2 tsp. butter .... 1 ounce chocolate
16 marshmallows .... 1/4 pound
1 cup uncooked rice .... 4 cups cooked
3 1/2 cups confectioner's sugar .... 1 pound
2 1/4 cup brown sugar .... 1 pound
1 tablespoon cornstarch .... 2 tablespoons flour
1 cup whipping cream .... 2 cups whipped cream
5 whole eggs.. 1 cup
1 pound flour, sifted .... 4 cups
1 lemon .... 2 to 3 tablespoons juice
1 orange .... 1/3 to 1/2 cup juice

194

SALT SUBSTITUTIONS

Basil .... Add 1/4 to 1/2 teaspoon to 2 cups green vegetables; 3/4 to 1 1/2 teaspoons to 1 1/2 pounds pork chops or roast; 1/8 to 1/4 teaspoon to 2 tablespoons butter or margarine for basting 1 pound fish or 1 1/2 pounds chicken.

Chili Powder .... Add 1 to 2 tablespoons to ground beef, noodle or rice skillet dishes (about 8 cups); 1 to 2 tablespoons to 4 pounds pot roast; 1/2 to 3/4 teaspoon to 8 cups popped corn (1/3 cup corn, unpopped).

Curry Powder .... Add 1 to 2 tablespoons to 2 pounds lamb chops; 1 tablespoon to 2 pounds ground beef; 1 1/2 teaspoons to 1 cup uncooked regular long grain rice; 1/2 teaspoon to tuna salad using 6 1/2 to 7-oz. can tuna.

Dill Weed .. Add 1/4 to 3/4 teaspoon to 2 cups green vegetables; 1/2 to 1 teaspoon to 4 cups cooked noodles.

Nutmeg .... Add dash to 1/4 teaspoon to 2 cups mixed vegetables, carrots, spinach; 1/8 teaspoon to 1 pound ground beef; dash to 1/8 teaspoon to 4 cups creamed chicken or tuna.

Oregano .... Add 1/4 to 3/4 teaspoon to 4 eggs for egg salad; 1/8 to 1/4 teaspoon to 3/4 cup butter for basting fish; 1/4 to 1/2 teaspoon to 2 cups spinach, green beans or 3 cups tomatoes.

Paprika .... Add 1/2 teaspoon to 1/4 cup flour for dredging chicken or meat; 1/2 teaspoon to 1/4 cup butter for seasoning vegetables.

Parsley Flakes .... Add 2 to 4 teaspoons to 4 cups cooked noodles or 3 cups cooked rice; 2 tablespoons to 2 pounds ground beef; 1/4 to 1/2 teaspoon to 1/4 cup butter for vegetables, fish, meats.

Tarragon .... Add 1/4 teaspoon to 1 pound fish; 1 teaspoon to 3 pounds chicken, 1/4 to 1/2 teaspoon to 1/4 cup butter for basting steak or chops.

Thyme .... Add 1/4 to 1/2 teaspoon to flour for dredging 3 pounds chicken.

Does Your Recipe Call For: Then You'll Need

Bread
1 cup soft crumbs.. 2 slices
1 cup small cubes .... 2 slices
2 cups ready-mix bread stuffing .... Half an 8 ounce package
Cereal
1 cup crushed cornflakes... 3 cups
2 cups cooked cornmeal.. 1/2 cup
Crackers
1 cup fine graham cracker crumbs .... 12 crackers
1 cup coarse saltine crumbs........................... 20 cracker squares
Macaroni-Rice products
4 cups cooked spaghetti .... 8 ounce package
2 cups cooked elbow macaroni .... 1 c. uncooked or 4-oz. pkg.
3 1/2 cups cooked noodles .... 8 ounce package
4 cups cooked rice .... 1 cup uncooked
Meats
3 cups diced cooked meats .... 1 pound, cooked
2 cups ground cooked meat .... 1 pound, cooked
4 cups diced cooked chicken .... 1 five pound stewing hen
Fresh Fruits, Juices and Peels
4 cups sliced apples .... 4 medium
2 cups sliced strawberries .... 1 pint
3 cups pitted cherries.. 4 cups unpitted
4 cups sliced fresh peaches .... 2 pounds or 8 medium
1 cup orange juice .... 3 medium oranges
1 teaspoon grated orange rind .... 1/2 orange
3 tablespoons lemon juice .... 1 lemon
1 1/2 teapoon grated lemon rind....................................... 1 lemon
1 cup mashed banana.. 3 medium
Nuts
1 cup blanched whole almonds .... 5 ounce can
1 cup toasted slivered almonds .... 5 ounce can
1 cup walnuts.. 4 ounce can
1 cup pecans.. 3 ounce can
1 cup cashew nuts .... Approx. 4 ounce can
Fresh Vegetables
4 cups sliced raw potatoes .... 4 medium
1 cup chopped onion .... 1 pound
2 cups canned tomatoes .... 1 pound can
Cheese and Eggs
4 cups shredded cheese .... 1 pound processed cheese
1 cup egg yolks... 12 to 14 eggs
1 cup egg whites .... 8 to 10 eggs

Favorite Recipes

Recipe Name   Page No.

_____

_____

_____

_____

_____

_____

_____

_____

_____

_____

_____

_____

_____

_____

_____

_____

_____

_____

_____

_____

_____

_____

_____

INDEX

You now own a fine cookbook printed by

RECORD PRINTING COMPANY

Please note the excellent quality of your book. We are aware of no other company that manufactures cookbooks with the pride and workmanship that are characteristic of our product. Produced at reasonable prices, all materials used in the production of your book were of top grade to insure durability for its many years of use.

If you know of some other organization interested in the same fine quality books that you have, please give them the postpaid reply mail card below. Thank-you, and enjoy cooking with your new book!

RECORD PRINTING COMPANY

TOLL FREE 1-800-658-3241

Box 530   Cairo, NE 68824

Record Printing Co.

For information on Record Printing Co. cookbooks please fill out and mail this postpaid card.

Name _____

Address _____

City_____State_____Zip_____

Phone _____